C000085682

Butterworths Student Companion

EQUITY — TRUSTS AND WILLS

First Edition   1996
Second Edition   1999
Third Edition   2008

Butterworths Student Companion

EQUITY — TRUSTS AND WILLS

Third Edition

Thomas Gibbons
LLB (Hons), BSocSc (Waikato)
Associate, McCaw Lewis Chapman, Hamilton

Wellington
LexisNexis
2008

Members of the LexisNexis Group worldwide

NEW ZEALAND	LexisNexis NZ Limited, Level 1, 181 Wakefield St, PO Box 472, Wellington
AUSTRALIA	LexisNexis Butterworths, SYDNEY
ARGENTINA	LexisNexis Juris Prudencia, BUENOS AIRES
AUSTRIA	LexisNexis ARD Orac GmbH & Co KG, VIENNA
BRAZIL	LexisNexis, SAO PAULO
CANADA	LexisNexis Butterworths, LexisNexis Quick Law, MARKHAM, Ontario
CHILE	LexisNexis Ltd, SANTIAGO
CZECH REPUBLIC	Nakladatelství Orac sro, PRAGUE
FRANCE	Juris-Classeur Groupe LexisNexis, PARIS
GERMANY	LexisNexis, FRANKFURT
HONG KONG	
GREATER CHINA	LexisNexis Butterworths, HONG KONG
HUNGARY	HVG-Orac Publishing Ltd, BUDAPEST
INDIA	LexisNexis, NEW DELHI
IRELAND	LexisNexis, DUBLIN
ITALY	Dott Giuffrè Editore SpA, MILAN
JAPAN	LexisNexis, TOKYO
KOREA	LexisNexis, SEOUL
MALAYSIA	Malayan Law Journal Sdn Bhd, KUALA LUMPUR
POLAND	Wydawnictwo Prawnicze LexisNexis, WARSAW
SINGAPORE	LexisNexis Butterworths, SINGAPORE
SOUTH AFRICA	Butterworths Publishers (Pty) Ltd, DURBAN
SWITZERLAND	Staempfli Verlag AG, BERNE
TAIWAN	LexisNexis, TAIWAN
UNITED KINGDOM	LexisNexis Butterworths Tolley, LONDON, EDINBURGH
USA	LexisNexis Group, NEW YORK, New York LexisNexis, MIAMISBURG, Ohio

National Library of New Zealand Cataloguing-in-Publication data
Gibbons, Thomas.
Equity : trusts and wills / Thomas Gibbons. 3rd ed.
(Butterworths student companion)
Previous ed.: written by Rebecca Irving. Butterworths, 1999.
ISBN 9780408718738
1. Trusts and trustees—New Zealand—Cases.
2. Trusts and trustees—Cases. 3. Wills—New Zealand—Cases.
4. Wills—Cases. I. Irving, Rebecca, 1971- Equity. II. Title.
III. Series.
346.9305—dc 22

ISBN: 9780408718738
© LexisNexis NZ Limited 2008

PREFACE TO THE THIRD EDITION

Those with some knowledge of the field of asset planning will no doubt agree it is apposite to begin a book about trusts and wills with an "acknowledgment of debt" — in this case, to Rebecca Irving, the author of the first two editions of this book. She established the template for both the style and content, and my additions are largely just an update of a text that remains primarily hers. My role has been as trustee to her settlor, exercising some discretions but remaining mindful of the purpose and intended beneficiaries of the trust.

The law of trusts operates as a fascinating mediator between a range of areas of law; most notably, family and commercial law. The "family" in family trusts is clear in a number of the cases noted in this book; so too are the commercial considerations which often guide the settlement of trusts. As trusts become an increasingly common device in the asset planning field, litigation relating to the creation, operation and winding up of those trusts is only likely to increase. This is no doubt good news for students contemplating a career in law.

The reality is that many spheres of law require a good understanding of the law relating to trusts and wills. Lawyers still draft wills, as they have done for years, and help clients settle trusts and wind up estates. But these actions are rarely devoid of context. These days, it is common for business people to place their assets in trusts to protect against their personal liability as directors; for property developers to use trusts to avoid tainting between different projects; and for family lawyers to need to pick apart trusts when relationships end. Even in an age of increasing specialisation among practitioners, a sound knowledge of the law of trusts and wills is essential to any law graduate.

Some comment on trends over the past few years must be made. Most additions to this book are focused on a few key areas, and these provide some indication of where the attention of trust lawyers will go in the future:

- There is an entirely new section on sham and alter ego trusts, traversing family and commercial law and indicating the key principles that apply when the validity of a trust is challenged.
- There have been significant developments in the field of Family Protection Act claims. New kinds of claims have been brought, and other claims have been decided, then appealed, to clarify provisions whose scope remains uncertain over 50 years after they were passed.

- There have been a number of important cases on the role of trustees — their duties, decisions and discretions. Consequential to this, there have been a number of cases on the rights of beneficiaries.
- Charitable trusts have been the subject of a number of cases, including some asking the key question of "what is charitable?", but also others concerning the administration of charitable trusts. This litigation is likely to continue in future, as the Charities Act 2005 changes the regime under which charities operate, and as many charities grow as businesses of a sort.
- Certain specialist fields of trust law have also had attention from the Courts. Most notably, cases relating to energy trusts and superannuation trusts occupy a number of pages of this edition.

These developments all illustrate that the law relating to trusts and wills remains in steady flux.

This book also has its limitations. As Irving noted in the first edition, no summary can ever be a real substitute for reading the actual case. Most cases have valuable insights for students and practitioners in the fields of trusts and wills, and these insights are discussed only very briefly in this book. This book also has a restricted subject-matter: it has little to say about the vast field of commercial equity, including such rich topics as the fiduciary duties of joint venturers, although a few cases of note have been included, It also does not delve very deeply into the field of family law, which has been overhauled in recent times by the passage of the Property (Relationships) Act 1976. Some of these cases involve commercial and family law issues, of course, but the overall focus is on how these cases are relevant to the law of trusts and wills. The new Wills Act 2007 was passed too late in the play for any cases on it to make it into this book, although some references to particular sections of that Act have been added to assist those using the book.

There are plenty more people to thank. Helen Scott of LexisNexis played the key role of commissioning me to this project, while editor Robyn Mackay and a reviewer made a number of helpful comments which have improved the book. My employers, the Partners of McCaw Lewis Chapman in Hamilton, have all helped develop my legal career and encouraged my publications, even when only tangentially related to the practice of law. Special mention must go to Don Shirley and Phil Harris, for involving me in so many interesting problems relating to the law of trusts, family, commercial, charitable and otherwise. Gerard Rennie and Julie Hardaker have expanded my understanding of statutory trusts and the role of trusts in relationship property claims respectively, while Brendan Cullen and Mike Talbot have involved me in some weighty charitable trust matters. Among other staff members, Neil Davidson, Charlotte Isaac and Meenal Duggal have all provided particular support to my sometimes rather esoteric academic interests; although really the whole firm must be thanked for providing such a collegial and enjoyable place to work. Outside the firm, Sue Tappenden and Jessica Palmer, of the Universities of Waikato and Otago respectively, provided useful assistance as to content. My parents, Joan and Peter, and my mother in law, Janice, have all supported the project, my writing, and my career.

But ultimate thanks must go to my lovely, patient, graceful and tolerant wife Natasha for all her love and support, and for perhaps not appreciating the time this project would take when I committed to it; and to my wonderful daughters Chloe and Emily, who are a constant joy and whom I hope never have the need for detailed knowledge of the Family Protection Act — at least not as claimants. Tash, Chloe and Emily, this book (or the additions that are mine, at least) is for you.

Thomas Gibbons
26 November 2007

TABLE OF CONTENTS

	Page
Preface	v
Table of Cases	xi
FORMAL REQUIREMENTS	1
Inter vivos trusts of real property	1
Inter vivos trusts of personal property	3
Secret and half-secret trusts	4
THE THREE CERTAINTIES	15
(1) Certainty of intention	15
(2) Certainty of subject-matter	21
(3) Certainty of object	23
(4) Court's exercise of control	32
THE BENEFICIARY PRINCIPLE	37
General	37
Anomalous exceptions	39
Trusts for the maintenance of animals	39
Trusts for the saying of masses	39
Trusts for the erection and maintenance of monuments and graves	40
Miscellaneous exceptions	41
Trusts in favour of unincorporated bodies	43
"Quistclose" trusts	49
CHARITABLE TRUSTS	57
Definition of a charity: the four heads	57
Public purpose	58
Public benefit	62
Able to be controlled by the Court	63
The four heads	64
(1) Relief of poverty	64
(2) Advancement of education	68
(3) Advancement of religion	74
(4) Other purposes beneficial to the community	75
Schemes for the administration of charitable trusts	79
RESULTING TRUSTS	87

CONSTRUCTIVE TRUSTS 99
    General principles 99
    De facto property 116

TRUSTEES...127

NATURE OF A BENEFICIARY'S INTEREST 151

TRACING 165

COMPLETELY AND INCOMPLETELY CONSTITUTED TRUSTS.....183
    Sham Trusts and Alter Ego Trusts 189

PERPETUITIES 199

SUCCESSION — WILLS...203
    Formal and statutory requirements......................................203
    Gifts to attesting witnesses 208
    Incorporation by reference 209
    Mental requirements...210
        Animus testandi 210
        Undue influence, fraud and duress 213
    Mutual wills 217
    Revocation 219
    Family Protection Act 1955 221
    Law Reform (Testamentary Promises) Act 1949 239

FIDUCIARY DUTIES...245

TABLE OF CASES

(The number(s) in bold in parentheses after the case citation represents the paragraph number(s) where the case summary is found.)

Page

Adams v Kensington Vestry (1884) 27 Ch D 394 **(13)**..................................16
Amelia Bullock-Webster, Re [1936] NZLR 814 **(68)**................................79
Anne Myfanwy Fulton Trust, Re (HC, Auckland M706/88,
    4 December 1989, Eichelbaum CJ) **(102)**................................130
Archer, Re [1990] 3 NZLR 737 **(191)**................................240
Archibald, Re [1992] 2 NZLR 109 **(172)**................................219
Attorney-General for Hong Kong v Reid [1992] 2 NZLR 385 **(89)**................................107
Attorney-General v Blake (Jonathan Cape Ltd, third party)
    [1998] 1 All ER 833 **(91)**................................110
Auckland City Mission v Brown [2002] 2 NZLR 650 (CA) **(185)**................................232
Auckland Medical Aid Trust v CIR (1979) 1 NZLR 382 **(58)**................................70
Baden's Trust Deed (No 2), Re [1973] Ch 9 **(23)**................................30
Banicevich v Gunson [2006] 2 NZLR 11 (CA) **(116)**................................147
Bank of New Zealand v New Zealand Guardian Trust
    Company Ltd [1999] 1 NZLR 664 (CA) **(106)**................................136
Banks v Goodfellow (1870) LR 5 QB 549 **(166)**................................212
Barclays Bank Ltd v Quistclose Investments Ltd [1968] 3 All ER 651 **(38)**................................49
Bayley v Public Trustee (1908) 27 NZLR 659 **(3)**................................3
Begum v Ali (Family Court Auckland, FP 2001-004-866,
    10 December 2004, Judge O'Donovan) **(146)**................................191
Belton v CIR [1959] NZLR 1372 **(15)**................................18
Bendien, Re (1991) 8 FRNZ 108 **(178)**................................226
Blackwell v Blackwell [1929] AC 318 **(4)**................................4
Boardman v Phipps [1967] 2 AC 46 **(83)**................................99
Boyce v Boyce (1849) 16 Sim 476 **(19)**................................22
Bravda, Re [1968] 2 All ER 217 **(161)**................................207
Brown v Pourau [1995] 1 NZLR 352 **(11)**................................13
Budge, Re [1942] NZLR 350 **(30)**................................41
Burns v Steel [2006] 1 NZLR 559 (HC) **(123)**................................157
Buschau v Rogers Communications Inc [2006] SCJ 28,
    [2006] 1 SCR 973 (SCC) **(127)**................................161
Cadell v Palmer (1833) 1 Cl & F 372, 6 ER 956 **(151)**................................199
Cain, Re [1950] VLR 382 **(34)**................................43
Canterbury Orchestra Trust v Smitham [1978] 1 NZLR 787 **(59)**................................70
Carreras Rothmans Ltd v Freeman Mathews Treasure Ltd
    [1985] 1 All ER 155 **(40)**................................50
Carrigan v Redwood (1910) 30 NZLR 244 **(28)**................................39

Casson v Dade (1781) 28 ER 1010 **(157)** 205
Centrepoint Community Growth Trust v CIR [1985] 1 NZLR 673 **(63)** 74
Centrepoint Community Trust, Re [2000] 2 NZLR 325 (HC) **(72)** 83
Chase Manhattan Bank NA v Israel-British Bank
    (London) Ltd [1981] Ch 105 **(136)** 175
Chirnside v Fay [2007] 1 NZLR 433 (SCNZ) **(196)** 247
CIR v Medical Council of New Zealand [1997] 2 NZLR 297 **(66)** 77
Colin Cooper, Re [1939] Ch 811 **(9)** 11
Colling, Re [1972] 1 WLR 1440 **(158)** 205
Collinge v Kyd [2005] 1 NZLR 847 (HC) **(111)** 143
Compton, Re [1945] Ch 123 **(44)** 58
Conservative and Unionist Central Office v Burrell (Inspector of Taxes)
    [1982] 1 WLR 522, [1982] 2 All ER 1 **(33)** 43
Cook's Estate, Re [1960] 1 All ER 689 **(156)** 204
Corbett v Newey [1996] 2 All ER 914 **(164)** 210
Cossey v Bach [1992] 3 NZLR 612 **(97)** 119
Coulthurst's Will Trusts, Re [1951] 1 All ER 775 **(53)** 66
Cunnack v Edwards [1896] 2 Ch 679 **(76)** 88
Denley's Trust Deed, Re [1969] 1 Ch 373 **(31)** 41
Dickie v Torbay Pharmacy (1986) Ltd [1995] 3 NZLR 429 **(194)** 245
Densham, Re [1975] 3 All ER 726 **(79)** 93
Dingle v Turner [1972] AC 601 **(46)** 60
Diplock, Re [1948] 2 All ER 318 **(133)** 169
Duke of Norfolk v Howard (1863) 1 Vern 163; 23 ER 388 **(152)** 200
Dupree's Will Trust, Re [1944] 2 All ER 443 **(56)** 68
Elders Pastoral Ltd v Bank of New Zealand [1989] 2 NZLR 180 **(87)** 105
Endacott, Re [1959] 3 All ER 562 **(26)** 38
English & American Insurance Co Ltd, Re [1994] 1 BCLC 649 **(41)** 52
Flathaug v Weaver [2003] NZFLR 730 (CA) **(187)** 236
Foreman v Kingstone [2004] 1 NZLR 841 (HC) **(122)** 157
Fortex Group Ltd (In Receivership and Liquidation) v
    MacIntosh [1998] 3 NZLR 171 (CA) **(93)** 113
Foskett v McKeown [1997] 3 All ER 392 **(138)** 179
Foster v Spencer [1996] 2 All ER 672 **(107)** 139
Fox v Harvey [1968] NZLR 394 **(141)** 185
Gailey v Gordon [2003] 2 NZLR 192 (HC) **(125)** 159
Gartside v IRC [1968] AC 553, [1968] 1 All ER 121 **(120)** 153
Genc v Genc [2006] NZFLR 1119 (HC) **(147)** 191
Gerbich, Re [2002] 2 NZLR 791(HC) **(112)** 143
Gillies v Keogh [1989] 2 NZLR 327 **(96)** 118
Gillingham Bus Disaster Fund, Re [1958] Ch 300 **(75)** 87
Glass v Hughey [2003] NZFLR 865 **(145)** 190
Golay's Will Trusts, Re [1965] 1 WLR 969 **(20)** 22
Goldcorp Exchange Ltd (In receivership), Re:
    Kensington v Liggett [1994] 3 NZLR 385 **(137)** 177

Table of Cases

Gormack v Scott[1995] NZFLR 289 **(99)**..125
Grant's Will Trusts, Re [1979] 3 All ER 359 **(37)**.....................................46
Gulbenkian's Settlement Trusts, Re [1970] AC 508 **(21)**...........................23
Gwyon, Re [1930] 1 Ch 255 **(51)**...64
Hall v Hall (1868) LR 1 P&D 481 **(168)**...213
Hallett's Estate, Re (1880) 13 Ch D 696, [1874-80] All ER Rep 793 **(130)** 165
Hardie, Re [2002] NZFLR 229 (HC) **(183)**..230
Hawkins v Public Trustee [1960] NZLR 305 **(189)**.....................................239
Hooper, Re [1932] 1 Ch 38 **(29)**..40
Hotung v Ho [2002] 3 HKLRD 641 **(129)**..163
Hummeltenberg, Re [1923] 1 Ch 237 **(49)** 63
Hunter v Hunter [1938] NZLR 520 **(101)**...128
In bonis Truro (1866) LR 1 P & D 201 **(163)**..209
In the Matter of the Esteem Settlement (Abacus (CI) Limited as Trustee)
    Grupo Torras SA and Culmer v Al Sabah and Four Others
    ("In Re Esteem Settlement") [2003] JLR 188 **(149)**............................194
Incorporated Council of Law Reporting v Attorney-General
    [1972] Ch 73 **(57)**...69
IRC v Pemsel [1891] AC 531 **(43)** 57
Johns v Johns [2004] 3 NZLR 202 (CA) **(128)** 162
Jones v Lock (1865) 1 Ch App 25 **(12)**...15
Joseph Rowntree Memorial Trust Housing Assn Ltd v
    Attorney-General [1983] 1 All ER 288 **(52)**......................................65
Kain v Hutton [2004] 2 NZLR 318 (HC) **(114)**..145
Karsten, Re [1950] NZLR 1022 **(162)**...209
Kayford Ltd, Re [1975] 1 WLR 279 **(14)** 17
Keech v Sandford (1726) 2 Eq Cas Abr 741, 25 ER 223 **(82)**......................99
Keelan v Peach [2003] 1 NZLR 589 (CA) **(184)**..231
Keen, Re [1937] 1 Ch 236 **(6)** 7
Korkontzilas v Soulos (1997) 146 DLR (4th) 214 **(92)** 112
LAC Minerals Ltd v International Corona Resources Ltd
    (1989) 61 DLR (4th) 14 **(90)**..108
Lankow v Rose [1995] 1 NZLR 277 **(98)**..112
Latimer v CIR [2004] 3 NZLR 157 (PC) **(67)**...78
Leonard, Re [1985] 2 NZLR 88 (CA) **(175)**..222
Letterstedt v Broers [1881-5] All ER Rep 882 **(100)**..................................127
Lewis v Cotton [2001] 2 NZLR 21 (CA) **(171)**...217
Lindsay Sangster Rogers, Re (HC, Hamilton, M 4/95,
    19 May 1995, Hammond J) **(71)**..82
Lipinski's Will Trusts, Re [1976] Ch 235 **(32)**..42
Lipkin Gorman v Karpnale Ltd [1987] 1 WLR 987 **(85)**............................102
Lister & Co v Stubbs [1890] 45 Ch D 1 **(88)**..107
Little v Angus [1981] 1 NZLR 126 (CA) **(174)**...221
Lucas, Re [1922] 2 Ch 52 **(50)** 64
MacIntosh, Re (1990) 7 FRNZ 580 **(176)** 223

Manukau City Council v Lawson [2001] 1 NZLR 599 (HC) **(109)** 141

McElroy Trust, Re [2003] 2 NZLR 289 (CA) **(73)** 84

McIntosh, Re [1976] 1 NZLR 308 **(55)** 68

McLaren v McLaren [1919] GLR 287 **(160)** 206

McLean, Re [1991] 8 FRNZ 321 **(177)** 225

McPhail v Doulton [1971] AC 424 **(22)** 27

Mendelssohn and Schmid v Centrepoint Community
　　Growth Trust [1999] 2 NZLR 88 (CA) **(103)** 131

Milroy v Lord (1862) 4 De G F & J 264 **(139)** 183

Mitchell, Re [1963] NZLR 934 **(54)** 67

Morice v Bishop of Durham (1804) 9 Ves Jr 399 **(25)** 37

Mothew v Bristol & West Building Society [1996] EWCA CIV 533,
　　24 July 1996 **(195)** 246

Motorola New Zealand Superannuation Fund, Re
　　[2001] 3 NZLR 50 (HC) **(126)** 160

Mountain v Styak [1922] NZLR 131 **(1)** 1

Mulligan (Deceased), Re [1998] 1 NZLR 481 **(105)** 134

National Anti-Vivisection Society v IRC [1948] AC 31 **(48)** 62

Naumann, Re (HC, Dunedin A17/83, 16 December 1991,
　　Roberston J) **(170)** 216

Neagle v Rimmington [2002] 3 NZLR 826 (HC) **(110)** 142

Neville Estates Ltd v Madden [1962] Ch 832 **(35)** 44

New Zealand Dairy Board v New Zealand Co-operative
　　Dairy Co Ltd [1999] 2 NZLR 355 (HC) **(24)** 32

New Zealand Society of Accountants v CIR [1986] 1 NZLR 147 **(47)** 61

Niak v Macdonald [2001] 3 NZLR 334 (CA) **(108)** 140

Northern Developments (Holdings) Ltd, Re
　　Unreported, Ch D, 6 October 1978 **(39)** 50

Nottage, Re [1895] 2 Ch 649 **(64)** 75

Oatway, Re [1903] 2 Ch 356 **(131)** 167

Official Assignee v Wilson [2006] 2 NZLR 841 (HC) **(148)** 192

Oliver v Bradley [1987] 1 NZLR 586 **(95)** 116

Ontario Securities Commission v Greymac Credit Corpn
　　(1986) 30 DLR 4ed 1 **(134)** 172

Oppenheim v Tobacco Securities Trust Ltd [1951] 1 All ER 31 **(45)** 59

Ottaway v Norman [1972] Ch 698 **(5)** 5

Palmerston North Halls Trust Board, Re [1976] 2 NZLR 161 **(69)** 80

Panapa, Re [1993] 1 NZLR 694 **(173)** 220

Parker v Felgate (1883) 8 PD 171 **(167)** 213

Pascoe v Turner [1979] 2 All ER 945 **(142)** 186

Paul v Constance [1977] 1 WLR 527 **(16)** 19

Pecore v Pecore [2007] SCJ 17, 2007 SCC 17 (SCC) **(81)** 97

Perpetual Trust Ltd v Roman Catholic Bishop of Christchurch
　　[2006] 1 NZLR 282 (HC) **(154)** 201

Pettingall v Pettingall (1842) 11 LJ Ch 176 **(27)** 39

Pinion: Westminster Bank Ltd v Pinion, Re [1965] 1 Ch 85 **(62)** 73

Powell v Public Trustee [2003] 1 NZLR 381 (CA) **(192)** 241

Powell, Re [2000] NZFLR 269 (HC) **(186)** 234

Prime v Hardie [2003] NZFLR 481 (HC) **(144)** 189

Recher's Will Trust, Re [1972] Ch 526 **(36)** 45

Rochefoucauld v Boustead [1898] 1 Ch 550 **(2)** 2

Rose, Re; Rose v Inland Revenue Commissioners
    [1952] 1 All ER 1217 **(140)** 184

Royal Brunei Airlines v Tan [1995] 3 All ER 97 **(86)** 104

Ryan v Public Trustee [2000] 1 NZLR 700 (HC) **(193)** 242

Saunders v Vautier (1841) 4 Beav 115 **(118)** 151

Schmidt v Rosewood Trust Ltd [2003] 3 All ER 76 (PC) **(121)** 155

Schroder's Wills Trusts, Re [2004] 1 NZLR 695 (HC) **(113)** 144

Securitibank Ltd, Re [1978] 1 NZLR 97 **(135)** 173

Sepsy, Re (HC, Dunedin, CP 65/87, 12 August 1994,
    Robertson J) **(181)** 228

Shalson v Russo [2005] Ch 205, [2003] EWHC 1637 (Ch) **(150)** 196

Shaw, Re: Public Trustee v Day [1957] 1 WLR 729 **(61)** 72

Shaw's Will Trusts, Re: National Provincial Bank Ltd v
    National City Bank Ltd [1952] 1 Ch 163 **(60)** 71

Sinclair v Brougham [1914] AC 398 **(132)** 168

Smith v Hugh Watt Society Inc [2004] 1 NZLR 537 (HC) **(94)** 116

Smith, Re: Public Trustee v Smith [1932] 1 Ch 153 **(65)** 76

Speight v Gaunt (1883) 9 App Cas 1 **(104)** 133

Spencer's Will, Re (1887) 57 LT 519 **(7)** 9

Sprange v Barnard (1789) 2 Bro CC 58 **(18)** 21

Stephenson (Inspector of Taxes) v Barclays Bank Trust Co Ltd
    [1975] 1 WLR 882, [1975] All ER 625 **(119)** 151

Stewart, Re (HC, Auckland A389/85,
    17 December 1991, Tompkins J) **(155)** 203

Stewart, Re [2003] 1 NZLR 809 (HC) **(188)** 237

Tanner v Public Trustee [1973] 1 NZLR 68 **(169)** 214

Tonge, Re (HC, Whangarei, M 23/8621, 13 March 1990,
    Robertson J) **(179)** 227

Twigger, Re [1989] 3 NZLR 329 **(70)** 81

Twinsectra Ltd v Yardley [2002] 2 All ER 377 (HL) **(42)** 53

Vandervell's Trust (No 2), Re [1974] 1 Ch 269 **(77)** 89

Villar, Re: Public Trustee v Villar [1929] 1 Ch 243 **(153)** 200

Walsh, Re (1911) 30 NZLR 1166 **(8)** 10

Welch, Re [1990] 3 NZLR 1 **(190)** 240

Wellington Harness Racing Club Inc v Hutt City Council
    [2004] 1 NZLR 82 (HC) **(143)** 187

West Sussex Constabularies Widows, Children and Benevolent
    (1930) Fund Trusts, Re [1971] 1 Ch 1 **(78)** 91

Westdeutsche Landesbank Girozentrale v Islington London

Borough Council [1996] 2 All ER 961 **(80)**...94
Westpac Banking Corporation v Savin [1985] 2 NZLR 41 **(84)** 100
White v White (1909) 28 NZLR 129 **(17)** 21
Whyte, Re [1969] NZLR 519 **(165)**...211
Williams v Aucutt [2000] 2 NZLR 479 (CA) **(182)** 229
Wilson Home Trust, Re [2000] 2 NZLR 222 (HC) **(74)**...84
Wong v Burt [2005] 1 NZLR 91 (CA) **(115)**...147
Wrightson Ltd v Fletcher Challenge Nominees Ltd
     [2002] 2 NZLR 1 (PC) **(124)**..158
Young, Re [1951] 1 Ch 344 **(10)**...12
Young, Re [1969] NZLR 454 **(159)** 205
Youyang Pty Ltd v Minter Ellison Morris Fletcher [2003] HCA 15,
     212 CLR 484, 196 ALR 482, 77 ALJR 895 (3 April 2003) **(117)** 149

FORMAL REQUIREMENTS

Inter vivos trusts of real property

1   *Mountain v Styak*
         [1922] NZLR 131

In 1889 a property, "Oaklands", was purchased by Susannah Styak. The property was vested in the name of her daughter-in-law, Maria, but the understanding was that the land was to be held on trust for Maria's two children, Alfred Styak and Mabel Mountain. The only written evidence of any trust in connection with land was a letter written by Maria to her son Alfred in 1912 which said "I am most anxious that your dear old grandmother's wishes should be carried out, which were that when she bought this property in my name that it was to be secured after our death equally to you and your sister".

Susannah died in 1898, and Maria in 1918. Maria's will left all her property to her daughter Mabel Mountain. Mabel denied there was any trust and said that it could not be proved in writing under s 7 of the Statute of Frauds. Her brother Alfred challenged this.

The New Zealand Court of Appeal considered two issues in deciding whether or not there was a trust: whether the language used in the letter was sufficient to create a trust; and whether the fact that the letter was written by the mother, not the grandmother, defeated any trust.

As to the first ground, the Court was of the opinion that the language used in Maria's letter was sufficient to create a trust. It was noted that in declaring a trust of personal or real property no special form of words is necessary: the Court should consider the intension of the writer in each particular case. Here they were satisfied beyond reasonable doubt that the letter established Susannah's definite wish that the property should go to Mabel and Alfred in equal shares.

The second ground relied upon s 7 of the Statute of Frauds (now s 49A of the Property Law Act 1952). This section relevantly provides that all creations of trusts of land shall be manifested and proved by some writing signed by the party who is, by law, able to declare such trust. On a literal construction this would mean the writing should be signed by Susannah, the settlor of the trust,

1

as opposed to Maria, the trustee. The Court considered, however, that the decisions on this point established that, the apparently definite provisions of the section notwithstanding, a trust manifested and proved in writing signed by the trustee is sufficient to enable a Court to enforce the trust against them.

Accordingly, the trust was established. It was held that Mabel held Oaklands upon trust for herself and her brother.

2   *Rochefoucauld v Boustead*
[1898] 1 Ch 550

In 1873 the Comtesse de la Rochefoucauld found herself in financial difficulties. The Comtesse was registered owner of a large number of coffee estates in Ceylon, which were mortgaged to a Dutch company. The Dutch company wished to call in the mortgage, and the Comtesse was afraid that they might transfer the mortgage to her estranged former husband, who would then foreclose on her. To avoid this situation she entered into an agreement with Mr Boustead. Boustead was to buy the estates at auction in his name, but on behalf of the Comtesse, as trustee for her. The land was to be subject to a charge in his favour in respect of the purchase price, and of expenses he incurred in managing the estates. This scheme was put into effect. The estates were conveyed absolutely to Boustead, with no mention of any alleged trust in favour of the Comtesse.

Some years after this, without consulting with the Comtesse, Boustead sold the estate. The proceeds of sale were more than sufficient to repay all that Boustead was owed in respect of the sum he paid for the estates, and their subsequent maintenance. The Comtesse claimed that the surplus on the sale should be paid to her. Boustead disagreed. He argued that the estates were conveyed to him as beneficial owner, and that the trust alleged by the plaintiff could not be proved by any writing.

The English Court of Appeal disagreed. The Court held that the Statute of Frauds did not prescribe that any trust should be declared by writing at the time of its creation. It would be sufficient if it could be evidenced by some writing signed by the trustee. The date of the writing would be immaterial. It was also held that the Statute cannot itself be used as an instrument of fraud; and that it is a fraud on the part of a person to whom land is conveyed as trustee, and who knows this, to deny the trust and claim the land beneficially. Consequently, it was possible for a person claiming land to prove it was conveyed upon trust by offering oral evidence as opposed to evidence in writing.

The Court found that correspondence between the plaintiff and defendant could have been enough to satisfy the Statute of Frauds. Whether or not this was so, oral evidence was admissible in order to prevent the statute from being used to commit fraud. This evidence proved the plaintiff's case completely. It was held that Boustead had held the property on trust for the Comtesse, and thus was required to account to her for the profit he had made upon its sale.

Inter vivos trusts of personal property

3   *Bayley v Public Trustee*
(1908) 27 NZLR 659

Mrs Gaisford had three sons, Edward, John and Henry, and a daughter Muriel. In 1906 she made her will in which she divided her property amoung her three sons, and then noted "I desire and request my ... sons ... respectively during their respective lives to pay the following annual sums to my daughter Muriel".

Apart from not having much faith in her daughter's ability to manage property, Mrs Gaisford apparently also had qualms about her son Henry's ability to look after himself. In early 1906 she had talked to a Mr Bayley and discussed buying a property for Henry. Mrs Gaisford intended to give Mr Bayley £5000 with which to buy a suitable place for Henry so he could not lose the money or be swindled out of it. She mentioned this to Mr Bayley several times, and gave him the £5000. Believing that she had effectively provided for her son Henry, Mrs Gaisford then altered her will, reducing the interest he was given in the estate.

Mrs Gaisford died in November 1906. Two problems arose from her will: whether the £5000 given to Mr Bayley constituted a valid trust in favour of Henry; and whether a trust had been created in favour of Muriel with respect to the sums her brothers were to pay her.

In relation to the first question the Supreme Court held that in order to render a voluntary settlement valid and effectual the settlor must have done everything which was necessary to transfer the property and render the settlement binding upon the trustees. Mrs Gaisford had defined the purposes for which she placed £5000 in the hands of Mr Bayley, and Mr Bayley had accepted this money. In the opinion of the Court there had been a valid declaration of trust. The money was personal property, and an oral declaration of trust is sufficient to create a trust. Accordingly, the Court held Mr Bayley held the money upon trust to purchase a property for the use of Henry and to permit him to receive the rents and profits of it during his lifetime.

The next question was whether the provision in Mrs Gaisford's will expressing her desire and request that her sons should pay life annuities to her daughter Muriel was enforceable. The question was whether a precatory trust had been created in favour of Muriel. (For further discussion of a precatory trust, see *Adams v Kensington Vestry* **(13)**.) The Court held that the words of the will did not create such a trust. It was not apparent from a consideration of the whole will that it was intended to be mandatory, and although the object of the trust was certain, the subject and duration of it were not, and its administration would cause confusion.

Secret and half-secret trusts

4   *Blackwell v Blackwell*
         [1929] AC 318

This House of Lords case deals with a question which in various forms has for over 200 years been the subject of vexed controversy. The key issue for the Court to determine was to what extent it is possible to give effect to testamentary intentions that are not contained in a will.

A testator by a codicil (a codicil is an "add on", or amendment to a will) left £12,000 on trust to five persons. A large proportion of the principal and income from the £12,000 was to be applied "for the purposes indicated by [the testator] to [the trustees]" together with a power to pay over the sum of £8000 "to such person or persons indicated by [the testator] to [the trustees]". The deceased, Mr Blackwell, had entered into this arrangement because he had had a son to a woman who was not Mrs Blackwell. Consequently, Mr Blackwell was concerned not to have all of the sordid details recounted in his will, but nevertheless wished to make provision for both his son and his mistress after his death. Mrs Blackwell and her son brought an action against the trustees and executors in order to test the validity of the purported secret trust.

The House of Lords was unanimous in affirming the decision of the lower Court, and rejecting Mrs Blackwell's appeal.

The difficulty which arose in this case, was that nowhere in the will, or codicils, was there mention of the beneficiaries of the alleged secret trust. As a consequence, oral (or parol) evidence was necessary in order to establish the secret trust.

Lord Buckmaster stated that a testator, having been induced to make a gift on trust in his will in reliance on the clear promise of a trustee that the secret trust will be executed in favour of certain named persons, the trustee will not be at liberty to renounce the secret trust and thereby destroy the whole object of its creation — in effect, to commit a fraud upon the beneficiaries of the secret trust. To support his view, His Lordship traversed authorities dating back over two centuries, and observed that in none of those cases was there anything to support Mrs Blackwell's challenge to the secret trust.

Although there was some confusion in previous case law, the Court held that as the secret trust had been constituted on the face of the will (albeit with some details omitted), Mrs Blackwell was not entitled to defeat the claim of the beneficiaries of the secret trust, and her appeal was accordingly dismissed.

5 *Ottaway v Norman*
[1972] Ch 698

Harry Ottaway's first wife died in 1919. His second wife died in 1928. After the death of his second wife, Harry had a succession of housekeepers, the last being Eva Hodges, who came into Harry's house, "Ashcroft", in 1931. The two lived together as husband and wife for over a quarter of a century, but did not marry.

Harry was keen to see that Eva was looked after when he died. Consequently, Harry advised his son, William Ottaway, that he would leave "Ashcroft" to Eva, but upon Harry's death, she was to immediately make a will leaving the property to William.

Harry kept his side of the bargain, and in his will left "Ashcroft" to Eva.

During discussions with Eva, Harry and William, it was decided that Ashcroft would be left to William and his wife for their benefit once Eva had shuffled off this mortal coil. With Harry out of the picture, Eva (initially) kept her side of the agreement. She duly executed a will leaving "Ashcroft" to William and his wife.

By 1966, however, Eva had formed a strong relationship with Mr Norman, the defendant. She changed her will in June 1966 appointing Norman as the sole executor and bequeathing "Ashcroft" to Mr and Mrs Norman.

In 1968 Eva died, and the arguments began. Norman claimed his right to "Ashcroft" pursuant to Eva's later will. William Ottaway and his wife issued proceedings against Norman as executor, seeking a declaration that "Ashcroft" was held by Norman upon trust for them.

Brightman J in the Chancery Division of the High Court began by stating the general principle outlined in *Blackwell* **(4)**:

> It has long been settled that if a gift be made to a person or persons in terms absolutely but in fact upon a trust communicated to the legatee and accepted by him, the legatee would be bound to give effect to the trust, on the principle that the gift may be presumed to have been made on the faith of his acceptance of the trust, and a refusal after the death of the testator to give effect to it would be a fraud on the part of the legatee. Of course in these cases the trust is proved by parol evidence, and such evidence is clearly admissible.

Brightman J defined the person upon whom a secret trust is imposed as a "primary donee", and a beneficiary under that trust as "the secondary donee". The essential elements which had to be proved to exist in order to succeed on a claim under a secret trust were outlined as follows:

1. The intention of the testator to subject the primary donee to an obligation in favour of the secondary donee.

2. Communication of that intention to the primary donee.

3. The acceptance of that obligation by the primary donee either expressly or by acquiescence. That is relevant whether the elements as outlined precede or succeed the will of the donor.

The fundamental principle underpinning the doctrine of a secret trust is the obligation imposed on the conscience of the primary donee. The Court held that there was nothing material in the machinery by which the donor intended that the obligation should be carried out.

In defence, it was argued that (on authority), in order to succeed, not only must there be evidence of a secret trust, but also evidence that the primary donee acted "malo animo" (or fraudulently). This argument was rejected by the Court. If correct, it would lead to the surprising result that if a primary donee faithfully observed the obligation imposed on him or her on the face of the will, there would never be a secret trust at any time in existence. His Honour stated, however, that clear evidence would be needed before the Court would assume that a testator did not mean what he or she had said in a will.

6   ***Re Keen***
      [1937] 1 Ch 236

This interesting case discusses and distinguishes ***Blackwell* (4)**.

A testator appointed three people to be his executors of his will. A clause of the will provided that £10,000 would be paid to the executors to be disposed of "by them among such person, persons or charities as may be notified by me to them during my life time, and in default of notification [the money] shall fall into my residuary estate".

Mr Evershed was one of the trustees and executors. He was told by the testator that he wished to leave a legacy to a person whose name he did not wish to be published in the will, but was given no further information. The testator did say that he would leave a short note with his will, giving the name of the person, address, and the amount which would be paid to the mystery person. On the testator's death, the mystery envelope was opened (a bit like "It's In The Bag"), and that note advised that the sum of £10,000 should be paid to a Miss Griffiths.

Evershed brought a summons to determine whether a validly constituted secret trust had arisen, or whether the £10,000 should fall into the testator's residuary estate.

Farwell J felt there was no need to investigate the law relating to secret trusts. The evidence indicated that none of the trustees or executors of the will had been notified of the recipient of the gift during the lifetime of the testator. As there was an absence of notification required in order to entitle any person to take under the secret trust, then as a necessary consequence the moneys fell into the residuary estate.

Miss Griffiths appealed. The Court of Appeal came to the same conclusion as Farwell J, but for quite different reasons.

Lord Wright felt that Farwell J's decision put too narrow a construction on the word "notified" as used in the will. To take a parallel, a ship which sailed with sealed orders, is still sailing under orders, although the exact terms are not ascertained by the captain until later. Relying on that analogy, His Lordship found that the trustees had the means of knowledge whenever necessary to complete the requirements of a trust. It followed that the trustees and executors had "notification" of the beneficiary of a proposed secret trust within the terms of the testator's will.

That left two questions for the Court to answer:

1.   How far was parol evidence (oral evidence of the meaning and intention of a written document which is generally inadmissible) admissible to define the alleged secret trust? and

2.   How far would such evidence, if admissible, be excluded on the basis that it was inconsistent with the will?

The Court considered that cl 5 of the will (which referred to the sum of £10,000 payable to a party to be notified to the trustees), referred to a trust which had not at the date of the will been established, and which between the date of the will and the date of the testator's death might never be established. The clear principle in relation to secret trusts was that such trusts are created by an expression of the testator's wishes, communicated to and accepted by the trustee. This was so even though in the express terms of the will no such trust arose. Secret trusts are therefore altogether outside the scope of the will.

Blackwell was authority for the admissibility of parol evidence in order to prove the existence of a secret trust. It was clear, however, that in *Blackwell's* case there was no conflict between the express terms of the will, and the actual trusts intended. The evidence in *Blackwell* was not admitted to add to, or vary or contradict what the will said "or to fill-up blanks in it or to specify what was left vague". There was an important qualification upon the common law principles relating to secret trusts which was set out in *Blackwell* itself: a testator cannot reserve to himself or herself a power of making future unwitnessed wills by merely naming a trustee and leaving the purposes of the trust to be supplied afterwards. If people were permitted to dispose of testamentary property in this way, then it would defeat the whole purpose of the Wills Act (UK), which requires that a will be duly executed in front of two witnesses.

Clause 5 of the will in this case contemplated future dispositions, and purported to reserve to the testator the power to make dispositions, without a duly attested codicil, simply by notifying during his lifetime the trustees and executors of his will. This was clearly in breach of the principle laid out by Lord Sumner and was held to be fatal to the appellant's claim.

Just to make things worse for Miss Griffiths, His Lordship held that there was a further objection to the claim for a secret trust. The alleged secret trust was inconsistent with the express terms of the will. Clause 5 referred to a future notification of the beneficiary of the purported secret trust. It was also held that the letter notifying the trustees of the beneficiary *pre-dated* the date of the will. It followed that the purported secret trust was inconsistent with the language with cl 5 of the will.

This case is difficult to distinguish from *Blackwell*. The rule in *Blackwell* did not apply because it was stated that an exception to the rule of secret trusts would arise where a testator purported to reserve a power to establish a secret trust at some time after he or she had executed a will. This hardly seems distinguishable from the situation where a testator purports to establish a secret trust prior to the execution of a will. The objection remains the same — that a testator is avoiding the requirements to have a will properly witnessed and attested. Arguably, the decision in *Re Keen* is incorrect when viewed in light of the broad principle in *Blackwell*.

7 *Re Spencer's Will*
(1887) 57 LT 519

Jonas Spencer died in 1885. In his will he bequeathed to his friends Charles Bradlaugh and George Payne the sum of £500 "upon their applying the said sum in or towards the object or objects privately communicated to them" by him.

In contrast to the other cases so far dealing with secret trusts, neither Charles nor George were appointed as executors of the will. So when Jonas died, Charles and George had to apply to the executors in order to obtain the £500. The executors refused to pay the money on the basis that it was given upon a secret trust. A motion was accordingly made for payment of the legacy.

George filed an affidavit in support of the application for payment of the money. The executors filed affidavits in opposition alleging that the purpose of the legacy was for "the erection of a building for the propagation of socialistic opinions". (In other words, the age-old peril of the dreaded communist hordes.)

Viscount Bristowe in the Court of Appeal held that the evidence of both executors, George and Charles, was admissible. This was because evidence of a gift pursuant to a will on trust was admissible either to establish the existence of a valid secret trust, or in order to challenge the bequest on the basis that it did not conform with the general principles of testamentary disposition. Indeed, this case is limited only to a consideration of the admissibility of parol evidence in investigating the existence, and validity of a secret trust.

In this case, the evidence was not admitted for the purpose of construing the will (which would have been inadmissible); rather it was admitted to show that there were circumstances which induced the testator to make the bequest on conditions, and which would enable the Court to attach to George and Charles an obligation or secret trust. Ample authority for that proposition was found in *Russell v Jackson* (1852) 10 Hare 204. In that case a will conferred upon the legatees an absolute gift for their own benefit. Parol evidence was admissible to prove that the bequest was not an absolute gift, but was made upon conditions arising from the instruction of the testator. That created a secret trust, and the parol evidence was admissible to establish that trust.

In this case, the Court held that it was bound to admit parol evidence. That evidence was admissible to investigate whether the circumstances attendant to the communication by the testator to the legatees of his wishes were such as to enable the Court to enforce the instructions, as a secret trust.

8   *Re Walsh*
(1911) 30 NZLR 1166

The Reverend Michael Walsh made a will leaving all of his property to the Reverend Keenan "according to instructions to be given hereafter". Reverend Walsh subsequently died, and Rev Keenan was appointed executor under the will. On the day before Walsh's death, he instructed Keenan as to how his property was to be disposed. The instructions were taken down, but never signed or witnessed. The instructions directed a small payment to Keenan, another to Walsh's niece, a sum for "masses for the repose of Reverend Walsh's soul", and the balance to be divided equally among a number of named charities.

The issue was whether, in terms of the will, Keenan as executor took the beneficial interest in the estate property for the purposes outlined by Walsh, or, alternatively, as a trustee for Walsh's next of kin. In determining this issue, the Court was required to examine the wording of the will alone, without reference to any outside circumstances or expression from the testator.

It was clear from the will on its face that it imposed an obligation on the executor to apply the estate in such a way as the testator might at a later stage direct. It followed that the plain language of the will negatived any intention that the executor should take a beneficial interest. If the testator had died before he had given any instructions, then the trust intended to be created would have failed. It followed that if the testator had died without giving any instructions, the executor would have held the estate as trustee for the next of kin of Walsh, according to the rules of intestacy. This was an important issue because if the will had given Keenan an absolute beneficial interest, then there was sufficient authority for the proposition that the later instructions would have made Keenan a trustee of a secret trust for the persons outlined in the instructions. Unfortunately, the effect of the will was not to give Keenan a beneficial interest, but to give him the testator's estate upon trust to be declared at some later stage.

In this situation, the will failed to establish a properly constituted trust in favour of those parties named in Walsh's instructions. As a consequence, a resulting trust arose in favour of the next of kin of Walsh in accordance with the rules of intestacy. If the will had given Keenan as executor the absolute beneficial interest in the estate, then the later instructions (accepted by Keenan) would have amounted to an agreement on his part with the testator to hold the estate property upon trust for the parties outlined in Walsh's instructions. In short, no secret trust could arise as the property had not been correctly vested in the primary donee.

9 *Re Colin Cooper*
[1939] Ch 811

Colin Cooper, the testator, appointed Mr Le Neve-Foster as an executor and trustee of his will, together with Messrs Wilson and Troughton. In his will, Mr Cooper bequeathed to Le Neve-Foster and Wilson £5000 "upon trusts which I have already communicated to [my executors and trustees]". Before executing the will, Cooper had advised Wilson that the £5000 would be held and the income from it paid to a widow and her children, and after her death, to fall into Cooper's residuary estate.

Cooper went on a big game shooting expedition in Africa, and contracted a horrible disease from which he died. Two days before his death, he made a further testamentary disposition. In his last will, Cooper increased the £5000 to £10,000 noting that his trustees knew his wishes regarding the sum. The matter came to Court, where the issue was whether the increase in the bequest was valid.

Lord Greene MR lost no time in concluding that it was not possible to give effect to Cooper's obvious desires, "because he has not taken the steps which the law requires to enable that desire to become effective". While recognising that there was a clear intention to establish a secret trust, it was necessary that the intention of the testator be communicated to the trustees, that the trustees accept the instructions of the testator, and that acting on the faith of that acceptance, Cooper made a gift to the trustees. Following *Blackwell* (4), His Lordship held that the necessary elements which are required to be established are intention, communication, and acquiescence.

In the present case there was no question that when the initial legacy of £5000 was bequeathed to the two trustees the requirements of a secret trust had been complied with. The terms had been communicated, the trustees had acquiesced, and the testator made his will upon the faith of that acquiescence. The only trust contemplated at that time was, however, defined by a sum stated as £5000. That was the legacy to which the intention to bequeath related, and also that which was communicated to the trustees.

The Court treated the purported increase in the original bequest as a second bequest, and second purported secret trust for another £5000. In respect of the second bequest, the secondary elements had not been made out. Consequently, the gift of the additional £5000 failed.

10   *Re Young*
[1951] 1 Ch 344

Roger Pilkington Young left his estate to his wife; however, there were conditions on the grant. Roger stated in his will that "it being a condition of this will that after my wife's death she makes a new will leaving my estate for the purposes she knows I desire it to be used — for the permanent aid of distressed gentle folk and similar purposes".

The issue was whether Young had communicated his wishes to his wife during his lifetime, and thereby established a valid trust which was effective to bind the estate.

In an affidavit, Mrs Young stated that before executing his will, Young had discussed with her the devolution of his estate after his death, and that she knew his wishes. Young had explained that he wanted £2000 to be given to his chauffeur and that his land agent and personal friend (a seemingly incongruous relationship) should also receive a further legacy.

Danckwerts J held that there was no doubt what the testator's intentions really were. The question was whether Young had adopted a method of establishing a secret trust which was legally effective. His Honour concluded that the trusts were secret trusts established by parol evidence given by Mrs Young, and that they were effective in respect of the estate. His Honour observed that the trusts were communicated to Mrs Young during the testator's lifetime, and before the date of the will, that they were only communicated to her, and not to her co-executor. Even though the communication of information establishing the secret trust had only been made to one of the executors (that is Mrs Young) the omission to inform the other executor was not material in this case, and did not upset the existence of a secret trust.

11 *Brown v Pourau*
[1995] 1 NZLR 352

Sophie Douglas was a traditional Maori kuia, or elderly woman. She died in 1977. At the time of her death she owned and lived on a ten-acre block of land in Whangamata. Sophie left the Whangamata property absolutely to Emma, her eldest daughter. Emma died in 1986, and she left the property to her son, Mark Pourau, the first defendant in this case.

Proceedings were issued in the High Court in order to upset Sophie's will, in particular, the transfer of the Whangamata property to Emma. The plaintiffs, who were all members of the Douglas' extended family, claimed that the apparently absolute bequest to Emma was impressed with a secret trust "for the family". Therefore, proceedings were issued in order to constitute Emma as a constructive trustee of the property on behalf of herself, and her 11 other brothers and sisters as tenants in common in equal shares.

This appears to be the only reported New Zealand case dealing with secret trusts. Hammond J examines the cases dating from last century, and their application to modern New Zealand. Where the elements of a secret trust have been made out, the Courts protect the beneficiaries' interest by way of a remedial constructive trust. Turning to the standard of proof required in cases of secret trusts, His Honour observed that there had been a lot of debate on whether the very high standard required for proof of fraud was appropriate; whether some intermediate standard was appropriate; or whether the usual civil standard of proof on the balance of probability is applied. It was clear that the three elements of a secret trust "must be established to the reasonable satisfaction of the Court" (see *Blackwell* **(4)**).

The necessary elements required in order to establish a secret trust are intention, communication, and acquiescence. Such requirements are conjunctive. A fully secret trust of land was still valid, independent of the requirement of written evidence under the Contracts Enforcement Act 1956, but in the case of half-secret trusts (that is, secret trusts where part of the trust is evident on the face of the testamentary instrument), such trusts would not be enforceable without further written evidence.

An interesting question which proved to be of difficulty during the course of the trial was whether, once the elements of a secret trust had been made out, uncertainty in respect to the identity of the beneficiaries of the secret trust would prove fatal. In this regard, His Honour held that in such a case the secret trustee could not take beneficially whether or not the terms of the trust were uncertain.

Although there were a number of factors tending to establish the existence of a trust, on the evidence as it stood there was no more than "a state of equipoise". That was not sufficient in a claim of this kind, even on the civil standard of proof, and therefore His Honour found that an intention to create a binding trust in law had not been established.

THE THREE CERTAINTIES

(1) Certainty of intention

12   *Jones v Lock*
(1865) 1 Ch App 25

Robert Jones was an ironmonger who went away on business to Birmingham. When he returned home he was confronted by his infant son's nurse. She said to him "you have come back from Birmingham and have not brought baby anything". Jones replied "Oh, I gave him a pair of boots and now I will give him a handsome present". He then went upstairs and got a cheque for £900 which he had received a few days earlier as repayment for a loan he had given. Jones said "Look you here, I give this to baby; it is for himself".

Jones then put the cheque in the baby's hand. His wife then expressed some concern about the baby tearing it and Jones replied "never mind if he does; it is his own, and he may do what he likes with it". He then took the cheque from the child and locked it in an iron safe.

When he had received the cheque shortly before, Jones had said to his solicitor, Mr Lock, that he intended to add £100 to it and invest it for the benefit of his infant son. Subsequently, he met Lock and said "I am coming to your office on Monday to alter my will so that I can take care of my son" but he died the same day. Lock was an executor of the will. He found the cheque in the iron safe and obtained payment of the money as part of the estate.

Jones already had a will which gave an annuity to his wife and gave the rest of his property for the benefit of his other children by an earlier marriage. His wife brought a claim against the estate on behalf of the infant son for the £900.

At first instance it was held that there had been a valid declaration of trust by the father for the infant and the £900 should be given to him. The decision on appeal was different. Lord Cranworth LC held that Jones, by his actions, had not intended to declare that he held the property in trust for the child. At most his giving the note to the child was symbolic, but it was not his intention to enable the child to bring an action for the £900. He merely meant to say that he would make provision for the child and what he subsequently said to his solicitor was quite consistent with this approach. Jones would have been very surprised if he had been told that he had parted with the £900 and could no longer dispose of it.

In order to create an express private trust, each of the three certainties must be present. Here, there was no certainty of intention. Although it was possible to create a trust orally, it was not certain from Jones' words that he intended to create a trust in favour of his infant son. Moreover, Jones may well have intended to make a gift to his infant son but he had not actually done so. It is well accepted that equity will not correct an incorrectly made gift by holding there to be a trust instead.

13   *Adams v Kensington Vestry*
(1884) 27 Ch D 394

This case involved two appeals, only the second of which is considered here. The outcome of a fairly complicated dispute over who had title to a particular piece of land depended on whether or not George Smith had left land to his wife Harriet absolutely, or whether she got a life interest in the property but otherwise was to hold it on trust for her children.

If the land was simply left to her, then she could do what she liked with it and, in particular, she could sell it to one Charles Adams, who could then sell it on to the Kensington Vestry. If Harriet Smith held it on trust for her children then she could only sell it with their consent.

The provisions of George Smith's will included the following:

> I give, devise, and bequeath all my real and personal estate and effects whatever and wheresoever unto and to the absolute use of my dear wife Harriet Smith, her heirs, executors, administrators, and assigns, in full confidence that she will do what is right as to the disposal thereof between my children, either in her lifetime or by will after her decease.

Baggally LJ began his judgment by noting that were it not for a particular line of authority, the interpretation of the will would not be at all difficult. The authority he was referring to had established the notion of the "precatory trust". Where a testator had left property to another expressing his or her confidence, belief, desire, hope, recommendation, or similar such words that the property would be used in a particular way, it had been held to establish a precatory trust. The Courts had previously been very quick to find such expressions to indicate the intention of the testator to create a binding trust.

Baggally LJ "thoroughly and entirely" concurred with the decision in *Lambe v Eames* (1871) LR 6 Ch 597, in which it was said:

Now the question is, whether those words create any trust affecting the property; and in hearing case after case cited, I could not help feeling that the officious kindness of the Court of Chancery in interposing trusts where in many cases the father of the family never meant to create trusts, must have been a very cruel kindness indeed. I am satisfied that the testator in this case would have been shocked to think that any person calling himself a friend could file a bill in this Court, and, under pretence of benefiting the children, have taken the administration of the estate from the wife.

Cotton LJ said that the old authorities had gone a great deal too far in holding that certain words appearing in a will were sufficient to create a trust. It is necessary to look at the whole of a will in order to see the true effect of its words and what the intention of the testator was. In the present circumstances, George Smith's intention, as he plainly says, was to leave the property to his wife absolutely. The fact that he expressed the confidence that Harriet would do what was right was merely a confidence and did not impose a trust on his wife.

14   *Re Kayford Ltd*
[1975] 1 WLR 279

Kayford Ltd carried on a mail order business in bedding, quilts, stretch covers for chairs and such like. Its customers either paid in full in advance or paid a deposit. Kayford began experiencing difficulties in getting supplies and it entered into an arrangement with a manufacturing company named Monaco Manufacturing (Household Textiles) Ltd.

After a particularly successful advertising campaign by Kayford, it found itself again unable to obtain supplies to meet all its orders. Monaco, which had become Kayford's main supplier, had found itself in serious financial difficulties, even though Kayford had already provided it financial support to the extent of some £80,000. The managing director of Kayford became concerned for his customers, who had sent, and were still sending, money for goods ordered. If Monaco went into liquidation, it would affect not only Kayford's ability to deliver the goods but also its solvency.

The managing director of Kayford was advised by accountants to set up a separate bank account to be called "Customers' Trust Deposit Account". All further money paid by customers for goods not yet delivered would be paid into this account and withdrawn only when the goods had been delivered. Thus, if Kayford had to go into liquidation, these sums of money could be refunded to the customers who had paid them.

The managing director then spoke to Kayford's bank manager, and they agreed that a deposit account in Kayford's name which had not been used for some time should be used for this purpose. The account was £47 in credit. Subsequently, £37,872.42 was deposited by Kayford, all of it being money paid in advance by customers.

Monaco stopped making deliveries. Kayford then resolved to go into voluntary liquidation. The accountants discovered that their advice had not been followed to the letter: a new bank account had not been opened, only an old one had been used. The account was also not called "Customers' Trust Deposit Account".

The question for the Court was whether the money in the bank account, apart from the £47 and the interest on it, was held on trust for those who paid it or whether it formed part of the general assets of the company. If the money was held on trust for the customers, then they got it back. If it formed part of the general assets of the company, then the customers had to stand in line with all the other unsecured creditors of the company and they probably wouldn't get anything at all.

Despite the fact that the accountant's advice was not strictly followed, Megarry J held that there was clearly an intention that there should be a trust. He said that it was well settled that a trust can be created without using the words "trust" or "confidence" or the like. The question is whether in substance a sufficient intention to create a trust has been manifested. In the present circumstances, the intention to create a trust had been made clear and accordingly the customers got their money back.

15   *Belton v CIR*
[1959] NZLR 1372

Mr Belton was in trouble with the tax department. He had been assessed additional income tax for the years 1948 to 1956 for the sale and purchase of certain sheep. Mr Belton claimed that the income he had received was as a trustee for his infant children under a trust which he had set up. In 1957 he had entered into a formal trust deed in which he declared the trust which, he claimed, had existed since 1948.

In 1948 he had purchased 60 hoggets in his infant son's name and his instructions to stock and freezing companies were that the sheep purchased were to be charged to his young son and that the proceeds of their sale were to be credited to the same person. Further, he obtained a safe deposit box at the Bank of New South Wales in the son's name. When he had more children, he opened further accounts in their names. Apparently he grazed the sheep in a separate part of the farm and when his elder son began to show an aptitude for the piano, he bought him a piano out of the money in the fund.

Belton had "borrowed" all the money from the fund at one time. But his accountant had recorded it as a loan without interest in Belton's balance sheet and Belton had paid it back.

In determining whether a trust had been created, the Court held that no specific words were required to do so. A trust can be created by any language which is clear enough to show an intention to create it. It may even be inferred from conduct, at least in so far as conduct may be taken into account along with such words as there may be for determining the settlor's intention. In the present circumstances, factors such as the safe deposit box and the purchase of the piano out of the specific funds supported the existence of a trust. While there were no specific words declaring a trust, it could be inferred from all the circumstances that a trust had been created.

16   *Paul v Constance*
[1977] 1 WLR 527

Dennis Constance separated from his wife Bridget in 1965. In 1967 he met Doreen Paul. They lived together but did not marry. Dennis Constance died in 1974.

In 1969 Constance had been injured at work and he successfully claimed compensation from his employers. He received damages in the sum of £950. Dennis discussed with Doreen what to do with the money and they decided it should go into a bank account. They went to see the bank manager and discussed opening a new account. At some stage in the interview Constance revealed that they were not married and the bank manager then said to him "Well, it will be in your name only then?" and Constance replied "Yes".

Constance then asked the manager what could be done about allowing Mrs Paul to draw on the account. Doreen could draw on the account if she used a note with Constance's signature on it authorising the withdrawal.

Between opening the bank account and Constance's death some 13 months later, other sums were paid into the account, in particular, their bingo winnings. Nevertheless, when the account was closed on the death of Constance, the balance consisted largely of the initial sum of £950. There had also been one withdrawal of £150, the remainder of which was apparently divided between Constance and Mrs Paul after it had been used to buy

Christmas presents and food. Apparently Constance had also said on more than one occasion, "The money is as much yours as mine".

Constance died intestate and, under the law relating to intestacy, all his property was to go to his estranged wife, Bridget. Mrs Paul claimed that the money in the bank account had been held on trust for the benefit of both her and Constance jointly. Bridget Constance claimed, however, that the whole of the fund was the property of Constance at the time of his death and as such became part of his estate after it.

In order to resolve this dispute, the Court examined whether there had been a sufficient certainty of intention manifested by Constance to create the trust claimed by Mrs Paul. It was acknowledged that Constance never said anything remotely like "I am now disposing of my interest in this fund so that you, Mrs Paul, now have a beneficial interest in it". Counsel for Mrs Paul was quick to remind the Court that it was dealing with simple people, unaware of the subtleties of equity, but understanding their own domestic situation very well. Counsel for the Mrs Constance argued that, although a person may say in clear and unmistakable terms that he or she intends to make a gift to another person, that does not necessarily mean there has been a declaration of trust. This is in accordance with the well-settled principle that equity will not perfect an imperfect gift.

The Court ruled that there was no suggestion of a gift by transfer in the present circumstances. The question for the Court was essentially one of fact and the trial Judge had decided that it was the intention of Constance to create a trust in which both he and Mrs Paul were interested. The question on appeal was therefore whether there was sufficient evidence to justify this conclusion of fact.

The English Court of Appeal held that the words used by Constance, the interview with the bank manager when the account was opened, the deposit of bingo winnings into the account and the one withdrawal from the account for the benefit of both Constance and Mrs Paul were sufficient evidence to support the trial Judge's conclusion. Scarman J noted, however, that this may very well be a borderline case, since it was difficult to pinpoint a specific moment of declaration.

17   ***White v White***
          (1909) 28 NZLR 129

Daniel White was not a learned man, if the following document of his is
anything to go by. He wrote:

> Mr White desire That Mr Pisey get his gold chain and green stone and to stop the
> note that Monday and Sim has got regarding property make it now void the
> property to be carried on the same as it is, when it become free the property to be
> between Lizzie and Danney and Willies two sones and Mary to have a small
> portion of what left.

On Mr White's death, proceedings were brought before the Supreme Court of
New Zealand to ascertain what on earth this document was and what it was
supposed to mean. The first question was whether it was intended to be
testamentary, since Mr White's solicitors held a will which was executed prior
to the above document. As Mr White had had the document witnessed in
accordance with the requirements of the Wills Act and given that Mr White
wrote it before he was about to undergo an operation, the Court held that in
the circumstances the document was testamentary and effected a revocation of
the earlier will.

The Court further held, however, that the bequest to Mary was void for
uncertainty. A person may express his or her intention to create a trust in the
clearest of terms, but will fail to do so if he or she does not describe what
property is to be the subject of the trust with sufficient precision. There must
be some identifiable property to which the trust can attach. In this case, "a
small portion of what is left" was held to be too vague to provide the requisite
certainty of subject-matter. It was impossible for the trustees to identify
properly how much it was that Mary was supposed to get.

(2) Certainty of subject-matter

18   ***Sprange v Barnard***
          (1789) 2 Bro CC 58

Susannah Crapps left the following will:

> This is my last will and testament at my death, for my husband Thomas Sprange,
> to be willed to him the sum of £300, which is now in the joint stock annuities,
> for his sole use; and, at his death, the remaining part of what is left, that he does
> not want for his own wants and use, to be divided between my brother John

Crapps, my sister Wickenden, and my sister Bauden, to be equally divided between them.

At Susannah's death, her husband filed for the £300. Susannah's brother and two sisters argued that he could not have it all, that he was only to have it for his life and that he could only use it for necessities.

Lord Arden stated that in order to raise a trust, the property of the trust must be certain. In the present case it was impossible to execute the particular trust. The phrase "the remaining part of what is left, that he does not want for his own wants and use" was too vague. It did not relate to any identifiable property and certainly could not restrain Sprange from spending the money in whatever way he chose. Therefore Sprange was entitled to the £300 absolutely.

19   *Boyce v Boyce*
(1849) 16 Sim 476

Richard Boyce made a will in which he left two houses to his trustees on trust. They were to convey one to his daughter Maria "whichever she may think proper to choose or select". The other house was then to go to his other daughter Charlotte. Maria died before her father and accordingly did not make a choice about which house she wanted. The question for the Court was whether the other daughter, Charlotte, was able to get one of the houses.

The Vice-Chancellor held that the gift in favour of Charlotte was a gift not of all her father's freehold houses but of all his other freehold houses which Maria did not choose. It was only a gift of the house that would remain provided that Maria chose one of them. No choice had been or could have been made by Maria and it was therefore impossible to ascertain with any certainty the property which was the subject of the gift in favour of Charlotte. Accordingly the gift had to fail.

20   *Re Golay's Will Trusts*
[1965] 1 WLR 969

Adrian Golay left a will in which he directed his executors to allow "Tossy" (Mrs Florence Bridgewater) to "enjoy one of my flats during her lifetime and to receive a reasonable income from my other properties".

The executor of the will sought a declaration about exactly what he should do in relation to these directions. One of the questions the Court had to determine was whether the gift of reasonable income failed for uncertainty. The essential difficulty was that no person had been specified to quantify what a reasonable income was.

The Court thought the answer lay in whether Mr Golay had given a sufficient indication of his intention to provide an effective determinate of his intentions so that the Court, in applying that determinate, could give effect to his intentions. There needed to be an objective yardstick.

The Court thought that the yardstick indicated by the testator was not what he or any other specified person subjectively considered to be reasonable, but what is identified objectively as a reasonable income. Ungoed-Thomas J thought that the Courts were constantly involved in making such objective assessments of what is reasonable and accordingly the direction in the will was not defeated by uncertainty.

(3) Certainty of object

21 *Re Gulbenkian's Settlement Trusts*
[1970] AC 508

Calouste Gulbenkian, while loving his son dearly, did not trust him with money. Accordingly, he made a settlement expressed to be in consideration of his natural love and affection for Nubar, but including what is commonly described as a "spendthrift" clause. The idea behind such a clause is that a wise and fiscally responsible person is made trustee of certain money, invests it and distributes the income for the benefit of the silly and capricious child. The silly and capricious child cannot blow it all themselves.

Unfortunately, Calouste Gulbenkian's solicitor was not the most gifted of commercial drafters. He had simply taken a standard form settlement straight out of a law journal and used that. Clause 2 of the settlement provided that the trustees "shall", during the life of Nubar Gulbenkian:

> At their absolute discretion pay all or any part of the income of the property hereby settled in the investments for the time being representing the same (hereinafter called the Trust Fund) to or apply the same for the maintenance and personal support or benefit of all or any one or more to the exclusion of the other or others of the following persons ...

Among these persons were (as well as Nubar himself, his wife and children):

> Any person or persons in whose house or apartments or in whose company or under whose care or control or by or with whom the said Nubar Sakis Gulbenkian may from time to time be employed or residing.

The sole question for the House of Lords was whether the clause was void for uncertainty in that it did not describe the recipients of the intended settlement in sufficiently certain terms. Lord Upjohn gave the leading speech of the House.

He began by noting that it was agreed by everyone that the trustee's discretion to distribute the fund's income was a "mere" or "bare" power, or a "power collateral". The trustees could exercise their discretion to distribute the money to any of the beneficiaries they chose, but they did not have to do so. If they did not exercise the power, then the money would eventually fall by means of a default clause to be held on trusts under a separate part of the settlement. (The same outcome would eventuate if the clause was void for uncertainty as well.)

Lord Upjohn then commented that it was odd that there was no long line of authority on the right test for deciding whether a mere power is void for not being able to ascertain the class of potential beneficiaries with sufficient certainty. However, cases recent to that time had established this test:

> Can you say with sufficient certainty whether any given individual is or is not a member of the class?

The point of this test is that you do not have to able to list every member of the class in advance. Lord Upjohn then went on to consider whether the clause satisfied this test for certainty, although he did not decide at that point whether it was in fact the right test.

He said that the first task is to attempt to ascertain the settlor's intention by reading the clause literally and in accordance with the ordinary rules of grammar. Sometimes, however, the drafter is more or less illiterate and this approach is not particularly helpful. It is then for the Court to give a reasonable meaning to the language if it can do so by "judicial knowledge", "experience", and "innate common sense".

In the present situation, the part of the clause causing the most difficulty was the second excerpt quoted above. Lord Upjohn paraphrased it as follows:

> [A]nd any person or persons by whom the son may from time to time be employed and any person or persons with whom the son from time to time is residing whether in the house or apartments of such person or persons or whether in the company or under the care or control of such person or persons.

Lord Upjohn thought that, although the clause created difficulty, mere difficulty was something the Court of Chancery dealt with all the time. He did not think that the clause was so difficult that it could not meet the test that he had postulated.

The Court of Appeal, however, had been propounding a weaker test than that which Lord Upjohn had applied (without deciding whether it was the right one) in this case. As the clause had met the strong test, it was not really necessary for the House of Lords to consider whether it would have met the weaker one: there was enough for the House of Lords to decide the case and dispose of the appeal.

Nevertheless, Lord Upjohn felt that he should examine the weaker test and see whether it was the right one for future cases. This test was:

> Can you say any one person is clearly within the class of beneficiaries, even though it may be difficult to say about other people whether or not they are in the category?

The argument supporting this test is that, with a mere power, as soon as the trustees have at least one person to whom they can distribute the money, then they should be able to do so if they want to. It doesn't matter that there are other people about whom it might be difficult to say whether or not they are potential recipients as well.

Lord Upjohn rejected this approach. It was unsupported by authority and, he claimed, unsupported by principle as well. He gave his essential reason for this at the end of the judgment. Those people who received money by means of the default clause, in the event that the trustees did not exercise their power to distribute the money, were able to restrain the trustees by means of legal action from choosing someone out of the defined class. Therefore, the trustees, or the Court, must be able to say with certainty who is within and who is outside the class.

While it is all fine and well if the trustees decide to give the money to somebody obviously within the class, what if they decide to give it to somebody who does not obviously fit the criteria of the class? The fundamental point is that the question of whether the clause is certain must be decided before the trustees start applying it. Certainty cannot depend on to whom the trustees decide to give the money. Lord Reid put it this way:

> If the donee of the power (whether or not he has any duty) desires to exercise it in favour of a particular person it must be possible to determine whether that particular person is or is not within the class of objects of the power. And it must be possible to determine the validity of the power immediately it comes into

operation. It cannot be valid if the person whom the donee happens to choose is clearly within the objects but void if it is doubtful whether that is so.

Lord Upjohn also considered the proposition that the test for certainty in relation to trust powers (where the trustees *must* distribute the money, although they can choose to whom) should be the same as that for mere powers (where they *can* distribute the money but they don't have to). The test for trust powers had been whether it was possible to draw up a complete list of members of the class. Lord Upjohn decided that it should not change and he made some general observations.

He began by stating that if a settlor directs his or her trustees to make provision for "John Smith" then it must be possible to identify who "John Smith" is. If the settlor knows three John Smiths then neither the trustees nor the Court can guess which John Smith should get the money. The clause must fail for uncertainty.

Then, what if the settlor directs that an amount of money should be equally divided between members of a particular class? The Court and the trustees must be able to identify the class just as much as they must be able to identify "John Smith"; they can't take a guess at it. For example, if the settlor directs his or her trustees to divide an amount of money equally between "my old friends", unless the use of the term "my old friends" is some special code for certain clearly identifiable people of which the trustees are aware, then the clause is void for uncertainty.

The reason for this is that if two or three people turned up who could show they were the settlor's "old friends", the trustees could not pay them either the whole or any defined part of the fund and say that they were acting in accordance with the settlor's intentions. To claim the whole fund the friends would need to prove that they were the only members of the class of the settlor's "old friends". Nor could they claim a defined part of the fund. It would be impossible for the trustees to ascertain the number of shares to be divided equally. The trustees do not have any authority to distribute to a smaller class than that stated by the settlor.

If the settlor does not direct an equal division of the money among the class but gives a power of selection to the trustees, then the same principles must apply. The trustees have a duty to select the recipients of the money from among the class defined by the settlor. They have no authority to select the recipients from a smaller class than that, such as merely those who have put their hand up. So if the class is insufficiently defined, then the clause must fail for uncertainty.

Lord Upjohn was careful at this point to draw a distinction between uncertainty in terms of an ambiguous definition of the class by virtue of the settlor's language, and uncertainty in actually drawing up a list because it is uncertain where members of the class are or if they are still alive. This distinction has been coined the distinction between "conceptual" or "linguistic" uncertainty and "evidential" uncertainty. In the case of linguistic or conceptual uncertainty, the clause is void. In the case of evidential uncertainty, the clause is valid, and the trustees can simply pay the share of the money for those people they are not sure about into Court.

The essential difference between trust powers and mere powers is that with trust powers (unlike mere powers) the trustees must distribute the money to people in the class and there is no default clause if they do not do so. If the trustees do not exercise the power then the Court will exercise it for them. This is not the case with mere powers, because the trustees do not have to distribute the fund to the members of the class but can leave it to fall to the default trust. Lord Upjohn concluded by stating that this essential difference meant that the principles applicable to mere powers should not be applied to trust powers. Accordingly, the old authority stood and, in order for a trust power to be sufficiently certain, it was necessary for the Court to be able to draw up a complete list of members of the class.

22   *McPhail v Doulton*
[1971] AC 424

Bertram Baden established a trust fund for the benefit of the staff of Matthew Hall & Co Ltd. If the trust failed, then Robert McPhail and two others got the trust money as residuary trustees. They went to Court to get a ruling that the trust deed was void in that it did not describe the potential beneficiaries with sufficient certainty. Peter Doulton and several others (comprising the trustees of the trust fund, the company itself and some of the staff) attempted to stop them.

The crucial clauses of the trust deed were as follows:

9(a) The trustees shall apply the net income of the fund in making at their absolute discretion grants to or for benefit of any of the officers and employees or ex-officers or ex-employees of the company or to any relatives or dependants of any such persons in such amounts at such times and on such conditions (if any) as they think fit and any such grant may at their discretion be made by payment to the beneficiary or to any institution or person to be applied for his or her benefit and in the latter case the trustees shall be under no obligation to see to the application of the money.

(b)   The trustees shall not be bound to exhaust the income of any year or other period in making such grants as aforesaid and any income not so applied shall be dealt with as provided by clause 6(a) hereof.

[6(a)   All moneys in the hands of the trustees and not required for the immediate service of the fund may be placed in a deposit or current account with any bank or banking house in the name of the trustees or may be invested as hereinafter provided.]

(c)   The trustees may realise any investments representing accumulations of income and apply the proceeds as though the same were income of the fund and may also (but only with the consent of all the trustees) at any time prior to the liquidation of the fund realise any other part of the capital of the fund which in the opinion of the trustees it is desirable to realise in order to provide benefits for which the current income of the fund is insufficient.

10   All benefits being at the absolute discretion of the trustees, no person shall have any right title or interest in the fund otherwise than pursuant to the exercise of such discretion, and nothing herein contained shall prejudice the right of the company to determine the employment of any officer or employee.

The first question for the House of Lords involved the proper categorisation of the trustees' powers. Were they "mere" or "bare" powers or were they trust powers? The second question arose if the House of Lords decided that the powers were trust powers. On the authority at that time, the tests for the validity of mere powers and trust powers were different. The test for the certainty of objects for trust powers was whether a complete list of all possible beneficiaries could be drawn up. The test for the certainty of mere powers was that laid down by Lord Upjohn in *Re Gulbenkian's Settlement Trusts* (21).

Lord Wilberforce began by noting that the distinction between trusts and mere powers was often artificial and that it was unsatisfactory that the validity of a disposition should turn on such distinctions. He agreed that the basic difference was that there was no obligation to exercise a mere power but that a trust power was mandatory. However, that proposition did not contain an exhaustive comparison of the respective duties.

Lord Wilberforce gave the example of a trustee of an employee's benefit fund with a mere power to distribute money. Such a trustee exercising this power can be controlled by the Court if he or she exercises it capriciously or outside the scope permitted by the trust. Moreover, such a trustee would surely find out the permissible area of selection and consider responsibly, in individual cases, whether the purported beneficiary was within the power and whether, in relation to the other claimants, a particular grant was appropriate.

A trustee with a duty to distribute among an extremely large class would almost certainly not draw up a complete list of names but would approach the matter by way of categorisation. Lord Wilberforce thought that if such a trustee acted diligently in this manner then it could be hardly said that he or she was not carrying out the trust.

In short, it is possible to underestimate the fiduciary obligation of the trustee with a mere power and to overstate the responsibilities of the holder of a trust power. The difference between mere powers and trust powers is probably more one of degree than principle.

In deciding the nature of the relevant powers accorded to the trustees in the present case, Lord Wilberforce stated that none of Their Lordships had much doubt about the fact that they were trust powers.

Lord Wilberforce then went on to consider the appropriate test for the validity of trust powers. The difficulty was the decision of the English Court of Appeal in *IRC v Broadway Cottages Trust* [1955] Ch 20. In that case, it was held that in order for a trust power to be valid, it must be possible to draw up a complete list of the members of the class. The reason for this was that if the trustees failed to perform their function, the Court must step in and do so. The Court can only distribute the trust fund by ordering an equal distribution among all the beneficiaries, according to the maxim "equity is equality", and it was necessary for the Court to have a complete list of beneficiaries in order to do this.

Lord Wilberforce was critical of this approach. It was not necessary for the Court to execute a trust power only by an equal distribution. In fact, often that is the last thing the settlor intended: equal division among all would probably produce a result beneficial to none. Lord Wilberforce then examined a number of older authorities, which were termed the "relation" cases, in which the Court did not distribute equally but exercised some kind of discretion or judgment.

Lord Wilberforce noted that nowhere in Lord Upjohn's speech in *Re Gulbenkian* was there an endorsement of *Broadway Cottages*. Moreover, the passages in Lord Upjohn's speech which appeared to support *Broadway Cottages* were apparently merely leading up to a rejection of the broader test for the validity of powers propounded by the Court of Appeal.

Accordingly, Lord Wilberforce rejected the *Broadway Cottages* reasoning and adopted the *Gulbenkian* test for validity in respect of mere powers as the correct test for the validity of trust powers. Therefore, a trust is valid if it can be said with certainty that any given individual is or is not a member of the class. If the Court is called upon to exercise a trustee's trust power in the event of his or her default, it will do so in a manner designed to best give effect to the settlor's intention. This might be by appointing a new trustee, or by directing representatives of the different classes of beneficiaries to draw up a scheme, or even directing the trustee to distribute in a particular manner if the basis on which to do so is evident.

Lord Wilberforce concluded by emphasising the value of Lord Upjohn's linguistic/evidential certainty distinction. He then noted that there might be a third case where the meaning of the trust deed is patently clear but that the class of beneficiaries is so hopelessly wide that it does not really form a class at all. Such a trust may be "administratively unworkable" and may fail for that reason. Lord Wilberforce gave the example of "all the residents of Greater London". The majority view, then, was to send the case back to the Court below to apply the right test.

Lords Hodson and Guest dissented. Both agreed that the trust deed created a trust power but they fundamentally disagreed with the assimilation of the test for validity with that used for mere powers.

Lord Hodson stated that the Court could not assume the kind of powers suggested by Lord Wilberforce in executing a trust when the trustees failed to do so. It could only distribute equally; it could not exercise a discretion which had been placed on the trustees only. Moreover, he stressed that the trustees have no authority to select the recipients from a smaller class than that defined by the settlor. The test for validity of mere powers meant that the trustees would be selecting from this narrower class.

23   *Re Baden's Trust Deed (No 2)*
[1973] Ch 9

The question of the validity of Bertram Baden's trust deed was referred back to the first instance Court for the application of the new test for the validity of trust powers after the decision in *McPhail v Doulton* **(22)**. The decision of Brightman J was appealed to the English Court of Appeal.

It is fair to say that Sachs LJ was a little unhappy with the amount of time the matter had spent before the Courts — some ten years in fact. He noted also that McPhail and the others were probably fortified by the fact that their costs were coming out of the trust funds. Sachs LJ said with a slight hint of sarcasm:

> At the patent risk of this judgment being in due course attacked as emotive — in other words, of my having lifted my eyes from the delectably refined arguments

put before us to look at the background situation in which they have been adduced — I feel impelled to observe that the situation lacks attraction.

After getting this off his chest, he went on to apply the test set down in *McPhail*: "can it be said with certainty that any individual is or is not a member of the class?".

Counsel for McPhail argued that the Court must always be able to say whether any given individual is *not* within the relevant class as well as being able to say whether he or she is in it. In response to this argument, Sachs LJ said that it was essential to bear in mind the difference between the question of conceptual certainty and evidential difficulties.

The Court is never defeated by evidential uncertainty. Once the class of persons to be benefited is conceptually certain then it becomes a question of fact to be determined on evidence whether any individual has, on inquiry, proved to be within that class. Sachs LJ said that the suggestion that the trusts could be invalid because it might be impossible to prove of a given individual that he or she was not in the relevant class is wrong.

Sachs LJ went on then to consider whether the terms "dependants" and "relatives" were conceptually uncertain. He noted that once the Court reached a conclusion that the widest meaning attributable to those words did not produce uncertainty then the trust was not void for uncertainty. As for the word "dependant", Sachs LJ thought that the definition "any one wholly or partly dependent on the means of another" would do. As regards "relatives", he said that a person is a relative of another if both trace legal descent from a common ancestor.

Megaw LJ substantially agreed with Sachs LJ. He thought too much emphasis had been placed on the words "or is not". He considered that the test was satisfied if, as regards at least a substantial number of objects, it can be said with certainty that they fall within the trust. Sachs and Megaw LJJ therefore appear to alter the test slightly. It is apparently sufficient if it can be said of any given individual that he or she is:

1. within the class;

2. outside the class; or

3. it is not proven whether he or she is in the class or out of it.

Stamp LJ disagreed, stating that one had to be able to say with certainty of any individual whether they were in or out. Any other approach would introduce by the backdoor the test which was rejected in *Re **Gulbenkian's Settlement***

Trusts **(21)**. Stamp LJ gave a narrower definition of relations, being "nearest blood relations" and therefore the trust deed was still sufficiently certain.

(4) Court's exercise of control

24   *New Zealand Dairy Board v New Zealand Co-operative Dairy Co Ltd*
[1999] 2 NZLR 355 (HC)

This case concerned the validity of deeds entered into by the NZDB and three other parties relating to the ownership of trademarks or brands. The three other parties were NZCDC, who owned the "Anchor" brand, TCCDC, who owned the "Fernleaf" brand, and MP who owned the "Mainland" brand.

The trade marks were assigned to the NZDB so that it could market the brands internationally on behalf of the whole dairy industry. The three other parties wished to protect the value of the trade marks and consequently each entered into a similar, but independent, set of arrangements with the NZDB.

The arrangements comprised a series of deeds entered into over a period of time, one of which was a "pool deed". It arose out of the fact that the NZDB had spent a lot of money promoting the trade marks. They were concerned that the benefit of this expenditure should be available to the whole dairy industry in the event of re-assignment of the trade marks. Consequently, the pool deed provided that each of the other parties was to hold the respective trade marks on trust for itself and other dairy companies. A dairy company was "any other person or company engaged in the manufacture of dairy produce for export". The deed provided for the establishment of a marketing pool for the brands in order to utilise the international rights under the trade marks.

The dairy industry was subsequently concerned that the value of the trade mark would not be adequately protected by the arrangements contained in the pool deed. So the NZDB and the other three parties agreed on three "cancellation deeds" which would cancel all the respective earlier deeds. It was intended that the cancellation deeds would provide for the NZDB and its successors to hold the full international rights to the various brands free of all obligations under the earlier deeds.

All the co-operative dairy companies who both at the time and in the past had supplied the NZDB with dairy products for export consented to the cancellation deed.

The Court noted that in each case the pool deeds could be construed as having created rights for dairy companies other than those directly involved, and for persons entering the field or companies which might be formed in the future. This was a problem because if the effect of the deeds was to create enforceable rights for third parties who were not yet in existence, and if the NZDB and the other parties needed to get the consent of those parties for whom the benefit of the deeds was intended, then the cancellation deed would be ineffective.

This gave rise to several issues. The first was one of privity: whether persons named but not parties to the deed were able to enforce their rights under them. If they were not, it was argued that the parties to the arrangements were free to alter or cancel them without the need for consent.

It should be noted that in relation to two brands the Contracts (Privity) Act 1982 had not been enacted at the time the deeds were entered into and therefore it did not apply.

The Court considered whether or not the contemplated beneficiaries could rely on the status of being a beneficiary under an alleged trust to avoid the requirement of privity. It referred to the proposition made in some earlier cases that, where a contract involves the conveyance of property to a recipient to hold in trust for a third party, the rule of privity does not apply. It then endorsed the proposition that a person not in existence at the time of the creation of a trust may still acquire rights under the trust. This rule was, however, subject to considerations such as the rule against perpetuities.

The Court held that, in light of the intentions expressed in the deeds, prima facie a trust had arisen (or an obligation that equity would enforce). This was because neither party to the original deed was free to dispose of the property and there was a clear covenant to hold the property concerned on trust in the event of a contingency occurring. It was therefore necessary to consider the other preconditions of an effective trust.

While the plaintiff raised arguments to the contrary the Court held that the trust property was both in existence and clearly defined. The plaintiff also contended that there was a lack of certainty as to the third parties qualifying and the beneficial interests of the cestuis que trust, as there was no indication as to the extent of each beneficiary's beneficial interest. Both these arguments failed on the interpretation of the agreements.

The Court accepted the argument that the trust should fail because there was insufficient provision for the management or administration of the trust property in the terms and conditions of the various deeds. The Court considered that the nature of the property concerned was such that it required a considerable amount of investment. Additionally, commercial and subjective decisions needed to be made in order to maintain the value of the property and satisfy the needs of the industry.

It was noted that traditionally the Courts had not permitted trustees to carry on businesses unless this was clearly provided for in the setting up of the trust. In addition, the execution of the trust is under the control of the Court and the trust therefore must be defined in such a way that the Court can control or enforce it. It would be very difficult for the Court to exercise control in this case.

Further, the Court considered that it was not appropriate to confer the statutory powers of the NZDB, in the event that Parliament had removed those powers, on one of the other three parties who were the only possible trustees (in the event of the contingency arising). Also these third parties would have substantial commercial interests of their own which would give rise to conflicts of interest.

The Court distinguished the situation where "the ordinary principles of trust management provide a degree of guidance to a trustee and which allow the Court to have confidence in the management of such a trust", from the situation in this case where questions of policy arise "which are not determinable on undisputed principles".

The trust having thus failed for want of certainty in relation to its administration, the Court held that the NZDB and other the parties were free to modify or cancel the agreements.

In obiter, the Court noted that the NZDB and other parties would also be free to alter or cancel the agreements because of the rule against perpetuities. At common law a trust must vest "within a life in being and 21 years". The Court considered that a corporation could not be regarded as a "life in being" and therefore the trust would be void at common law. However, the effect of the Perpetuities Act 1964 was that, rather, the class of persons in whom the benefit of the trust would vest had to be ascertained within 21 years from the date of the pool deed. This period had passed in relation to the "Anchor" and the "Fernleaf" brands by the time the case was heard. Thus all the possible beneficiaries were ascertained, and as they had consented to the cancellation deed, the Court held that it should be valid.

In relation to those deeds executed after the Contracts (Privity) Act the beneficiaries contemplated by the deeds were considered to be entitled to have enforceable interests by virtue of the Act. The deeds were nevertheless regarded as void for uncertainty for the same reasons as the other deeds.

These deeds gave rise to further considerations. Because of their timing, the 21-year period had not expired and therefore the parties were not all ascertained; as there may still be dairy companies which had not yet come into existence. So this alternative solution available in respect of the other brands was not available in relation to this brand.

The Court decided to approve the cancellation deed under s 7 of the Contracts (Privity) Act.

THE BENEFICIARY PRINCIPLE

General

25   *Morice v Bishop of Durham*
(1804) 9 Ves Jr 399

Little is known of Ann Cracherode except that when she died in 1801 her will, after giving several legacies to her next of kin, directed that all her personal estate should be bequeathed to the Bishop of Durham upon trust to dispose of it to such objects of benevolence and liberality as the Bishop, in his discretion, should approve. The next of kin, unhappy with the legacy, brought an action to have the bequest to the Bishop declared void.

The Master of the Rolls analysed the general principles of the law of trusts, and stated that there can be no trust over which the Court cannot assume control: that is, there must be somebody in whose favour the Court can decree performance. This means that every trust must have a definite object. The exception to this is charitable trusts. Where a charitable purpose is expressed, however general, the bequest shall not fail on account of any uncertainty of the object.

The question then became whether Ann Cracherode's trust was a trust for charity. Do purposes of "liberality and benevolence" mean the same as objects of charity? Here the Court decided that the words "charity" and "charitable" did not occur in the will, and, moreover, the words used were not synonymous with those. For these reasons it was decided that the trust could not be said to be for charitable purposes, and as it was too indefinite to be disposed of to any other purpose it followed that the trust failed. The residue was ordered to be distributed among the next of kin.

This establishes the classic rule of the beneficiary principle: that a trust must have a beneficiary, and if there is no beneficiary the trust must fail. This principle, is of course subject to exceptions.

26   *Re Endacott*
[1959] 3 All ER 562

Mr Endacott made a somewhat unusual gift in his will. After making several bequests to his son he concluded his will by stating that he left the residue to the North Tawton Devon Parish Council for the purpose of providing some useful memorial to himself. Quite what he had in mind is not clear. The question before the English Court of Appeal was whether that residuary gift could take effect.

Lord Evershed noted that a trust must, in English law, have ascertained or ascertainable beneficiaries. The exception is if the trust is charitable; or if it is uncharitable, but public in nature, making it enforceable by the Court. Such exceptions could be classified as:

1.   trusts for the erection or maintenance of monuments or graves;

2.   trusts for the saying of masses;

3.   trusts for the maintenance of particular animals;

4.   trusts for the benefit of unincorporated associations (although this group is more doubtful); and

5.   miscellaneous cases.

His Lordship noted that these anomalous exceptions ought not to be extended.

Although Mr Endacott's gift was specific in the sense that it indicated a purpose capable of expression, it was far too wide and uncertain to fall within any of the above categories, which would exempt it from the beneficiary principle.

The Court of Appeal also held that the purported trust did not fall within the charity exception to the beneficiary principle. The mere fact that the gift was to the Parish Council did not render it charitable because the activities of the Parish Council were not limited to charitable purposes. Accordingly the trust was held invalid. And so, sadly, North Tawton Devon Parish Council does not have a park bench or drinking fountain in memory of Alfred Endacott.

Anomalous exceptions

Trusts for the maintenance of animals

27   *Pettingall v Pettingall*
(1842) 11 LJ Ch 176

A testator made the following bequest in his will:

> Having a favourite black mare, I hereby bequeath that, at my death, 50 shillings per annum be paid for her keep in some park in England or Wales; her shoes to be taken off, and she is never to be ridden or put in harness; and that my executor consider himself in honour bound to fulfill my wish, and see that she be well provided for, and removable at his will. At her death all payments to cease.

It was admitted by all that a bequest in favour of an animal was a valid purpose trust. Two questions arose however: whether a trust had been established; and what was to happen to any surplus funds.

The Court held that the mare should be maintained as the testator wished, and that the executor was entitled to any surplus.

If the mare was not being properly attended to, any parties interested in the residuary estate could apply to the Court to enforce the trust.

Trusts for the saying of masses

28   *Carrigan v Redwood*
(1910) 30 NZLR 244

Mary Sellars, a Roman Catholic, died in Palmerston North in the early 1900s. Her will requested that her trustee should expend one-half of her estate in having weekly masses offered up for her soul in the Parish of Palmerston North until her estate was expended. The question came before the then Supreme Court as to whether this trust was valid.

Cooper J spend an inordinate amount of his judgment considering whether certain statutes of Henry VIII and Edward VI (passed in England as part of the reformation of the English Church and the break from the Roman Catholic Church) applied in New Zealand. After reaching the conclusion that they did not, meaning that gifts and bequests to religions other than the Church of

England could be valid, he then went on to consider whether the bequest in question in this case would be a good charitable use: or in other words whether it would be an exception to the beneficiary principle. In this case the Court was satisfied that it was. An effective charitable use may be defined to be a bequest for the advancement of religion. As the Roman Catholic faith is a lawful religion a bequest to that church for masses for the dead is an effective charitable use. Accordingly, the trust was valid, and masses were said for the soul of Mary Sellars as she wished.

Trusts for the erection and maintenance of monuments and graves

29   *Re Hooper*
[1932] 1 Ch 38

When Harry Hooper died in December 1927, he appeared to have outlived most of his immediate family. This fact is borne out by a clause in his will which provided that £1000 of his estate was given to his trustees upon trust for the care and upkeep of the graves and monuments in the Torquay Cemetery of his father, mother, wife and two daughters; and also the grave and monument in Shotley Churchyard near Ipswich where his "gallant and only son" was buried. He was also keen to look after the tablet in St Matthias' Church at Ilsham to the memory of his wife and children, and a window in the same church to the memory of his father. It seems his mother must have missed out on her memorial window. Harry's next of kin disputed the validity of this trust, and the matter came before Maugham J in the Chancery Division to decide the point.

Maugham J noted that he would have felt difficulty in deciding this case had it not been for the decision in *Pirbright v Salwey* [1896] WN 86 where it was decided that gifts for the erection and maintenance of monuments or graves are valid purpose trusts. Accordingly, he concluded that the trust for the maintenance of the graves and monuments in the churchyard or in the cemetery were valid for a period of 21 years from Harry's death; while the tablets and windows in St Matthias' Church were good charitable gifts, and therefore the rule against perpetuities did not apply to them. Thus that trust was valid indefinitely.

30 *Re Budge*
[1942] NZLR 350

When Mary Budge died, her will, after leaving all her personal effects to her sister, directed her executor to apply the residue of her estate to erecting a suitable monument over her grave, paying for her funeral expenses, and keeping her grave and its surroundings in a neat and tidy state. The whole of the residue of the estate which was available for carrying this out was approximately £150. The matter was heard before the Supreme Court in Auckland to determine whether or not this bequest was valid. The validity of the provision had initially been questioned on the ground that there was no one in the position to enforce it and thus it was in breach of the beneficiary principle. This ground was clearly untenable as such a bequest was an exception to the general rule. The main issue in the case then became whether or not the trust infringed against the rule of perpetuities.

The Court held that there was nothing in the will to indicate that the testatrix contemplated the trust should continue in perpetuity. She may have meant it to continue for a reasonable time, such as the lifetime of her executor; for 21 years; or until the fund was exhausted. None of these periods expressly contemplated a period greater than 21 years, and thus for that period, the trust was valid.

Miscellaneous exceptions

31 *Re Denley's Trust Deed*
[1969] 1 Ch 373

By a trust deed made in 1936 a company conveyed land upon trust to Harry Denley and other trustees to hold for the use and purpose of a recreation or sports ground primarily for the benefit of the company's employees, or such other persons as the trustees allowed to use it. The trust deed was drawn up so as not to offend the rule against perpetuities.

The trustees took out an originating summons to have the question of validity decided. Goff J held that the beneficiary principle was confined to purpose trusts which are abstract or impersonal. The objection is not that the trust is for a purpose or object per se, but that there is no beneficiary or cestui que trust. Where, then, the trust, though expressed as a purpose, is directly or indirectly for the benefit of an individual or individuals, it seemed to Goff J that it would, in general, be outside the mischief of the beneficiary principle, and thus should be allowed. However, this was subject to the proviso that where a purpose trust, the carrying out of which would benefit an individual or individuals, has a benefit that is so indirect or intangible or which gives nobody any standing to apply to the Court to enforce the trust, then the beneficiary principle would apply to invalidate the trust, quite apart from any question of uncertainty or perpetuity.

The present case escaped the workings of the principle and the proviso. The trust deed expressly stated that the employees of the company should be entitled to the use and enjoyment of the land, and accordingly they would have standing to enforce the trust. As the trust was also limited in time so as to avoid any infringement of the rule against perpetuities, and was for the benefit of individuals then it did not offend against the beneficiary principle and was a valid trust.

32   *Re Lipinski's Will Trusts*
[1976] Ch 235

Harry Lipinski died in May 1969. He had been a widower for some years and for most of his life had taken an active part in various Jewish organisations in Hull. In his will he left one-half of his residual estate to the Hull Judeans (Maccabi) Association in memory of his late wife to be used solely for constructing new buildings for the association and/or improvements to the buildings; one-quarter for the Hull Hebrew school; and the remaining one-quarter for the Hull Hebrew Board of Guardians to construct new buildings for the association. These bequests were challenged by his next of kin.

Counsel for the next of kin argued that the gifts in the present case were purpose trusts, and failed both for that reason, and because they infringed the rule against perpetuities.

After considering the question of trusts in favour of unincorporated associations, Oliver J applied the decision of Goff J in *Re Denley's Trust Deed* (31). In that case it was held that a trust which benefits individuals was outside the mischief of the beneficiary principle and thus enforceable. In the opinion of Oliver J this approach accorded with both authority and common sense. Adopting this as the correct principle, he concluded that the evidence did not show the testator had any specific building in mind when he left the funds to the association, and thus his words meant that the association was to have the legacy to spend for the benefit of its members.

No question of contravention of the rule against perpetuities arose, and that the fact that the beneficiary was an unincorporated non-charitable association made no difference to the matter. In the judgment of Oliver J, the gift was valid. The association's members were the persons who were entitled to enforce the purpose of the trust.

Trusts in favour of unincorporated bodies

33 *Conservative and Unionist Central Office v Burrell (Inspector of Taxes)*
[1982] 1 WLR 522, [1982] 2 All ER 1

The Conservative and Unionist Central Office was a political party in Great Britain. In the late 1970s demand was made on it to pay tax under the Income and Corporation Taxes Act on the basis that it was an unincorporated association, and thus fell within the definition of a "company" contained in the Act. The party appealed against that assessment, contending it was not a company as there was, as a matter of law, no unincorporated association in existence to which party funds belonged.

The English Court of Appeal held that an unincorporated association means two or more persons bound together for one or more common purposes, not being business purposes, by mutual undertaking, each having mutual duties and obligations. The organisation must have rules which identify those in control of the organisation and its funds, and which identify procedures for joining. It was noted that the bond between members of an unincorporated association has to be contractual.

On the facts, nothing contractually or directly linked the members of the party, and accordingly it lacked the characteristics of an unincorporated association for the purposes of the tax legislation.

This is a case which does not involve a trust or a gift to an unincorporated association. It is, however, the touchstone for such a body's definitive characteristics, and has often been cited.

34 *Re Cain*
[1950] VLR 382

The will of Walter Cain made a number of bequests to a large number of organisations and institutions: one was made to the Victorian Council for Mental Hygiene; and another to the Victorian Vocational Guidance Centre.

In respect of the first bequest, a gift of one-quarter of the residue of the estate to the Victorian Council for Mental Hygiene, the Court held that, as the objects of the Society were charitable, in the legal sense the gift was effective.

The second caused more problems. The Victorian Vocational Guidance Centre was an unincorporated body which had a written constitution setting out its objects and providing for membership. Its functions were to advise people on job and occupation choices. As was noted by the Court, this was no doubt a most useful activity, but was non-charitable. The gift made no reference to any purposes for which it was to be used. This led Dean J, in the Supreme Court of Victoria, to ask whether a gift to an unincorporated body is one which creates a trust binding the members to apply it to the purposes of the body. If so, and if such purposes are not charitable, the gift will fail. This was not the case here however. The gift was taken to be a gift to the members, who might, by agreement, dispose of the money, divide it among themselves, divert it to other uses, or dissolve their body on such terms as they think fit.

This case was concerned with testamentary gifts to such societies, and dicta suggested that if a society holds the gift upon trust to apply it to the objects or purposes set out in the constitution of the Society, unless those purposes are charitable that trust is void because there is no beneficiary.

35   *Neville Estates Ltd v Madden*
[1962] Ch 832

On 1 June 1959 the trustees of the Catford synagogue in London (Mr Madden and others) entered into a contract to sell two pieces of vacant land adjoining their synagogue to Neville Estates Ltd. The sale price was to be £10,000. The agreement also provided that the contract was subject to the consent of the Charity Commissioners, so far as it was required. The Commissioners refused to give their consent to the sale, and an unhappy Neville Estates applied to the Court for a declaration that the land be sold without the Commissioners' consent, and for specific performance of the contract.

The plaintiff claimed consent was not needed because, among other arguments, the land in question was not held on a charitable trust, but remained the property of the synagogue in the same way as the property of a club remains the property of its members.

Cross J stated that a gift to, or in trust for, unincorporated associations could take effect in three ways:

1. It may be a gift to the members of the association at the relevant date as joint tenants. Any member then can sever their share and claim it whether or not they continue to be a member of the association; or

2.   It may be a gift to the existing members subject to their respective contractual rights towards one another as members of the association. In such case a member cannot sever their share. Upon death or resignation the gift will accrue to the remaining members; or

3.   The gift may not be at the disposal of the members, but is to be held in trust for, or applied for, the purposes of the association. In this case the gift will fail unless the association is a charitable body.

At issue in this case was therefore whether the members of the synagogue were legally able to divide its property, including the land, among themselves; and secondly, if they were not so able, whether the trusts on which the property of the synagogue were held were charitable.

His Honour was satisfied that on the facts the synagogue's property was held on trust to be applied for the purposes of the synagogue as a quasi-corporate entity. The existing members could not divide it among themselves. Following on from this, he then held that the trust here was a charitable trust. He noted that the synagogue was an association which was supported by its members for the purposes of providing benefits for themselves, and this would not normally be a charity. But he did not think that this principle could apply with its full force in the case of trusts for religious purposes. Trusts in such a context have to recognise that Church activity overflows from the Church itself. And the Court was entitled to assume that some benefit accrued to the general public from the attendance at places of worship by people who live in the world and mix with their fellow citizens.

The case also considered a number of other arguments raised by the plaintiff to seek specific performance of the contract. None were successful, and the action failed.

36   *Re Recher's Will Trusts*
[1972] Ch 526

Mrs Eva Recher, a lifelong animal lover, died in 1962. Her will, made in May 1957, left her husband a beneficial life interest, and then settled her residuary estate upon six named organisations in equal shares. All were to benefit animals. One of the named organisations was the "Anti-Vivisection Society" of Victoria Street, London. It was discovered at the trial that until a few months before Mrs Recher made her will, an unincorporated society named "The London and Provincial Anti-Vivisection Society" did conduct activities from Victoria Street; however, this society had amalgamated with another group, "The National Anti-Vivisection Society" of Palace Street, London from 1 January 1957. This raised the question of whether the National Society was entitled to the share of residue given to the "Anti-Vivisection Society". Further, Mrs Recher's executor was not entirely sure that the gift was valid.

Brightman J held that it was conceded that the purposes of the London and Provincial Society were not exclusively charitable — an argument against validity. Brightman J then summarised the three possible interpretations of gifts to unincorporated associations set out in *Neville Estates v Madden* **(35)**.

Counsel in this case submitted a fourth possible interpretation: that there could be a gift to the members of the association beneficially, on the basis that the subject-matter of the gift is dealt with in accordance with the rules of the association by which the members are contractually bound. Brightman J accepted that neither of the other alternatives applied in this situation. He noted that the members of the London and Provincial Society were bound together by contract, which they could vary or determine as between themselves. That contract set out how the members' subscriptions and the income of the association were to be spent.

His Honour thought that a donation, unaccompanied by words purporting to impose a trust, would take effect as an accretion to the funds of the association which are governed by the contract. It would be dealt with in the same way as funds subscribed by the members themselves. The same would be true with a legacy. Brightman J felt that any other conclusion would be contrary to common sense, making it difficult, if not impossible, for a person to make a donation to a club or association they wished to benefit.

The Judge was unable to avoid the conclusion that, in this particular instance, the gift to the London and Provincial Association would fail, as that association was no longer in existence at the time the will was made. This conclusion was reached with reluctance, and with some words of criticism for Mrs Recher's professional advisers who had allowed her will to be incorrectly drafted.

37   *Re Grant's Will Trusts*
[1979] 3 All ER 359

This case tells you all you ever wanted to know, and more, about the inner workings of the Labour Party in Great Britain. Mr Grant died on 6 June 1975. In his lifetime he had been a dedicated member of the Labour Party, and was in fact the financial secretary to his local constituency party in Chertsey. In 1959 this local party had bought a property which was held on trust for that constituency absolutely. In 1970 electoral boundaries changed, and with it the position of the ownership of the house became confused. Part of Chertsey was amalgamated into the constituency of Chertsey and Walton. The old constituency party was dissolved. Pending resolution of the problem of the ownership of the property, it was placed in the hands of a local property committee.

Grant's will left his entire estate to "the Labour Party Property Committee for the benefit of the Chertsey Headquarters of the Chertsey and Walton constituency Labour Party", with the proviso that if the headquarters did not remain in the Chertsey Urban District Council area, the estate was to go to the National Labour Party absolutely. It was common ground that in giving his estate to the Labour Party property committee, Grant meant the property committee that had managed the property purchased by the old Chertsey local constituency party. Beyond this, the will caused problems. The trustees of the trust deed applied to the Court to determine whether the request was a valid gift or was void for uncertainty, and if it was valid who was entitled to benefit.

Vinelott J felt constrained to hold that the gift in the will had failed. He noted that in the first category laid down in *Neville Estates v Madden* **(35)** an association becomes, in effect, a convenient label for a class of beneficiaries. Gifts within this category are relatively uncommon. More common is a gift to an association within the second category. There, the gift is to members of an association, but the property is given as an accretion to the funds of the association so the property becomes subject to the contract which governs the rights of the members between themselves. This was the situation envisaged in *Re Recher's Will Trusts* **(36)**. It is interesting to note that the Judge in this case felt this was part of the second category, whereas Brightman J considered it to be a fourth category in itself. The final *Re Recher's* categories are where a trust is imposed for present and future members indefinitely, or by giving the money to the association on trust for its purposes. In the former case the gift will fail for perpetuity, and in the latter will fail unless the purposes of the association are charitable.

Vinelott J made two further points. A testator may choose to make a gift to an association as a means of furthering its purposes in the expectation that the gift will be so used; however they do not have to impose a trust or obligation on the members. Secondly, Vinelott J felt it was a necessary characteristic of any gift within category 2 that the members of the association can alter their rules to provide that their funds can be applied for new purposes or even distributed among the members.

Grant's will was then considered. The Chertsey and Walton constituency party had argued that the gift was to the trust of the property held by the old Chertsey Party, or the proceeds of its sale. The Judge felt that the terms of the will were an insurmountable obstacle to this construction as Grant had clearly indicated that if the headquarters did not remain there his estate was to go to the National Labour Party absolutely. A second argument was that the gift should be construed as a gift to the members of the Chertsey and Walton Constituency Party with the direction that it should be used for its purposes.

The Judge considered that this too would fail because the rules which governed the Chertsey Constituency Party were capable of being altered by the National Labour Party. Accordingly, the Chertsey and Walton Constituency Party did not control any property given by subscription or otherwise to it. This conclusion was based upon an analysis of the terms upon which subscriptions to the party were treated: essentially subscriptions or other property given to the Constituency Party were not under its control. Further, the proviso with the gift over to the National Labour Party demonstrated that this bequest was not intended to be a gift to the members of the new Chertsey Constituency Party. Accordingly, the trust failed.

In the course of his judgment Vinelott J also criticised **Re Denley's Trust Deed (31)** holding that on a proper analysis of that case it falls altogether outside the categories of gifts to unincorporated associations and purpose trusts. In his opinion that trust should have failed.

"Quistclose" trusts

38   *Barclays Bank Ltd v Quistclose Investments Ltd*
[1968] 3 All ER 651

At the annual general meeting of Rolls Razor Ltd, on 2 July 1964, payment of a 120 per cent dividend to shareholders was approved by the company's directors. Rolls Razor had no liquid resources to enable it to pay this dividend, however, and was advised by its bankers that, as it was over its overdraft limit, they would be unable to help them. One of the directors succeeded in borrowing the money needed to pay the dividend from Quistclose Investments Ltd. The money was lent to Rolls Razor by Quistclose "for the purpose of that company paying the final dividend on July 24 next". A cheque was paid into a bank account in the name of Rolls Razor at Barclays Bank. The covering letter sent with the cheque stated that the amount would only be used to meet the dividend due on 24 July 1964.

Despite its ambitious plans to pay the dividend Rolls Razor went into voluntary liquidation in early July. Once the effective resolution for Rolls Razor's liquidation was passed on 27 August, Barclays Bank set off the credit balance in the dividend account against part of the debit balance in Rolls Razor's other accounts. This was followed by a demand by Quistclose Investments for repayment of this sum by Barclays Bank. The case for Quistclose was that the loan made to Rolls Razor was impressed with a trust in their favour in the event of the dividend not being paid.

The House of Lords had no doubt that the loan was made specifically in order to enable Rolls Razor to pay the dividend. Lord Wilberforce was certain that the mutual intention of Quistclose and Rolls Razor was that the sum advanced should not become part of the assets of Rolls Razor, but was to be used exclusively for payment of the dividend. He felt that a necessary consequence of this was that the money was to be returned to Quistclose if the dividend could not be paid. The main argument for Barclays Bank was that only an action for recovery of a debt existed between Rolls Razor and Quistclose. This, they argued, necessarily excluded the implication of any trust. Lord Wilberforce had no difficulty in recognising the co-existence in one transaction of both legal and equitable rights and remedies. In the present case he felt the intention was to create a secondary trust for the benefit of Quistclose, to arise if the primary trust, to enable payment of the dividend, could not be carried out. He saw no reason why the law should not give effect to this.

A secondary question arose as to whether Barclays Bank had sufficient notice of the trust alleged by Quistclose. Again Lord Wilberforce found there was no doubt that they had been told that the money had been provided on loan by Quistclose and was to be used only for the purposes of paying the dividend. This, in the opinion of the House of Lords, was sufficient to give them notice it was trust money, and not the assets of, Rolls Razor that they were receiving.

39   *Re Northern Developments (Holdings) Ltd*
Unreported, Ch D, 6 October 1978

Northern Developments was the parent company of a group of companies including one named Kelly. Kelly was in dire financial straits. Seventeen banks, who had other companies in the Northern group as their customers, formed a syndicate and agreed to advance a sum of money in excess of £500,000 in an attempt to rescue Kelly. The moneys were paid into an account in Northern's name for the express purpose of providing money for Kelly's unsecured creditors, and for no other purpose. The sum advanced was treated as an advance to the banks' other customers in the group. The funds sustained Kelly for some time, but it was then put into receivership. A little over one-half the fund contributed by the banks remained unexpended. One of the issues that arose was who was entitled to that balance.

Sir Robert Megarry V-C held that a *Quistclose* trust attached to the fund. He considered that it was a purpose trust enforceable by the banks as lenders; Kelly, for whose immediate benefit the trust fund was established, and Kelly's creditors. The Vice-Chancellor held that the fund was established not with the object of vesting the beneficial interest in them, but in order to confer a benefit on Kelly, and so consequently on the rest of the group and the bankers, by ensuring that Kelly's creditors would be paid. He held that the creditors had a right akin to the right of a beneficiary under a will to compel an executor to administer the estate properly.

40   *Carreras Rothmans Ltd v Freeman Mathews Treasure Ltd*
[1985] 1 All ER 155

Rothmans, the well-known cigarette manufacturer, employed Freeman Mathews Treasure (FMT) to promote its products in the UK. FMT handled all of Rothmans' placement work, buying space for advertisements in newspapers and magazines, and producing the artwork needed to supply those spaces.

Rothmans paid FMT an annual fee for their services, and also reimbursed FMT for their expenditure on production agencies. These agencies performed the technical services that enabled FMT to supply the newspapers and magazines with the actual advertisements. FMT would supply a monthly invoice to Rothmans for those disbursements, and Rothmans would pay each month.

In 1983, Rothmans became aware that FMT was in financial difficulty. The company decided to explore whether the large sums of money that they were expending on FMT could be protected, as they were concerned at the damage to Rothmans if FMT ceased trading and left the agencies unpaid. Accordingly, an agreement was reached to the effect that payments made by Rothmans to FMT to pay the production agencies would be paid into a special account for the purposes only of meeting those accounts. FMT agreed to this plan, and the special bank account was opened. The bankers were given notice of the purposes of the account. On 26 July a cheque for nearly £500,000 was paid into this account, and cheques drawn on it were sent out to the production agencies. A few days later FMT went into liquidation and all the moneys in their accounts, including the special account, were frozen by the liquidator. The cheques drawn on the special account bounced. Rothmans claimed that the moneys in the special account were trust moneys and asked the liquidator for confirmation that they would be applied to meet the production agencies' debts, or that they would be repaid to Rothmans. The liquidator refused to do so, and Rothmans brought proceedings seeking a declaration that the money was held on trust.

Peter Gibson J held that the account was intended to be little more than a conduit pipe, and it was clearly intended that moneys paid into it would never become the property of FMT. He felt it was manifest that FMT was intended to act in relation to those moneys in a fiduciary capacity only. He noted that Lord Wilberforce's description of the mutual intention of the parties in *Quistclose* **(38)** fitted in this case.

The liquidator and FMT sought to distinguish *Quistclose*, but Peter Gibson J was unimpressed with this. He felt it was unhelpful to overanalyse the *Quistclose* type of case. The overriding principle is that equity fastens on the conscience of the person who receives from another property transferred for a specific purpose only so that such a person will not be permitted to treat the property as their own or to use it for other than the stated purpose.

The Judge was also unimpressed with an argument that no trust could exist because the agencies would have no enforceable rights against the "trust fund". The Judge relied on *Re Northern Developments* **(39)** to hold that the beneficial interest was in suspense until payment was made. Accordingly, it was held that the trust was created by the agreement between the two companies, and Rothmans had an equitable right to compel FMT to carry out the trust.

41   *Re English & American Insurance Co Ltd*
[1994] 1 BCLC 649

In 1991 an agreement was entered into between the English & American Insurance Co (E & A) and the Structural Engineers' Professional Indemnity Association Ltd. The two organisations planned to cooperate to provide professional indemnity insurance for professional engineers. The Association, however, did not have the required authorisation to be an insurer, and it was accordingly agreed that until the authorisation was obtained, E & A would itself provide insurance to members of the Association.

The terms of the agreement provided for engineers who wished to be covered to pay their premiums to E & A on an interim basis until the mutual Insurance Association could be formed. It was a specific term of this agreement that all money received by E & A from engineers was to be segregated from all other income and assets, and was to be applied solely for the purposes of their insurance. When E & A became insolvent the company applied for directions as to whether or not the funds received from engineers under the scheme were held on trust for them, or formed part of the general assets of the company.

Harman J noted that the agreement between the two organisations was structured so that the company would have a separate fund of assets for the engineers' insurance. This, in his opinion, was held on a resulting trust. A resulting trust arises between one person and another when property is put into the hands of the recipient either with no purpose stated (in which case there is a straight resulting trust), or with a purpose stated. In the latter case a resulting trust arises if that purpose fails. His Honour then considered and applied *Quistclose* (38) and *Carreras Rothmans* (40).

The Court held that the essence of the agreement between the parties created a trust. The specific agreement to segregate the funds, together with the fact that E & A accepted that they were not to make any profit or loss on the scheme (thus indicating they did not hold the beneficial ownership of the money) led to the finding that a trust had been intended. This was so despite oddities and inconsistencies in the later documents and evidence. The Court held that these could not prevail against the clear evidence of the parties' earlier intention, and described them as merely "loose ends". As equity looks to substance rather than the form of any transaction the Court was satisfied in this instance that the parties had intended to create a trust.

- C E F Rickett, "Different Views on the Scope of the *Quistclose* Analysis: English and Antipodean Insights", Vol 107, LQR 608.

42 *Twinsectra Ltd v Yardley*
[2002] 2 All ER 377 (HL)

Leach was a solicitor in sole practice. In 1992 he was instructed by Yardley in relation to the purchase of some land at Bradford. Funding was to be through Barclays Bank, but this fell through and Yardley obtained short-term alternative funding from Twinsectra. Twinsectra made the loan on the basis that repayment was secured by a solicitor's undertaking, an unusual requirement. Leach refused to give this undertaking but Sims, another solicitor who owed Yardley some money, agreed to give the undertaking that Twinsectra sought. This undertaking stated that the Twinsectra loan would be used solely for the acquisition of property on behalf of Yardley, and for no other purpose, and that the undertaking was given in the course of Sims' firm's business as a solicitor. By this time, Barclays had agreed to provide finance and the Twinsectra loan was no longer required. However, Yardley and Sims proceeded with it anyway, with Sims using the loan to repay the moneys owed to Yardley. Sims' undertaking to repay, then, would be as principal debtor rather than guarantor. Twinsectra was not told of this.

The trial Judge found that Sims' letter was fundamentally untrue, as Sims was not acting for any client or acting in the usual course of his business as a solicitor. Before giving the undertaking, Sims had discussed matters with Leach and had become concerned that if the moneys were not used for the acquisition of property, then Sims would be in breach of his undertaking. Leach acknowledged this, but noted that the money had to be disbursed in accordance with Yardley's instructions. Leach was told by Yardley at this time that the money would in fact be used for various property acquisitions, and the bulk of the funds received from Sims were applied in this way. However, some sums retained for Leach's costs and paid to Yardley for non-property purposes were the subject of claims for "knowing receipt" and "dishonest assistance". Yardley for his part was found by the trial Judge to be dishonest in holding out to Twinsectra that Sims was his solicitor.

One issue was whether Sims' undertaking created a *Quistclose* trust. This was dealt with in most detail in the judgment of Lord Millett. While loan money normally became the property of the borrower, money advanced for a specific purpose where the borrower was not free to apply it to any other purpose gave rise to fiduciary obligations on the part of the borrower. Following the *Quistclose* **(38)** decision, the lender was entitled to prevent the money being applied to anything other than the stated purpose.

Twinsectra argued that Sims' undertaking created a *Quistclose* trust. Leach denied this, on the basis that Twinsectra lacked intention to create a trust and looked solely to Sims' undertaking; and also argued that commercial life would be impossible if trusts were lightly inferred from slight purpose. A loan for a specific purpose, it was argued, was not enough to create a trust: there must be something more, such as a requirement that it be held in a separate account. It was also argued that the objects (for the purchase of property) were too uncertain.

Lord Millett noted that a settlor must intend to create a trust, but that subjective intentions were irrelevant. Arrangements that had the effect of creating a trust bound a party that intended to enter into them, whether or not a trust was intended. Lord Millett observed that a *Quistclose* trust does not arise merely because money is paid for a particular purpose. The key question was whether the monies, once advanced, would be at the free disposal of the borrower. Following the *Quistclose* decision, Sims' undertaking made it clear that the loan moneys would be used for the acquisition of property and for no other purpose, and would be retained until so applied. This was not simply the case with a solicitor's undertaking — it was an essential principle of equity and this was a "classic situation" in which a fiduciary relationship arose.

Drawing on commentary on the *Quistclose* decision, Lord Millett found that a *Quistclose* trust was a simple commercial arrangement whereby money lent remained the property of the lender until applied in accordance with agreed purposes, or returned if not applied to these purposes. The money did not vest unconditionally in the borrower; nor was the lender enforcing the trust as a beneficiary or as settlor in the usual way. The trust arrangements were more than contractual. The *Quistclose* trust was ultimately a kind of resulting trust, with the borrower not a beneficiary but rather a trustee of the moneys for the lender, unless and until applied for the intended purposes. In addition, uncertain objects did nothing to help the borrower: if the objects of the trust were uncertain, then the trust failed and the borrower was obliged to return the moneys to the lender.

In Lord Millett's view, Sims' undertaking created a *Quistclose* trust. The money advanced belonged to Twinsectra, subject only to Yardley's right to apply it to the acquisition of property, and was never at Yardley's or Sims' free disposal. Sims' actions in paying the moneys to Leach were a breach of trust, but did not prevent the moneys being applied to the objects, which they were partially by Leach.

The majority found that Leach had not been dishonest. He believed the money was at Yardley's disposal, and that a breach of Sims' undertaking was not his concern. While this may have been wrong or misguided, if based on an honest belief, it was not dishonest. The trial Judge's finding that there was no dishonesty was upheld.

CHARITABLE TRUSTS

Definition of a charity: the four heads

43   *IRC v Pemsel*
         [1891] AC 531

By deeds of trust dated 1813 and 1815 Mrs Elizabeth Bates settled certain properties upon trust for the Church of the United Brethren, or the Moravians. The Moravians were to use the income from the trust to support missionaries in "heathen nations". Heathens were happily supported by the trust until 1886. Then the trust was refused taxation benefits on the grounds that the benefits were only available to trusts for charitable purposes, and the purposes to which the trust income was applied did not bring it into this exception. Consequently, the treasurer of the Church applied for a writ of mandamus to compel the Commissioners for Special Purposes of Income Tax to grant the exemption. If the purposes of Mrs Bates' trust were decided to be charitable within the meaning of the Income Tax Act 1842, the charity was entitled to the exemptions.

The background to this case is a little more complex. Lord Macnaghten noted that almost all tax legislation contains an exemption in favour of property dedicated to charitable purposes. Charitable purposes have never been defined in the Acts, and about three or four years before this case the Inland Revenue Board had discovered that there was no defined meaning of a charitable purpose. It concluded that the meaning of charity was to be gathered from popular usage, and they considered that the word had only one ordinary familiar and popular use: the relief of poverty. On this basis they then proceeded to refuse exemptions in cases in which they had been claimed and allowed for more than 40 years.

The difficulty was that the legal definition of charity was obviously much wider than the popular version. The Courts of Chancery had consistently relied upon the Statute of Charitable Uses 1601 (also known as the Statute of Elizabeth) which set out a number of objects of charity that do not fit into the popular definition. The Statute of Charitable Uses had been repealed by the Mortmain and Charitable Uses Act of 1888, but s 13(2) of that later Act had expressly preserved the preamble to the 1601 statute.

Lord Macnaghten did not doubt that the popular meaning of the words "charity" and "charitable" differed from the legal meaning. He then went on to define the legal meaning of charity. Charity, in its legal sense, comprises four divisions: trusts for the relief of poverty; for the advancement of education; for the advancement of religion; and for other purposes beneficial to the community not covered under any of the preceding heads. After this he then went on to hold that the expression "trusts for charitable purposes"; the Income Tax Act; and other Acts in which the expression "charitable" occurs must be construed according to English law and not by the popular and more restricted meaning.

Based on this reasoning, Mrs Bates' trusts were held to be valid charitable purposes and thus were exempt from the income tax provisions.

Public purpose

44   *Re Compton*
       [1945] Ch 123

The unknown testatrix in this case had provided in her will for a trust to be set up for the education of "Compton, Powell and Montague Children" until they reached the age of 26 years. The money was to be used forever to fit the children to be servants of God and serve the nation. "Compton, Powell and Montague Children" were then defined to be the lawful descendants of H C Compton, W Powell and William, Earl of Sandwich. The question arose as to whether this trust was a valid charitable bequest. When the matter came before the Court, there were 28 possible beneficiaries of the trust alive.

Lord Greene MR noted first, that the trust was to last forever and would therefore be against the rules of perpetuities unless it was a charitable trust; and secondly, the persons who were to benefit were the descendants of three named individuals.

Lord Greene felt it was fundamental that the law recognises no purposes as charitable unless they are of a public character. In other words, the trust must be for the benefit of the community or a section of the community. He then quoted with approval the words of the Privy Council in the case of *Verge v Somerville* [1924] AC 496: that the first inquiry into a trust must be whether it is for the benefit of the community or of an appreciably important class of the community. Private individuals, or a fluctuating body of private individuals cannot be the objects of a charitable gift. Lord Greene held this to mean that no gift can be charitable in the legal sense unless it has this necessary public character. Once a purely personal element is introduced to the qualification of the beneficiary (such as where the beneficiaries are defined by reference to a personal relationship to a named person) then, on principle, it cannot be a valid charitable gift. Here, the educational trusts were founded upon the fact of kinship to three individuals. Lord Greene was of the opinion that this vitiated any public character: it had to be regarded as a family trust and not a trust to benefit a section of the community.

Lord Greene was also of the opinion that the trust was not beneficial to the community because it was aimed at producing God-fearing men and women who would be good citizens for the country. In the opinion of His Lordship this could be obtained by an ordinary public school education in England.

45 *Oppenheim v Tobacco Securities Trust Ltd*
[1951] 1 All ER 31

A husband and wife set up a trust whereby Tobacco Securities Trust Co Ltd was to hold investments and property on trust, and apply the income in providing for the education of children of employees or former employees of British/American Tobacco Co Ltd. The question arose as to whether the trust was valid. It was clear that it created a perpetuity and thus would only be valid if it was charitable. It was established by the Court that the number of employees of the company and its subsidiary and allied companies exceeded 110,000 people.

Lord Simonds observed that a trust is not charitable unless it is directed to the public benefit. This means that the class of persons benefiting from such a trust must be able to be regarded as "section of the community". Lord Simonds felt that these words had no special sanctity, but indicated first, that the possible beneficiaries must not be numerically negligible, and secondly, that the quality which distinguishes them from other members of the community must be something which does not depend on their relationship to a particular individual. Here, the Court could find no justification for regarding employment as a quality which constitutes employees a section of the community. They could also make no distinction between children of employees and the employees themselves.

An employee/employer relationship is highly personal. Whatever the number of employees under the same employer, each still stands independently in this relationship to the employer. The large number of employees of the company in this case did not help the argument. The majority of the House of Lords considered that to admit this trust to the category of charities would be contrary to principle, and dismissed it as an invalid charitable trust.

Lord Simonds also noted that it had been suggested that the element of public benefit was not essential except for the charities falling within the fourth category outlined by Lord Macnaghten in *Pemsel* **(43)**. He noted that this is certainly wrong, except in the anomalous case of trusts for the relief of poverty.

46   *Dingle v Turner*
[1972] AC 601

In his will of 10 January 1950 Frank Dingle directed his trustees to invest the sum of £10,000 in investments upon trust to apply the income in paying pensions to poor employees of E Dingle & Co Ltd. The ultimate residue of his estate was also to be applied to this trust. E Dingle & Co Ltd was a department store owned by Frank Dingle. At the time of his death it employed over 600 people, but by the time the proceedings were started it had 705 full-time and 189 part-time employees.

The case eventually found itself before the House of Lords. Lord Cross considered the case law, including *Compton* **(44)**, and *Oppenheim* **(45)**. This led him to conclude that the *Compton* rule ought to apply to all charitable trusts; and that only "poor relations"; and "poor employees" cases are anomalous exceptions to that. Accordingly, he held that this trust was a valid charitable trust.

Lord Cross was inclined to draw a distinction between the merits of the *Compton* rule, and the reasoning by which Lord Greene had justified it. He considered that Lord Greene's reasoning — based on the distinction between personal and impersonal relationships — had never been satisfactory. He also noted the difficulties in the contrast between "a section of the public" and "a fluctuating body of private individuals" which the Courts had relied upon to clarify the meaning of a "section of the public".

Lord Cross considered that the question as to whether or not potential beneficiaries could be said to be a section of the public is a question of degree, and cannot by itself be decisive of the question as to whether or not the trust is a charity. In his opinion much must depend upon the purpose of the trust.

His Lordship also noted that, from a practical viewpoint, the validity of charitable trusts and the question of the fiscal benefits they enjoy, often go hand in hand. He felt that decisions in cases such as *Compton* and *Oppenheim* were influenced by the consideration that if the trusts were declared valid they would enjoy a possibly undeserved immunity from taxes.

47   *New Zealand Society of Accountants v CIR*
        [1986] 1 NZLR 147

As most of the general public would be aware, the New Zealand Law Society and Society of Accountants maintain fidelity funds to reimburse those people who lose their money through the activities of solicitors or accountants. The issue in this case was whether these fidelity funds constitute trusts for charitable purposes, and are thus exempt from income tax under the Income Tax Act 1976. The two respective professional councils both argued that the funds were held on trusts within the fourth head of Lord Macnaghten's classification in *Pemsel* **(43)**: namely trusts for purposes beneficial to the community. They were claimed to be beneficial to the community as potential clients had the benefit of knowing that the fund was there to safeguard and protect their interests.

The case was considered by the New Zealand Court of Appeal. Richardson, Somers and Casey JJ were all in agreement that the trusts were not charitable. Somers J felt that the prospective claimants of the fidelity funds did not constitute the public, or a sufficient section of it, to pass the test of a charitable purpose. The claimants would be only clients of solicitors or accountants who deposited money with them. These prospective beneficiaries would also extend to incorporated companies. Somers J was aware of no cases in which it had been held that trading companies may be the objects of charity, or form part of a section of the public. Richardson J reiterated his fellow Judge's point that the trusts were not for the benefit of a section of the public. He was also not impressed by the argument that the fidelity funds benefited the community as a whole. The public peace of mind seemed to him far too nebulous and remote to be regarded as a public benefit.

Public benefit

48   *National Anti-Vivisection Society v IRC*
         [1948] AC 31

The facts of this case are simple. The plaintiff's society had claimed exemption from income tax on its investments on the grounds it was established for charitable purposes only. The Commissioners for Income Tax disagreed. They felt that it had been proved conclusively that a large amount of medical and scientific knowledge was due to experiments on living animals; and this in turn had led to the discovery of valuable cures for disease which alleviated suffering both to human beings and to animals. They were satisfied that any public benefit by the advancement of morals and education through the prohibition of vivisection would be outweighed by the detriment to medical science and research, and to the public health. The Society appealed this decision, and the case eventually found itself before the House of Lords.

The Court recognised that trusts for the benefit of animals were charitable because they promote and encourage kindness, discourage cruelty and stimulate humane and generous sentiments in humankind towards the lower animals, and by these means promote feelings of humanity and morality generally.

But could the Court disregard the fact that this public benefit would be outweighed by detriment to the public benefit of medical science and research? The Court found that the main purpose of the society was the compulsory abolition of vivisection by Act of Parliament. To Lord Simonds it seemed strange and bewildering that the Court would look so far and no further, and ignore injurious results to the public. He felt that when a purpose appeared broadly to fall within one of the categories of charity, the Court would assume it to be for the benefit of the community unless the contrary were shown. And where the evidence before the Court showed that however well-intentioned the donor, the achievement of the object would be greatly to the public disadvantage, there could be no justification for saying that the trust was charitable. In this case he was satisfied, and the majority of the Court was satisfied, that the purpose could not be charitable given the end result of the intentions of the Society.

In reaching this decision the Court departed from the decision in *Re Foveaux* [1895] 2 Ch 501 where Chitty J had decided that if the intention was to benefit the community the trust would be valid; and whether the community would in fact be benefited is a question on which the Court should not express an opinion.

Able to be controlled by the Court

49   *Re Hummeltenberg*
       [1923] 1 Ch 237

Mr Hummeltenberg sought to set up a trust with the somewhat unusual aim of training and developing suitable persons as mediums. The executors of Mr Hummeltenberg's will brought proceedings to determine its status. It was argued on behalf of the London Spiritualist Alliance Ltd that this was a valid trust for the advancement of education, or, alternatively, for the benefit of the public. They also claimed that, as the testator had expressly stated that the trust was to benefit the community, the Court was not required to express any opinion on whether or not the community would in fact be benefited. The residual legatee, however, argued that the gift was void. The main objection was that there was no way a Court could properly administer this trust as it would have no way of knowing whether or not mediums were being properly trained.

Russell J agreed with the latter view. He considered that no matter which of the four classes in *Pemsel* **(43)** a gift fell into, it was still necessary to establish that a charity would operate for the public benefit and that its administration could be controlled by the Court if necessary. He felt wholly unable to say that this was such a trust. This in itself was reason for declaring the gift void.

Russell J also held that the donor of the gift could not be the sole arbiter of whether or not its purpose is beneficial to the public. The Judge regarded a trust to teach poodles to dance as but a mild example of the kind of trust such an approach might produce. Accordingly, it was appropriate for the Court to determine whether or not a trust or gift is for the public benefit.

The four heads

(1) Relief of poverty

50   *Re Lucas*
[1922] 2 Ch 52

Mr Lucas directed that, at his death, the income from his estate should go to his niece, Agnes, for her lifetime. Following her death his estate was to be invested and the income given to "the oldest respectable inhabitants in Gunville" in the amount of five shillings per week each. Agnes was a little miffed at this bequest, and took out a summons to discover whether the gift in favour of the oldest respectable inhabitants of Gunville was a good charitable bequest, or was wholly or partly void. It was argued for the Attorney-General that, as indicated by the amount of the gift, the word "oldest" as used in the will was equivalent to "poorest". The ingredient of poverty would make this a valid charitable trust.

Unluckily for Agnes, Russell J agreed with this approach. He noted that the gift was of income in perpetuity in favour of the oldest respectable citizens, and of course if the bequest was not charitable it would fail. He felt that the words by themselves did not connote poverty, but that the sum of five shillings a week indicated quite clearly that the beneficiaries would be those to whom five shillings a week would be a comfort and relief.

The Judge did not feel he could hold that the element of age alone would transform a gift into a valid charitable bequest, but felt that if a gift can be construed to mean that the beneficiaries are needy people, then that could introduce the element of poverty. This would render a gift which might otherwise be invalid into a good charitable gift.

51   *Re Gwyon*
[1930] 1 Ch 255

The Reverend John Gwyon had a dream. It is obvious from his will and its codicils that he envisaged hundreds of young boys in the parish of Farnham being provided with knickers bearing his name. To this end, he bequeathed his estate to his executor on trust to set up the "Gwyon's Boys Clothing Foundation". All the income of the foundation was to be used to provide boys between the ages of 10–15 years (but preferably being around 13) with knickers. By this he meant "ordinary and strong durable knickers such as were worn by boys everyday, but no sporting or fancy knickers of any kind such as football knickers, cricket knickers, military knickers, boy scout knickers etc". There were some limits on the Reverend's generosity. Applicants and recipients should, if at all possible, live in the district of Farnham. They could not be black boys, and the term "boys" in the trust meant exclusively boys and did not include "girls or other females". It was also a condition of eligibility that the boy in question should not belong to, or be supported by, any charitable institution.

The Attorney-General contended this was a good charity, while the Treasury Solicitor claimed the property went to the Crown as bona vacantia.

Eve J did not think it could be a trust for the benefit of the poor and needy. None of the conditions laid upon possible recipients necessarily imported a requirement of poverty, and nor could the possible recipients be described as a class of "aged, impotent or poor" persons. The Judge thought that on the true construction of the will the Reverend's benevolence was intended for all eligible boys apart from paupers, and there was no indication that the trustees would be justified in refusing an applicant on the grounds that his background was too affluent. In these circumstances he could not hold the trust was a legal charitable trust.

52   ***Joseph Rowntree Memorial Trust Housing Assn Ltd v Attorney-General***
        [1983] 1 All ER 288

The plaintiffs were charitable associations and trusts formed in the early 1900s under a deed made in 1904 by one Joseph Rowntree, a philanthropist and cocoa manufacturer. The associations were to provide city housing and accommodation for workers and persons of limited means.

In the 1970s the trusts had formed a scheme providing housing for the elderly by building small self-contained dwellings for sale on long leases. The purchasers would make a small capital payment to purchase a lease. Five schemes were proposed, differing essentially only in the nature of the houses to be built; the facilities within them; and the level of ability or disability of the intended occupants. The Charity Commissioners considered that the schemes would not be charitable at law. Accordingly, the trusts commenced proceedings, before the schemes were implemented, to see if they could properly put them into place.

The Charity Commissioners' objections were that the schemes could not be charitable because:

(i)   they provided for the elderly by way of bargain on a contractual basis rather than by way of a bounty;

(ii)   the benefits provided could not be withdrawn if the beneficiary ceased to be eligible to qualify;

(iii)   the schemes were for the benefit of private individuals, not a charitable class; and

(iv)   the schemes were a commercial enterprise capable of producing profit for the beneficiary.

Before dealing with these objections, Peter Gibson J looked at the scope of a charitable purpose. He considered the wording of the Statute of Elizabeth: that charitable trusts must be for the relief of "aged, impotent and poor people". After reviewing a number of authorities the Judge concluded that relief of the aged does not have to be relief of the aged poor. It is a sufficient charitable purpose to benefit the aged, *or* the impotent, *or* the poor. The Judge also felt that there must be a need attributable to the aged or impotent condition of the person to be relieved by the charitable gift.

The plaintiffs had not argued that the proposed schemes were charitable simply because they were to benefit the aged. They had, however, identified a particular need for special housing. It seemed to the Judge that on any view of the matter that would be a charitable purpose. All the objections made by the Charity Commissioners were then dismissed, and a declaration made that it would, in law, be charitable for the plaintiffs to carry out the proposed housing schemes.

53   *Re Coulthurst's Will Trusts*
[1951] 1 All ER 775

Mr Coulthurst, who died in 1949, gave his trustees a fund of £20,000 to be called "The Coulthurst Fund". The trustees were directed to pay the income from the fund to widows and orphaned children of employees and former employees of Coutts' Bank. Payments were to be made to those who, in the absolute discretion of the trustees, because of their financial circumstances, were most deserving of assistance. Battle was then joined between Mr Coulthurst's widow, who claimed the trusts were ineffective charitable dispositions, and the Attorney-General who argued that they were not.

In the Court of Appeal, Lord Evershed MR held that this was a good charitable trust. Poverty can be paraphrased as meaning persons who have to "go short" with regard to their status in life. He then considered that a class of orphans and widows would be, by its very nature, a class comprising those who may be in real need of assistance. Reference to them in the will would proceed from general benevolence towards persons suffering under circumstances of privation, and this was a strong argument that the fund was charitable. Lord Evershed read the words as being an expression of the testator's intention that the money should go to those who were poor within the meaning of the Statute of Elizabeth.

The added qualification, that those to benefit would be those most deserving of such assistance, emphasised that the trust was charitable. This was interpreted as an objective standard: that the beneficiaries were to be persons whose financial circumstances left them in want.

54   *Re Mitchell*
[1963] NZLR 934

George Mitchell, retired merchant of Governors Bay, set out in his will that his residuary estate was to be divided into five parts. Two of the five were to be given to the Salvation Army to apply the annual income on trust for the benefit of young women, married or unmarried, who had their first child in the Salvation Army maternity home at Christchurch. This, along with other matters arising from the will, was considered by Wilson J in the Supreme Court at Christchurch.

The Salvation Army submitted that the gift was a valid charitable trust, either for the relief of poverty; or as a benefit to the community. The latter was not accepted by the Court, but the former argument was successful. The evidence showed that, although admission to the maternity home was not restricted only to the poor, it was nevertheless clear that most women went there because of their poverty. The Court felt that the testator may have been presumed to have known this. Thus, the testator intended to provide assistance because of the poverty of the recipients. Thus, despite no express reference to poverty in the will, it was held to be a trust for the relief of poverty.

The question was also raised as to whether the class of beneficiaries was too restricted for the gift to qualify as a valid charitable trust. The Court held that there was an exception to the general rule, and that trusts or gifts for the relief of poverty can be valid even though they are of limited application.

55   *Re McIntosh*
[1976] 1 NZLR 308

The Otago Hospital Board had for many years held funds left to it under testamentary trusts, but found it impossible or impractical to carry out many of the trusts imposed by the respective wills. The Board sought the Court's approval of a scheme by which the Hospital Board could apply and use the money. In considering this scheme the Court reiterated the tests a purpose must satisfy to be charitable, namely: whether the Attorney-General could apply to the Court to enforce it; whether the purpose was, by analogy, within the spirit and intendment of the Statute of Elizabeth; whether the purpose fell within any of the divisions of charity derived from that statute; and whether the purpose was for the public benefit.

A question arose as to whether four bequests of money to provide comforts or extra comforts for patients, would be charitable trusts. It was confirmed that the words in the preamble of the Statute of Elizabeth are to be read disjunctively; that is "impotent persons" were a charitable class within themselves. Once that class was established, persons could be included in it although not qualifying under any other charitable purpose. For these reasons, and because other New Zealand authorities had held the provision of comforts for patients in specified wards were charitable gifts, the Court concluded that they were charitable. The whole scheme was approved.

(2) Advancement of education

56   *Re Dupree's Will Trust*
[1944] 2 All ER 443

The late Sir William Dupree had, in 1932, executed a deed of gift for £5000 which was to be held on trust. The four trustees (the Lord Mayor of Portsmouth, the Town Clerk of Portsmouth, the Chairman of the Portsmouth Education Committee, and the Headmaster of Portsmouth Grammar School) were to apply the income from the Trust by way of prizes for an annual chess tournament open to males aged under 21 years and resident in Portsmouth.

The prizes were not to be paid in cash but were to be provided as the trustees thought fit for the advancement in life and benefit of the winners. Evidence was called from several schoolmasters who taught chess and found it to have a real educational value by teaching concentration, foresight, self-reliance and reasoning.

Vaisey J found that the promotion of chess playing in this case was a valid charitable trust. The reasoning was: the trust was confined to Portsmouth; two of the trustees were closely connected with educational activities within that city; and because chess has definite educational value.

The Judge, doubtless a chess player himself, thought that even without the evidence presented, the conclusion could have been reached that chess is essentially a game of skill and one of educational value. He was unwilling to venture any opinion on the status of draughts, bridge or stamp collecting however.

57 *Incorporated Council of Law Reporting v Attorney-General* [1972] Ch 73

The primary object of the Incorporated Council of Law Reporting was the preparation and publication of reports of the judicial decisions of the Courts in England. The Charitable Commissioners for England and Wales had refused to register the Council as a charity. The Council appealed this decision. Foster J allowed the appeal, holding that the Council fell into the fourth category of *Pemsel* (43): a purpose beneficial to the community.

The Commissioner of Inland Revenue appealed, arguing that the Council's purpose was to service the interests of the legal profession. He claimed that the reports provided an essential tool for the practice of law which might be beneficial to the community, but which was not within the spirit of the Statute of Elizabeth. The Council further argued that it was a charity for the advancement of education — an argument rejected by Foster J.

The majority of the Court of Appeal, Sachs and Buckley LJJ, found that a substantial purpose of the law reports was to provide essential material for the study of the law. Accordingly, the Council was advancing education. Sachs LJ thought that it would be unusual if a library for the study of a particular subject did not prima facie fall within the phrase "advancement of education". The same reasoning should then apply to the texts used in that study. Where an institution provides these texts; the individual members make no financial gain; and profits are used to provide further and better material; the institution should be deemed charitable. Neither Judge considered that the fact that the Council provided the legal profession with the "tools of their trade" should detract from this finding.

Russell LJ dissented. He upheld Foster J's decision regarding the fourth category, but he did not find the purpose was for the advancement of education. Although the furthering of knowledge in "legal science" was a function of the Council, its main aim was to further the sound development and administration of the law. In his opinion that was a purpose beneficial to the community. Sachs LJ noted that if he had not found the Council's purpose was to advance education, he too would have found the Council to be charitable on this ground.

58   *Auckland Medical Aid Trust v CIR*
[1979] 1 NZLR 382

The objects of the Auckland Medical Aid Trust were to maintain a comprehensive reproductive health and welfare service, and to educate the public about the facts of reproduction and reproductive health. It aimed to provide hospitals, clinics and other related services. Fees were charged for its services but the trust was not run for profit.

The Commissioner of Inland Revenue argued that the purposes of the trust were not charitable, and that it was not exempt from the Income Tax Act. Chilwell J had to consider whether the trust fell within the relevant exemption provisions of the Act. One of the statutory tests was whether the income was ultimately applied to charitable purposes.

Chilwell J, relying on *Incorporated Council of Law Reporting v A-G* (57), found this to be an educational trust. This branch of the law is not confined to teaching in the conventional sense. It extends to all branches of human knowledge and its dissemination. He supported his conclusions with other New Zealand authorities relating to educative trusts in the medical arena which distributed pamphlets or funded research.

In any event, Chilwell J also considered that the trust could have fallen into the category of trusts for the relief of the sick. He found that the term is today used to mean broadly those requiring medical treatment. A non-profit hospital would be charitable because it provided this treatment.

59   *Canterbury Orchestra Trust v Smitham*
[1978] 1 NZLR 787

In Christchurch in the 1970s two groups of citizens both wished to promote a local orchestra, but disagreed as to how it should be done. In 1975 the Christchurch Civic Orchestra Foundation was registered as a charitable trust. According to the trust deed its purposes were to establish and promote an orchestra in Christchurch to perform orchestral compositions and concert works and generally to sponsor performance in orchestra. It also aimed to foster the training of musicians, conductors and theatrical technicians and to promote the study, practice and performance of orchestral and chamber works.

Some of those associated with the body who had opposed this move attempted to have the Orchestra Trust dissolved and called a board meeting to effect this. The parties were able to agree to have the matter heard as a special case which was removed directly into the Court of Appeal.

The real question was whether the present Orchestra Trust was for the advancement of education, or for another purpose beneficial to the community. The Court had no doubt that a trust for the advancement of musical education would be charitable, not only because it would educate and train the musicians; but also because the public would be educated. The trust would raise the standard of musical taste, and give the public an opportunity of hearing and becoming familiar with different types of music. However, a society formed to promote music merely for the amusement of its members would not be charitable.

Woodhouse J believed that the purpose of the trust could not be put at risk by the performance of compositions, whether ancient or modern, which some sections of the community might find unappealing. In any event, if, by some chance of drafting, the constitution of the trust included objects going beyond the scope of charity in the legal sense, it would clearly be saved by s 61B of the Charitable Trusts Act 1957. Accordingly, the Court of Appeal held that the trust was a valid charitable trust.

This was, however, merely one of the issues facing the Court of Appeal. A number of other matters had to be considered in relation to whether or not the opponents of the trust board could validly use the provisions of the deed to dissolve the trust. It was eventually decided that they could not.

60   *Re Shaw's Will Trusts: National Provincial Bank Ltd v National City Bank Ltd*
[1952] 1 Ch 163

Charlotte Shaw was the wife of George Bernard Shaw, the well-known author and playwright. Both she and her husband were of Irish origin, but had lived for many years in England. On her death in 1943 it was found that her will purported to set up a trust to promote the education of Irish people to be better citizens in the various departments of life. Some of its aims were to bring masterpieces of art within the reach of Irish people of all classes; to teach and encourage self-control, elocution, oratory, deportment, the art of personal contact and social intercourse; and to establish and endow educational institutions to achieve these purposes.

Vaisey J considered that Mrs Shaw had had in mind a sort of finishing school for the Irish people, and was prepared to hold that this could be a trust for the purposes of education. Education, according to Vaisey J, includes not only teaching, but also the promotion or encouragement of the arts and graces of life which he saw as perhaps the finest and best part of the human character.

It was held that Mrs Shaw's Trust was educational. The Judge felt, however, that he ought not to speculate how the people of Ireland would react to such intensive treatment as Mrs Shaw appeared to envisage, or indeed to what extent such treatment would in fact be beneficial. He noted the Court should not weigh the respective merits of particular educational methods — it would suffice if purposes are genuinely educational in their aim and scope.

61   *Re Shaw: Public Trustee v Day*
[1957] 1 WLR 729

When George Bernard Shaw died in June 1950 his will demonstrated that he was quite as enthusiastic a deviser of trusts as his late wife (see above). After a few pedestrian clauses appointing a trustee and executor and bequeathing his authorial rights, Shaw set up a somewhat unusual trust. In summary, he directed that the residuary funds of his estate be held on trust for a period of 21 years for two purposes. First, his trustees were to inquire into how much time could be saved by English language users if the current 26-letter alphabet was to be substituted with an alphabet containing at least 40 letters; and secondly, they were to employ a phonetic expert to transliterate his play "Androcles and the Lion" into this proposed 40-letter alphabet and to disseminate a number of copies of this. Then, by advertisement and propaganda, the trustees were to persuade the government, the public and the English-speaking world to adopt this alphabet.

The ultimate residual legatees, the British Museum and the Royal Academy of Dramatic Art, claimed that this so called "alphabet trust" was entirely void, and that they were entitled to the money. The Attorney-General, appearing to uphold the Trust, replied that it was a valid charitable trust. Harman J first considered whether or not the trusts could be considered to be for the purposes of education. He decided that the research and propaganda envisaged by Shaw would merely increase public knowledge with respect to the saving of time and money by the use of the proposed alphabet. He could not discern any element of teaching or education combined with this. Nor was he convinced that the propaganda element in the trust would do more than persuade the public that the adoption of the new alphabet would be a "good thing". In the view of Harman J that was not education.

The trust also failed to fall into the fourth category of *Pemsel* (43). In order to be persuaded that the trust was beneficial, the Judge felt that he would have to hold that the proposed adoption of the new alphabet would confer a benefit on the public. That, however, was the very purpose the trust had been designed to investigate. He also considered the objects of the alphabet trust analogous to trusts for political purposes, and such objects have never been considered charitable.

In the end, the trust was held to be void. Accordingly, the world may never know whether a 40-letter alphabet will work better than the current 26-letter version.

62   *Re Pinion: Westminster Bank Ltd v Pinion*
         [1965] 1 Ch 85

Arthur Pinion's will instructed that his former house, together with all its contents, was to be turned into a museum. His next of kin argued that this was not a valid charitable trust, and that they were entitled to the residue of his estate. The Attorney-General was left with the thankless task of persuading the Court of Appeal that this was a valid charitable trust.

The Attorney-General confined his arguments that the trust was charitable to the category of the advancement of education. He claimed that a museum is presumed to have an educational value and purpose. It was argued that such a presumption prevented the Court from inquiring any further. The Court of Appeal disagreed: they considered that a mere gift of chattels to form a public museum will not in itself establish a tendency to advance education without some inquiry being made into the nature of the goods and the museum. The Judges were not convinced by the nature of the goods that this could be an educational trust.

The goods in Mr Pinion's house consisted principally of a number of paintings, (both by Mr Pinion and others), items of furniture, and "objects of art". No period or particular style of manufacture was illustrated. Mr Pinion's own paintings were said by one witness to be "atrociously bad", and it was found that all the other pictures were, without exception, worthless. Unanimous expert opinion was that nothing beyond the third rate was to be found in any of the other items. In the opinion of Harman J no useful object could be served in foisting such a mass of junk upon the public: he considered it to have neither public utility or educative value. Davies and Russell LJJ were of a similar views, although less scathing in tone. The Court was unanimous in holding that Mr Pinion's trust should not be carried into effect, and that his next of kin were entitled to the residue of his estate, such as it was.

(3) Advancement of religion

63   *Centrepoint Community Growth Trust v CIR*
[1985] 1 NZLR 673

The Centrepoint Community Growth Trust was incorporated in 1977 under the Charitable Trusts Act 1957. Members of the trust formed a residential community situated north of Auckland. The community was founded upon the spiritual beliefs of Bert Potter, its leader. In addition to being a spiritual community, the trust was also involved in counselling and therapy for the wider community. Those benefiting from its services could either stay with the trust as visitors or attend courses held in the Auckland area. Small charges were made for courses run in Auckland, while those attending as visitors made a contribution to the trust if possible. Trust members ceded all their assets to the trust upon joining. While part of the community they were fed, clothed and housed by the trust, and paid an allowance of $1 per week.

In May 1981 the trust submitted an agreement for sale and purchase of land to the Inland Revenue Department. The department advised the trust that it would not be granted an exemption from conveyance duty pursuant to the Stamp and Cheque Duties Act 1971, as the Department had determined that the trust was not charitable. The trust sought a declaration that they were a trust for charitable purposes; and accordingly were exempt from the conveyance duty claimed.

Tompkins J considered all four of the heads of charity outlined in **Pemsel (43)**, but concentrated on the issue of whether the trust was for the advancement of religion. He adopted the criteria for a religion laid down in the Australian case of *Church of the New Faith v Commissioner for P T* (Vic) 83 ATC 4652 where it was held that the criteria were twofold: first, the organisation must demonstrate a belief in a supernatural being, thing or principle; and secondly, they must have an acceptance of canons of conduct in order to give effect to that belief. Wilson and Deane JJ looked at similar criteria but also thought that adherents should constitute an identifiable group or identifiable groups, and that the adherents should themselves see their collection of ideas and practices as constituting a religion.

One of the expert witnesses, a senior lecturer in theology, noted that contemporary theologians consider there are a number of elements which make up a religion. These include:

(i)   A belief in a god, or an ultimate being;

(ii) The observation of sacraments, symbols, ceremonies and rituals taking place within the community;

(iii) An ethical code of behaviour which is understood in most religions to be reflective of the nature of divine reality and of a god; and

(iv) The form of organisation and structure of the community in the institution itself.

Tompkins J then analysed the objects of the Centrepoint Trust in line with these statements. He accepted that the trust was religious in intent, and that it was not too uncertain for the Court to control if necessary. Further, he had no doubt that the members of the trust had a belief in the supernatural, and that standards and codes of conduct existed that were expected to be observed. These involved not only concrete ceremonies and rites, but also concepts such as an acceptance of total honesty in their interrelationships, and a commitment to the trust. Members identified themselves as a group, and considered that they constituted a religion. Therefore, one of the principal purposes of the trust was the advancement of religion.

Tompkins J also held that the Trust could be a charitable trust under the fourth head of *Pemsel* because of the counselling and psychological services they provided for the general public.

(4) Other purposes beneficial to the community

64   ***Re Nottage***
         [1895] 2 Ch 649

In his will, Charles Nottage bequeathed £2000 per annum to the Yacht Racing Association of Great Britain. His trustees were to purchase a cup from the annual income of this sum and present it each season to the most successful yacht. Mr Nottage expressly declared that his object in giving this cup was to encourage the sport of yacht racing. The executors of Mr Nottage's will tested its validity in Court.

The matter was originally heard before Kekewich J. He felt that in order to uphold the gift as charitable he would have to be convinced that it was, by itself, directly and necessarily beneficial to the community. Here, the gift was expressly and directly to encourage the sport of yacht racing. An indirect result of this would be to employ people to build and fit out yachts. It would also train a potential defence force for Great Britain. Had these aims been the direct objects of the gift, it would be valid. But Kekewich J could not bring himself to hold that the sport alone was beneficial to the community in the sense that he had outlined. Despite the fact that he felt that anything which upholds the reputation and promotes the maritime influence of England must be for the benefit of the community, in this situation the gift failed.

On appeal, the Court upheld Kekewich J's decision, with two of the three Judges in particular noting that a gift to encourage a mere sport or game, primarily calculated to amuse individuals apart from the community at large, could not be held to be charitable.

65   *Re Smith: Public Trustee v Smith*
[1932] 1 Ch 153

Theodore Smith left quite a short will. He directed the payment of his funeral and testamentary expenses, and then bequeathed all his estate to "his country England" to and for England's own use and benefit absolutely. The Public Trustee was appointed as his executor. It was argued by Theodore's next of kin that not only did the gift fall outside the definitions of charity, but also that it was void for uncertainty.

Lord Hanworth MR first considered the question of whether or not the trust would be void for uncertainty. He considered that England was an identifiable entity, being that part of the country that is not joined to Scotland and to Wales. His response to the second question took a little more time. He ran through a number of authorities which hold that a gift to an area with no purpose specified is a valid gift for the benefit of those living there. He also looked at the case of *Nightingale v Goulburn* (1847) 5 Hare 484, which held that a gift to the Chancellor of the Exchequer for the "benefit and advantage of Great Britain" was a valid charitable trust. These authorities meant that the bequest created a valid trust for the benefit of the public. The money was to be used for the advantage of the inhabitants of England.

The Judge also felt that a principle could be drawn from *Pemsel* **(43)** that those who have the responsibility for administering a non-specific gift, such as that at issue here, have an obligation to see that the gift is used for charitable objects in the proper sense of that word.

66 **CIR v Medical Council of New Zealand**
[1997] 2 NZLR 297

The Medical Council of New Zealand was established under the Medical Practitioners Act 1950. It was set up to register medical practitioners, and discipline or suspend them if necessary. The Medical Council argued that it was exempt from the Income Tax Act because it was a public authority; and an institution established exclusively for charitable purposes.

The Commissioner of Inland Revenue disagreed. The Commissioner argued that the Medical Council did not fit the definition of a public authority, and that registration conferred significant non-charitable benefits on medical practitioners.

The Court agreed with the Commissioner that the Medical Council was not a public authority. But they were split 3:2 over whether the council was established exclusively for charitable purposes.

The majority and minority judgments differed in their approach to "purpose". Gault J and Richardson P held that when determining the purposes of an institution established by statute, the focus is on the functions the institution was established to carry out under the statute, not the general object or purpose the legislature may have had in establishing it. The Medical Practitioners Act does not explicitly state what the purposes of the council are, so the Act as a whole must be looked at. They found the principal purpose of the council is to keep a register of qualified doctors. The Judges could find nothing charitable in this activity.

In contrast, the majority opinion of McKay, Thomas and Keith JJ distinguished "function" and "purpose". They accepted that a principal function of the council is to provide and maintain a register of qualified medical practitioners. However, it did not follow that these benefits were either the purpose of the legislation, or the purpose of the establishment of the council. The obvious and primary focus of registration was the protection of the public, by ensuring high standards in the practice of medicine and surgery. Any benefits to registered practitioners were incidental. They held that the Medical Council was exclusively established for the purpose of the protection and benefit of the public.

The majority then considered whether the purpose was charitable. The Court examined the fourth category of charity referred to in **Pemsel (43)** — trusts for other purposes beneficial to the community. Such trusts must fall within the spirit and intendment of the Statute of Elizabeth I. McKay J could not see that the protection of the public in respect of the quality of medical and surgical services could possibly be held to fall outside this broad category.

The only obstacle to the viewpoint of the majority was the case *General Medical Council v Inland Revenue Commissioners* (1928) 97 LJKB 578; 13 TC 819 (KB & CA). That case had almost identical facts to the present, but the Court of Appeal had held that the General Medical Council was not a charity for the purposes of exemption from income tax. The main object of the General Medical Council was to protect the public against bad doctors by a system of registration and discipline. This aim was held to be for the public good, but not charitable. The majority accepted that that case could not be distinguished on the facts, but declined to follow it, stating that the case was not based on any real analysis, and is singularly unpersuasive. McKay J added, "it is difficult to discern from these judgments any clear principle of law which could be regarded as persuasive precedent".

67   *Latimer v Commissioner of Inland Revenue*
[2004] 3 NZLR 157 (PC)

Trust law is often seen as private law, but it can of course involve public issues. Following the decision in *New Zealand Maori Council v Attorney-General* [1987] 1 NZLR 641, the Crown and Maori entered into negotiations about claims to forestry assets. An agreement was reached in 1989, under which the Crown would sell forestry assets to two Maori organisations subject to a licence to use the land and with a rental payable. The parties would also use their best endeavours to enable the Waitangi Tribunal to process all forestry claims within the shortest reasonable period. Following a Tribunal recommendation, the Crown was to transfer relevant land to a claimant with compensation for the land now being encumbered by the licences. The terms of this agreement were to be contained in a trust deed pursuant to the agreement and the Crown Forest Assets Act 1989.

The trust deed was signed by the Crown and established the Crown Forestry Rental Trust. This trust was to receive rental proceeds from licences, and use the interest from these proceeds to assist Maori in Waitangi Tribunal claims involving licensed land. The trust was subject to an 80-year perpetuity period, although the duration was expected to be shorter.

The IRD argued that the trust was not established for charitable purposes and that tax was payable on the trust's income. Assisting Maori claimants was charitable, but the IRD argued that the trust had not been established for charitable purposes as was required under the relevant tax legislation. The

Privy Council, however, agreed with the Court of Appeal that a trust was different from a society or organisation. A charitable trust had no individual beneficiaries capable of enforcing the purposes and it was not necessary that a trust be established for charitable purposes as long as the funds were applicable for exclusively charitable purposes. Here, income from the trust was not required to be distributed: it could be retained and would ultimately become payable to the Crown.

Their Lordships found that the Crown was not a charity. The Crown's funds were not held exclusively for charitable purposes, and were applied to many non-charitable purposes, albeit public ones: "not all public purposes are charitable purposes". A gift to the Crown might be subject to an implied trust in favour of charity, but the reversion of the income to the Crown was not a gift. In the Privy Council's view, the trust deed served much the same purpose as a *Quistclose* trust (see **Barclays Bank Ltd v Quistclose Investments Ltd (38)**): it allowed the Crown to make its funds available for a specified purpose, and, if not required for that purpose, to revert to the Crown. There was an express resulting trust.

In the Privy Council's view, the trust settlement (the forestry rental) was tax-exempt income. If not applied anywhere, this income became capital and beneficially the property of the Crown. The income was all either tax-exempt for charitable purposes, or beneficially the tax-exempt income of the Crown (as all the Crown's income was tax-exempt). There was no income that was not either the Crown's or for charitable purposes, and the IRD's claim for tax failed.

Schemes for the administration of charitable trusts

68   *Re Amelia Bullock-Webster*
[1936] NZLR 814

Mrs Bullock-Webster's will provided that her estate was to be held on trust to provide pensions for retired New Zealand clergymen; however, her will contained no directions as to how she wished these trusts to be carried out. The executors of her estate requested the Bishop of Christchurch to draw up a scheme of administration and distribution that would allow her wishes to be effected. The Bishop did so, and then had the suggested scheme considered by the Diocesan Committee, the Public Trustee, and a meeting of retired clergymen drawn from around the country. The resulting scheme was submitted to the Court to be approved. In response to a challenge by the

Attorney-General to the Court's jurisdiction to approve the scheme, a comprehensive memorandum was submitted by the Public Trustee outlining the Court's jurisdiction. Northcroft J approved the scheme submitted to him, and appended the memorandum to his judgment.

The memorandum sets out the statutory basis for the Court's jurisdiction, as well as traversing a number of the relevant New Zealand and UK cases on the subject. It notes that under s 15 of the Religious, Charitable and Educational Trusts Act 1908 (now superseded by s 32 of the Charitable Trusts Act 1957), a Court has power to define the objects or prescribe the mode of administering a charity by a "scheme". This is merely a term used to describe a document containing directions as to how to deal· with the trust. Schemes are of two kinds:

1.   To define more precisely the administration of a charitable bequest where the trust is ambiguous or insufficient; and

2.   To provide for the application of the bequest cy-près where a clear charitable intention is expressed but cannot be executed.

The Court will only order a cy-près scheme where no scheme can be devised to give effect to the testator's intention.

The scheme proposed in this case fitted into the first category, and was approved.

69   *Re Palmerston North Halls Trust Board*
[1976] 2 NZLR 161

The Palmerston North Halls Trust Board owned six pieces of land with halls erected on them. These had been acquired from money contributed by members of the Exclusive Brethren Fellowship. The trust deed declared that the halls were to be used exclusively for meetings of Christians. The Trust Board applied to the Supreme Court to amend the deed. They sought to make two main changes: first, to revise and modernise the administrative powers available to the trustees; and secondly, to amend the purposes for which the properties were held. The trustees wished to define them with more clarity.

The Court proceedings sought an exercise of the Supreme Court's inherent jurisdiction to redefine the trust. The Trust Board deliberately did not rely on the statutory provisions of the Charitable Trusts Act 1957, as they were anxious to avoid the expense involved in complying with the statutory regime. Under the Act, the proposed scheme must be precisely formulated, advertised for potential objections, and reviewed by the Solicitor-General on behalf of the Attorney-General. In particular, the Board was unwilling to publicise the matter as required.

Wild CJ held that the amendments that the Trust Board wished to make fell into the description of s 32(1) of the Charitable Trusts Act 1957, which provides that where a stated charitable purpose "is illegal or useless or uncertain", the Court may have recourse to the provisions of Part III of the Act and approve a scheme in respect of the trusts.

The Judge held that this was mandatory. The Court has no jurisdiction to deal with a trust falling into s 32(1) other than to comply with the statutory regime. The Court was not able to deal with the matter in its inherent jurisdiction.

70   *Re Twigger*
       [1989] 3 NZLR 329

In 1885 John Twigger left a substantial fortune to be held on trust. The income was to be divided between three charitable foundations in the Christchurch area: the Ashburton Home, the Female Refuge, and the Canterbury Orphanage.

By 1980, the latter two of these three beneficiaries had become defunct. The trustee, the Canterbury Hospital Board, drew up a scheme for the amended administration of the Twigger Trust. This provided that the successor to the Ashburton Home was still to receive one-third of the trust's annual income, but that 50 per cent of the annual income was to be paid to four organisations (a child and family guidance and psychiatric centre, the Christchurch Women's Refuge, Nurse Maude, and Birthright). At the discretion of the trustee the remainder of the yearly income was either to be reinvested with its income being paid to those four organisations, or was to go to the organisations outright. The trustee presented this scheme to the Court for approval under the Charitable Trusts Act.

Objections were filed by a number of charitable institutions around the Canterbury area, including a children's home and various organisations supporting women.

Tipping J was satisfied that it was now impossible to carry out Twigger's original purposes. Therefore, the requirements of s 32(1) had been met. In line with previous authorities, any substituted trust under a scheme should accord as closely as possible to the terms of the original trust. A trustee drawing up a scheme is exercising something akin to a trust power: they should inform themselves as fully as possible of those who may fall within the qualifying class and then measure their respective claims to be beneficiaries. Tipping J thought it would be a wise course for trustees to call for submissions from interested parties so as to enable them to discover the most appropriate beneficiaries.

In this case, Tipping J was not satisfied with the scheme proposed. In his opinion it did not accord as closely as possible to the Trust's original terms. He felt that the children's home was a worthy recipient of the third of the fund that had initially been earmarked for the Canterbury Orphanage; and that various women's charities were appropriate beneficiaries for the third that had gone to the Female Refuge. The latter had opened in 1864 for women who had "succumbed to the temptations incident to city life", operating mainly as a maternity hospital.

The Judge was unable to lay down a new scheme himself, and had no power to approve substantive changes. He considered that the legislation should be amended to enable objectors to lodge counter-schemes so that further Court proceedings would not be necessary. The Judge suggested an appropriate division, and noted that he would be favourably disposed towards approving a scheme broadly along the lines he had indicated.

71   *Re Lindsay Sangster Rogers*
High Court, Hamilton, M 4/95, 19 May 1995, Hammond J

Lindsay Rogers was a remarkable man. A doctor by profession, in World War II he worked in Ceylon, India, Tibet, the Middle East and the Balkans, parachuting into the latter location. After the war he was a Professor of Surgery in Iraq. On his return to New Zealand he and his family ran a dairy farm near Te Awamutu.

On his death in 1962 it was found that his will, after providing for his wife and sons, left the residue of his estate on trust for the Te Awamutu College. The money was to be used to provide hostels and boarding facilities for pupils of the college. Any surplus money was to provide student bursaries.

Following their mother's death in 1989, Roger's sons made a claim against their father's estate under the Family Protection Act. As a result of this they were awarded 51 per cent of the residuary estate. The remainder was to be held on the above trust.

The trustees had determined that the reduced money available to the trust would not be enough to build the hostel envisaged by Roger. Nor would it be economic to run. Accordingly, the trustees prepared a scheme whereby the funds would be used to provide courses in farming and agriculture at the college, with a power retained to build a hostel at some future time, if possible. The scheme came before Hammond J for approval.

Hammond J noted that this fell within the ambit of the Charitable Trusts Act, and that the planned substitution was for a legally charitable purpose. The scheme accorded as closely as possible with the original intention as stated in *Re Twigger* (70). He felt that this case was a good example of an appropriate compromise being found between the objectives of the settlor, and current socioeconomic realities. As the scheme had no objectors, and served the interests of both the beneficiaries and the public at large, it was approved.

72   *Re Centrepoint Community Trust*
[2000] 2 NZLR 325 (HC)

Charitable trusts can change and develop, and so can charitable purposes. The Centrepoint Community Growth Trust had been incorporated in 1977 for spiritual and religious advancement. Some years later, some members of Centrepoint, including its "spiritual leader", Herbert Potter, were convicted of offences for drug offending, perjury, and sexual offending. These convictions led to some internal disagreement over Centrepoint's operations and the Court took on a supervisory role in relation to the trust.

The Attorney-General undertook an investigation of the trust, and the Public Trustee was appointed as trustee of Centrepoint in 1997, under s 51 of the Charitable Trusts Act 1957 (CTA). Shortly afterwards, the Public Trustee applied to the Court for approval of a scheme to reform the trust under Part III of the CTA. Following further negotiations as to this scheme, the proposed objectives were fourfold: therapeutic and counselling; educational; the relief of poverty; and public benefit (specifically the environment and the establishment of communities to protect abuse victims). Spiritual objectives were intentionally left out because they were seen as central to the failure of the 1977 trust and had not been met.

An issue arose as to whether the new objectives could be regarded as charitable. The Public Trustee also applied for directions under s 66 of the Trustee Act 1956 for directions authorising payments under the "relief of poverty" head to a group loyal to Potter who supported the trust's original spiritual and religious objectives.

The Court noted its responsibility to consider whether the scheme was charitable. In the light of contemporary standards, the objectives of protecting the environment and establishing communities to support those who had been victims of the offending actions could be classified as for the public good and were therefore charitable. Further, payments for the relief of poverty did not need to benefit the public generally, or benefit only those in grinding need or utter destitution, or only those poor and "worthy". The "old believers" of the trust could therefore receive payments under the relief of poverty head. The Court made orders accordingly.

73   *Re McElroy Trust*
[2003] 2 NZLR 289 (CA)

In 1956, the McElroy brothers settled the McElroy Trust, with 404 acres of farmland in Warkworth to be held for: (i) homes for the elderly as to a one-half share; and (ii) homes for children as to a one-quarter share; and (iii) for the benefit of the Warkworth Parochial District (within the Anglican Church) as to a one-quarter share.

In 1998, the trustees sold the farmland because the farming operation had become unprofitable. This was within the powers of the trustees, although cl 18 of the trust deed provided that if the trustees did sell, the proceeds of sale were to be given to the charitable beneficiaries stated above in the shares stated above. The only identifiable beneficiary for the bulk of the trust's fund was the Selwyn Foundation.

The trustees applied to the High Court under s 32 of the Charitable Trusts Act for approval of a scheme of arrangement on the basis that it had become impossible, impracticable, or inexpedient to carry out the original charitable purposes. The term "inexpedient" was found to mean that the original charitable purposes had become "unsuitable, inadvisable or inapt", and was not to be given too narrow an interpretation. Giving effect to the term required a value judgment rather than simply an assessment of feasibility.

In this case, there was no inexpediency in the funds being paid to the Selwyn Foundation, as it was well placed to carry out the charitable purposes as originally determined by the McElroy brothers. The trustees' application was therefore declined.

74   *Re Wilson Home Trust*
[2000] 2 NZLR 222 (HC)

The Wilson Home for Crippled Children was a charity established in 1937 for the benefit of crippled children in Auckland. An endowment fund was also raised, partly from public contributions, and partly from members of the settlor's family.

The first part of the fund was to be used for the maintenance of crippled children in the home, while the income from the second part was to be used for maintenance of the property. The trust property was also divided into two parts: one, for the benefit of crippled children, and, if not fully utilised, for non-crippled convalescent children. The income of the endowment fund was not to be used for this secondary purpose. The second part was to be used for convalescent non-crippled children, with no obligation for the trustees to carry out this purpose. The trust's purposes were seen to be of their time, with polio prevalent and little government assistance available for crippled children.

By 1949 the second part of the trust's property was no longer required for convalescent non-crippled children. An application to Parliament led to the passage of s 28 of the Local Legislation Act 1949, which enabled the trust board to use the whole of the trust property for crippled children, or alternatively for convalescent non-crippled children if the facilities were not otherwise fully utilised. The successful application also amended the trust deed to provide that both income and capital were to be available for the purposes of the trust, though the capital could only be used for improvements of a capital nature.

Keeping in mind further changes in society and children's care since 1949, the board applied under Part III of the Charitable Trusts Act 1957 (CTA) for a number of variations to the trust. Most notably, the class of persons to be assisted was sought to be extended to "Children with Disabilities and/or their Families", the nature of the assistance was sought to be extended beyond institutional care, and some land was sought to be sold to allow provision of other facilities in outlying areas. The Attorney-General and the descendants of the settlor also supported the application.

The Court approved the application on the basis that, under s 32(1) of the CTA, it was now impossible, impracticable, or inexpedient to carry out the original purposes of the trust as modern needs had changed. In addition, the changes would not detract from the charitable nature of the trust, and the designation of the class of beneficiaries was close to the original trust beneficiaries.

There was also a jurisdictional issue: the Attorney-General had raised the issue that s 28 of the 1949 Act had made the trust a creature of statute, and that any amendment could therefore only be by statute. The Court held on this point that the legislature merely intended to augment the powers of the trust board on one point, and the legislation was not to be seen as a complete reformulation of the trust. The application related only to matters outside the scope of the 1949 Act. The Court therefore granted the orders for amendment sought.

RESULTING TRUSTS

75   *Re Gillingham Bus Disaster Fund*
[1958] Ch 300

In December 1951, in Gillingham, Kent a bus ran into a column of Royal Marine cadets marching along the roadside. Twenty-four were killed and a number injured. In response to public concern at the tragedy, three mayors of the surrounding area opened a memorial fund and published letters in national newspapers inviting donations for a fund to meet funeral expenses, to care for those cadets who had been injured, and to use in the memory of those boys who had lost their lives.

Unfortunately, in their concern for the dead and injured cadets the mayors had forgotten that each of them would have common law rights aplenty against the bus company. These were in due course asserted with the result that full compensation was paid to the injured cadets and the estates of the casualties. This left the three mayors in control of a fund slightly in excess of £2000, and with no idea of what to do with it. Three claimants to the surplus emerged: the donors; the Crown who claimed the fund as bona vacantia; and the Attorney-General who claimed the fund was a charity.

Harman J rejected the argument that the trust was a charity, considering that the real issue was whether the surplus should be paid to the Crown as bona vacantia, or be held on a resulting trust in favour of the subscribers.

The general principle is that when money is held upon trust, and the trusts declared do not exhaust the fund, it will revert to the donor or settlor under a resulting trust. The reasoning behind this is that the settlor or donor did not part with the money absolutely, but only so that their wishes should be effected. Once this has been achieved, any surplus still belongs to the settlor. A resulting trust arises automatically where those wishes are for some unforeseen reason not fulfilled.

The Crown had to show that the principle did not apply to the present case and cited a number of cases where funds had reverted to the Crown rather than the donors. It was also claimed that the difficulty of tracing the donors to the fund made a resulting trust impossible. In the view of Harman J, the fact that it would be difficult to trace the donors did not defeat the resulting trust argument. If those people could be found by inquiry the resulting trust could be executed in their favour. If they could not, then the Judge was unable to see how the money could suddenly change and become bona vacantia simply because the donors could not be traced. It would merely be money held upon trust for which no beneficiary could be found. The Judge ordered that the money be held on resulting trust, and that there should be an inquiry to discover who the donors were.

Harman J did note that this doctrine is not based on any evidence of the state of mind of the donor. Rather, it is an inference made by the law based on hindsight, for in most cases the donor would not consider the ultimate destination of his or her money, but would rather simply expect that the purpose would be satisfied. Most donors would indeed be very surprised to receive anything back under these principles.

76   *Cunnack v Edwards*
[1896] 2 Ch 679

In 1810 a group of men in the small town of Helston formed the Helston Equitable Annuitants Society. This was a form of quasi-life insurance: each of the members of the fund was to contribute an annual sum to a common pool which was to be used to provide annuities to their wives. On the death of a member his widow would receive £25 per year until her death. If a member died leaving no widow his contributions were to remain with the society and form part of its common fund.

The fund continued for a number of years, and it was not until 1892 that the last widow to be provided for died. On her death, £1250 remained in the care of the trustees of the society. The personal representative of the last surviving member, who had died in 1878, claimed that he, as survivor, was entitled to the whole fund. The trustees were not so certain, and the matter was heard by Chitty J. He held that there was a resulting trust in favour of all the personal representatives of those who contributed to the fund.

The Court of Appeal considered that the entire beneficial interest of donors to the fund had been exhausted. Each member had contributed a fixed sum of money to the common fund so that his widow would receive a fixed annuity. There never was, and never could be, any interest retained by any contributor beyond the fact that his wife, if she survived him, was entitled to the annuity. As the subscriptions were to remain with the society in the event that a member died without leaving a widow, it was plain that the members had intended to abandon their rights to the money they had contributed. There could therefore be no resulting trust in favour of the contributing members of the society, as they had no interest in the money.

Having put aside this question, the Court then considered whether the fund could be deemed charitable, or would fall to be considered bona vacantia. The Court did not find that an arrangement such as this could be regarded as charity, as each member was only aiming to benefit their own wife, rather than all the widows. The members also were not beneficiaries of the funds or any part of them, but simply persons who had paid money to secure a contractual benefit for their widows. In the circumstances the surplus was held to be bona vacantia and went to the Crown.

77   *Re Vandervell's Trust (No 2)*
[1974] 1 Ch 269

Mr Guy Vandervell decided in 1958 that he wanted to give the sum of £150,000 to the Royal College of Surgeons to found a chair in pharmacology. At the time he could have had no idea of the complications that this would cause. Vandervell was chairman, managing director and controlling shareholder of Vandervell Products Ltd, a highly successful engineering company. Vandervell himself held most of the shares in this company. There were no voting rights for 100,000 of the "A" class ordinary shares. Vandervell decided to use these shares to provide the College with the amount they needed to found the Chair. It was determined that the shares would be transferred to the College, and Vandervell's company could then declare dividends on the shares, which would provide the money needed. Once the required sum had been reached Vandervell's company would exercise an option to repurchase the shares for the sum of £5000. This scheme was effected.

Vandervell also had set up a company to act as trustee of trusts for both his children and employees of his company. It was proposed that the option to repurchase the company shares from the College should be granted to the trustee company. This was done by way of deed. Nothing in the deed indicated whether the shares, once acquired by the trustee company, would be held beneficially, or on trust, and if so on what trust. At a later meeting with the chairman of the trustee company it was proposed, and Vandervell approved, that the option should be held either on trust for his children or on trust for the employees of his company. He had not made up his mind which one should benefit. But it was clear that he thought that he himself had parted with all interest in the shares and in the option.

During the following years the Royal College of Surgeons collected the dividends as planned. However, the Inland Revenue claimed tax on the dividends payable to the College, and surtax on the dividends declared by Vandervell. This formed the basis of the first round of the Vandervell litigation.

In October 1961 the trustee company exercised its option. The 100,000 shares were retransferred to the trustee company. Vandervell had by now decided that the company should hold those shares on trust for his children alone, and dividends declared on these shares now were for the benefit of the children. In 1965, following further demands for surtaxes on the dividends declared by Vandervell's company, Vandervell executed a deed by which he transferred all rights, title and interest which he had on the option or the shares or on the dividends to the trustee company, and expressly declared that the company was to hold them on trust for his children. Soon after this, Vandervell died.

The Inland Revenue Department then claimed surtax from Vandervell's estate on the dividends declared from 1958 to 1961 (while the College held the shares), on the basis that Vandervell was the beneficial owner of the option and from 1961 to 1965 (when the trustee company held the shares) on the basis that Vandervell remained the beneficial owner of the shares. The department did concede that they had no claim against the estate for the period when Vandervell had expressly transferred all rights he had in relation to the shares and/or the option to the trustee company.

The Court of Appeal considered that the first round of Vandervell litigation had resolved the question as to whether Vandervell was liable for tax for the first period. The House of Lords had held that he was the beneficial owner of the option and thus was liable for surtax on dividends declared in that period.

The Court of Appeal, however, did not consider that Vandervell had remained the beneficial owner of the shares in the second period, while the option had been transferred to the trustee company, but before he executed the deed assigning all his rights to it. This was because the shares were held by the trustee company. The evidence was indisputable. However, before the option was exercised and the shares transferred from the College to the trustee company, a gap existed in the beneficial ownership of the shares. As there must be some owner of the beneficial interest there was therefore a resulting trust in favour of Vandervell. The legal interest had vested in the College, but the beneficial interest had to be held by someone. As the trustee company had declared no trust to the option, the only possible beneficiary was Vandervell himself. Thus, for the period that no trust was declared, Vandervell was the beneficial owner of the shares and was liable to pay the surtax. Once the trustee company exercised the option and took the transfer of the shares the position was very different. There was no gap between the legal and beneficial interests, and no longer any need for a resulting trust in favour of Vandervell to fill it. Once the resulting trust came to an end there was created a new valid trust of the shares for the children.

An alternative ground was that an equitable estoppel existed. Vandervell would have been estopped from attempting to enforce his strict rights under any continuing resulting trust once the option had been exercised because of the dealings which had taken place between the parties.

The Court of Appeal was satisfied that this result was in accordance with the justice and reality of the case. Vandervell's estate was only liable to pay surtax on the dividends declared before the option was exercised, and while the College still held the shares.

While the Court of Appeal did differ from Megarry J in his findings of facts, they did not disturb his comments on the difference between a presumed and an automatic resulting trust. In a presumed resulting trust a transfer is made to one person without any form of declared trust. In such a case there is a rebuttable presumption that the transferee holds the property on a resulting trust for the transferor. The question is one of presumption because the property has been transferred to the transferee, and from the absence of consideration and any presumption of advancement the transferee is *presumed* to hold the beneficial interest for the transferor absolutely. This establishes both that the transferee has to take on trust and also what the trust is.

An automatic resulting trust, which is the type in Vandervell's case, arises where the transfer is made on trust, but which leaves some or all of the beneficial interest undisposed of. Here the transferee automatically holds on resulting trust for the transferor that part of the beneficial interest that has not been carried to them or others. The resulting trust does not here depend on any intention or presumption but is the *automatic* consequence of the transferor's failure to dispose of what is vested in him or her.

78   *Re West Sussex Constabulary's Widows, Children and Benevolent (1930) Fund Trusts*
[1971] 1 Ch 1

The West Sussex Constabulary initiated a fund for the purpose of granting allowances to widows and dependants of deceased members of the Police Force. Funds were collected from the members themselves, but revenue was also derived from other sources including the proceeds of raffles and sweepstakes, street collecting boxes, and donations from other members of the public, including legacies. On 1 January 1968 the Constabulary was amalgamated with other police forces. The fund then became superfluous. On 7 June 1968 a meeting of members of the fund resolved to amend the funds rules enabling them to wind up the fund and distribute its assets according to an agreed scheme.

This plan was challenged and the trustees asked the Court to determine whether they held the fund and its income on trust, and could use the fund in accordance with their resolution of 7 June 1968; or whether they held the money for the Crown as bona vacantia.

Goff J made a preliminary finding that following the amalgamation of the West Sussex Constabulary on 31 December 1967 there were no longer any members of the fund capable of holding a meeting, amending its rules, or winding up the fund. The purported meeting was therefore ineffective. The Judge then had to ascertain the ultimate destination of the fund. He first disposed of an argument that the money belonged in equal shares to all surviving members of the fund by finding that this was nothing but a pension fund. It was not at all akin to a club where members would have a right to receive funds of the club. The Judge was also swayed by the fact that this organisation existed for the benefit of third parties only: namely the wives and dependants of the members.

It was then argued that there was a resulting trust created of the fund. This was not however a simple resulting trust, as it would have to be divided into three parts: contributions from former members, from surviving members, and from outside sources.

Goff J considered that the doctrine of resulting trust was clearly inapplicable to the contributions of former and surviving members of the fund. The members had put their money into the fund on a contractual basis, and not one of trust. They had moreover received all that they had contracted for, either because their widows and dependants had received or were in receipt of the allowances, or because they had no widows or dependants.

The Judge divided money raised from external sources into three categories: first, the proceeds of entertainment, raffles and sweepstakes; secondly, the proceeds of the collecting boxes; and thirdly, the donations and legacies. The Judge considered that there could be no resulting trust arising from the proceeds of the entertainment and raffles. First, the relationship between donor and recipient was one of contract and not of trust; but secondly, and more importantly, there was no direct contribution to the fund at all. The fund received only the profit ultimately gained from the transaction, not the amount of the donor's contribution. The second category also failed, as the Judge considered that contributors to street collections must be taken to have parted with their money out and out. Goff J adopted the view of Lawrence J in holding that any other view would be inconceivable and absurd.

The third category, however, covering donations and legacies, was held to be a resulting trust. Goff J's reasoning was that a donor who gives both money and name in such circumstances intends to give his or her property for the particular purpose for which the donation has been solicited, and none other. If that purpose fails, then there will be a resulting trust in their favour. Goff J could see no justification for infecting this category with the weaknesses of all the other categories, and, accordingly, held that that portion of the fund attributable to donations and legacies was held on resulting trust for the donors or their estates. Beyond this, the fund was bona vacantia.

79 *Re Densham*
[1975] 3 All ER 726

Neil Densham was made bankrupt by his former employer after it was discovered that he had stolen some £13,000 from the company in the course of his employment. Mr Densham also found himself in prison for his troubles, but his trustee in bankruptcy sought a declaration that property registered in Neil Densham's sole name was indeed his property alone, and was now vested in the trustee. Mr Densham's wife resisted this. Mr and Mrs Densham had married in 1968. It was agreed that Mrs Densham would work to help them save money to buy a house and she did. From her income, £10 per week was saved and hidden under the carpet in their bedroom beneath the bed. In total £1170 was saved. The Denshams regarded this money as joint savings, because, although it represented the totality of Mrs Densham's earnings, her husband paid all their other outgoings. Once the Denshams found a house they wanted to buy Mr Densham used the money to pay the deposit on the house. The agreement for sale and purchase originally named both Denshams as purchasers, but the wife's name was later deleted and Mr Densham alone signed the agreement and transfer. It was on this basis that his wife claimed a beneficial interest in the property.

The first question was whether there had been an agreement between Mr and Mrs Densham that the house should belong to them jointly, and secondly, whether any such agreement could be effective. The Judge noted that the Court could infer from the circumstances and the parties' conduct that there was an agreement, and if it did so the Court would give effect to that agreement. In this situation, Goff J was satisfied that there was no doubt that the savings and purchase were treated as joint. There was a common intention at the time of the purchase of the house that the beneficial interest in it would be shared. However this agreement was void against the trustee in bankruptcy because it was a voluntary settlement made by Mr Densham, and the sums that Mrs Densham had contributed were insufficient to be valuable consideration which would have otherwise exempted this agreement under the Bankruptcy Act.

The question then became what share the wife had in the house apart from the agreement. The Court held that she must have some, because she had at least contributed to the deposit. Although she had saved £1170, this money was treated as joint. Accordingly, the Court credited her with half of this sum — £585 — approximately one-ninth of the total value of the house. Goff J referred to the judgment of Lord Diplock in *Gissing v Gissing* [1970] 2 All ER 780. In that case it was noted that a resulting, implied or constructive trust (Lord Diplock thought it was unnecessary to distinguish between the three) was created by a transaction between trustee and beneficiary when a trustee acquired a legal estate in land, whenever the trustee has so conducted himself that it would be inequitable to allow him to deny the beneficiary a beneficial interest in the land. This principle seemed directly applicable to the present case. It would be inequitable for Mr Densham to deny his wife's beneficial interest in the land acquired with her contribution of one-ninth of its value. Accordingly, a trust of some sort was created in her favour.

Goff J accordingly made no definitive finding as to the exact nature of this trust. However, this case has often been treated as an example of a presumed resulting trust under the distinction drawn in *Re Vandervell's Trusts* (77). In the event it was declared that when the house was sold by the trustee in bankruptcy, Mrs Densham was entitled to a one-ninth share of the proceeds.

80   *Westdeutsche Landesbank Girozentrale v Islington London Borough Council*
[1996] 2 All ER 961

This case concerned an English borough council that entered into an interest rate swap transaction with a foreign bank. "Swaps" are ridiculously complicated transactions, but they can be boiled down to three relevant facts in the present case. First, Westdeutsche (the foreign bank) paid £2.5 m to the council in 1987. Secondly, Westdeusche had been paid £1.3 m by the council between 1987 and 1989. And thirdly, in 1989 the House of Lords determined that all such swap transactions were ultra vires the local authorities who had entered into them, and accordingly were void.

The balance outstanding at the time the council and the bank became aware that the transaction between them was void was approximately £1.1 m. Westdeutsche brought proceedings against the council to recover that sum, together with compound interest.

At first instance, and in the Court of Appeal, it was determined that the council was required to repay that sum to the bank. The Court of Appeal also determined that compound interest was payable. The council eventually accepted that the money was repayable, but appealed to the House of Lords on the issue of whether the Court had jurisdiction to award compound interest.

To understand the issues regarding the claim for compound interest, it is necessary to know the basis on which the case had been decided in the bank's favour. At first instance it had been held that the bank could recover on two grounds. The first was a common law claim for money had and received, leading to a restitutionary remedy. The second was equitable.

The bank had paid the £2.5m under a purported contract which, although unknown at the time, was ultra vires. This meant the contract was void, as there had been no consideration given for the payment. On the basis of *Sinclair v Brougham* (132) the Court at first instance, and the Court of Appeal, held that Westdeutsche retained equitable title to the money it had paid. Therefore, the bank had an equitable proprietary claim to the money (it was still its money), and the council was trustee of the money for the bank.

Before this case came to the House of Lords, there was no dispute that compound interest is only available in equity when the claim is based on a relationship of trustee and fiduciary, or where there has been fraud. Whether this was correct became one of the issues considered by Their Lordships, as well as the question of exactly how to categorise the transaction between the bank and the council. Did it give the bank an equitable proprietary interest in the money paid?

The majority, lead by Lord Browne-Wilkinson, held that the bank's claim was not founded on a relationship of trustee and fiduciary in this case, and that therefore compound interest was not available. The limited equitable jurisdiction could not be extended.

Lord Browne-Wilkinson noted that the bank's argument was based on a resulting trust coming into existence. His Lordship rejected this theory. The payment was not subject to any trust when it was paid, and the Council did not hold it on constructive trust. None of the established grounds for a resulting trust could be made out. Further, Lord Browne-Wilkinson was not prepared to rely on *Sinclair*. He regarded that case as a bewildering authority, and felt it should be overruled. Accordingly there was no resulting trust, no equitable proprietary right, and therefore no ability to claim compound interest. His Lordship cautioned strictly against developing the law of trust against principle to give remedies even if they were felt to be deserved. He also noted that it was not the Court's role to usurp the power of Parliament to award interest in such circumstances.

Lord Slynn felt that the local authority was neither a trustee nor a fiduciary, so the Court of Chancery would not have awarded compound interest to it. Neither could the common law then, if not allowed by legislation, and the Courts did not have the power to go beyond the legislation.

Lord Lloyd was also in agreement. He felt that *Sinclair* was wrong, and should be overruled. If this is so then the grounds on which the lower Courts had agreed that compound interest should be payable were overruled.

The leading judgment of the minority was delivered by Lord Goff. He noted that he would not have made an equitable proprietary claim in the form of a trust available to the bank in this case but for the rule in *Sinclair,* and the equitable jurisdiction to award compound interest in cases where the defendant is a trustee. Lord Goff then approached *Sinclair*. He considered that it was not to be relied upon as a general precedent, as it was decided on its particular facts. Further, Lord Goff was not prepared to class the Council as trustee of the bank's money in order to base its claim in equity. It had been argued that a resulting trust should be available in cases of mistake, or failure of consideration, but Lord Goff felt that this was inconsistent with the traditional purposes of trust law. Also, there was no general rule that property in money paid under a void contract does not pass to the payee. Therefore, Lord Goff saw no basis for imposing a resulting trust in the present case. He found that the bank had no equitable proprietary interest and therefore no entitlement to compound interest.

Lord Goff, however, held that as the bank also had a common law restitutionary claim for the return of the money, the equitable remedy of compound interest should nonetheless be available to it as part of its restitutionary remedy.

In this ground-breaking view Lord Goff was supported by Lord Woolf. He agreed with Lord Goff's reasoning that compound interest should be available when one party is under a duty to make restitution to another. Both Lords recognised that there was no previous authority to support this conclusion, but here felt that such a claim was warranted in the present case.

The House of Lords judgment has cast considerable doubt on the decision in *Sinclair*. Four stated that they would overrule the authority, and Lord Goff made it quite clear that it is confined strictly to its own facts. This also casts doubt on the decision in **Chase Manhattan Bank NA v Israel-British Bank (London) Ltd (136).** That case, in reliance on *Sinclair,* held that the recipient of a payment made under a void contract held the funds as trustee for the payer, as equitable owner. Their Lordships' decision makes it clear that this is no longer to be regarded as good law.

The judgments in *Westdeutsche* cover a great many points relating to trusts, equitable proprietary interests, and restitution. They are discussed further in:
- David Friar "Equity, restitution and commercial common sense" [1996] NZLJ 447.
- Gareth Jones "Ultra Vires Swaps: the common law and equitable fall-out" *Cambridge Law Journal* 55(3) Nov 1996: 432-436.

81   ***Pecore v Pecore***
[2007] SCJ 17, 2007 SCC 17 (SCC)

Paula Pecore was one of three children, but the closest of the three to her father. While her siblings were financially secure, Paula had a number of low-paying jobs and cared for her quadriplegic husband Michael. Paula's father helped her family in various ways, including assistance for her children's education and for home improvements.

Following some financial advice, Paula's father began transferring some assets into his and Paula's joint names in 1994, with a right of survivorship. Following further tax advice in 1996, Paula's father wrote letters to the financial institutions holding his money stating that he was the 100 per cent owner of the relevant assets and no funds were actually being gifted to Paula. He continued to use and control the accounts after they were transferred into joint ownership, and paid all taxes on them, although Paula made some withdrawals with his consent.

By the time of his last will in 1998, Paula's father already held most of his assets in joint accounts with Paula. This will left specific gifts to Paula, Michael and her children, but did not mention the joint accounts. The residue of the estate was to be divided equally between Paula and Michael. Paula's father died later that year, after living with Paula and Michael for a while. Paula and Michael later divorced and a dispute arose. The trial and intermediate appellate Courts found that Paula obtained beneficial ownership of the joint assets through survivorship, meaning the joint account assets did not divest under Paula's father's will and Michael had no claim to them as a residuary beneficiary under the will.

The Supreme Court of Canada noted that the presumption of a resulting trust applies to gratuitous transfers; that is, where a transfer is made for no consideration the onus is on the transferee to show a gift was intended, as equity presumes bargains, not gifts. However, in the case of certain relationships between transferor and transferee (most notably, between husband and wife or parent and child), the presumption of advancement or gift would apply instead. The (rebuttable) presumption of advancement in the case of a transferor parent and transferee child dated back to *Grey (Lord) v Grey (Lady)* (1677) 23 ER 185, on the basis that a father had an obligation to provide for his sons, and no trust would arise. There was conflicting authority in Canada as to whether the presumption of advancement applied between parents and independent adult children, and the Court was inclined to the view that the presumption should not apply in such a case. The Court was also reluctant to apply the presumption to *dependent* adult children because "dependent" was such a loose and uncertain concept. In other words, the presumption of advancement should be limited to transfers by parents to minor children and the presumption of a resulting trust applied in this case, although this could be rebutted.

While there had been some instances where assets had been transferred to a joint account with the transferor retaining exclusive control until death, the SCC found that the rights of survivorship, both legal and equitable, vested when the joint account was opened. The resulting trust presumption did, however, mean that the onus was on the survivor to show that the right of survivorship was intended to apply to the assets remaining in the joint account.

On the facts, particularly Paula's reliance on her father and her father's concern with providing for Paula, the SCC found the intention to gift a right of survivorship at the time the accounts were set up. The assets were not intended to form part of Paula's father's estate. Michael's claim to the joint assets as a beneficiary under Paula's father's will was dismissed.

CONSTRUCTIVE TRUSTS

General principles

82   *Keech v Sandford*
(1726) 2 Eq Cas Abr 741, 25 ER 223

The owner of a lease on profits from a market decided to give the benefit of the lease to his child and accordingly conveyed it to a trustee to hold the lease on the child's behalf. Prior to the expiration of the lease, the trustee applied to the lessor to have the lease renewed for the child. The lessor refused on the basis that the child could not be bound by the terms of the lease and, if it were to become necessary, no remedy could be obtained against him. The trustee applied for the lease himself and was given it.

The small child eventually brought an action to have the lease assigned to him and for the trustee to account to him for the profits. Lord King LC held that the trustee held the lease as a constructive trustee for the child. The Lord Chancellor held that if that were not the case, the consequences would be that very few trustees would renew the lease on behalf of their beneficiaries. Accordingly, the trustee still held the lease on the child's behalf and had to account to him for the profits gained since the renewal.

83   *Boardman v Phipps*
[1967] 2 AC 46

Mr C W Phipps died in 1944. The trustees under the will were his senile wife, his daughter, Mrs Noble, and an accountant named Mr Fox.

C W Phipps' residuary estate included 8000 of the 30,000 shares in a private company called Lester & Harris Ltd. Mrs Noble was one of the residuary legatees; she was entitled to a three-eighteenths share. A share was also left to Mr Phipps's sons. Thomas Phipps was entitled to a five-eighteenths share and John Phipps was entitled to the same.

Mr Boardman was the solicitor for the trustees. In 1956, he and the accountant, Mr Fox, decided that the accounts of Lester & Harris were not up to scratch. Boardman and Thomas Phipps accordingly went to the annual general meeting of the company armed with proxies of Mrs Noble and Mr Fox. They asked some questions and did not like the answers. Boardman and Thomas Phipps then decided, with the full knowledge of Mrs Noble and Mr Fox, to attempt to obtain control of Lester & Harris by making an offer for the remaining 22,000 shares. The trustees themselves did not have the power to invest trust money in shares of the company without the sanction of the Court. Boardman also asked each member of the Phipps family whether he or she objected to the acquisition of the shares by him and Thomas Phipps, but it seems he did not tell them the full story.

Boardman and Phipps eventually managed to acquire 21,986 of the remaining shares in the company. During negotiations for the acquisition of the shares, Boardman, acting on behalf of the trustees, became aware of valuable information about the company's assets and the purchase price of shares. That information would not have been available to him if he had been an ordinary member of the public.

Once Boardman and Phipps gained control of the company, they set about restructuring it. They sold off some of its assets at a considerable profit and returned a lot of capital to the shareholders. The shares in the company eventually increased in value and they made a profit. They always acted honestly and, for a time, at considerable risk to their personal finances.

Despite this, John Phipps brought an action claiming that Boardman held the shares as constructive trustee on the trust's behalf. A majority of the House of Lords agreed. It was held that Mr Boardman had obtained confidential information by virtue of his fiduciary relationship with the trust and that he had profited from the use of that information. The information amounted to trust property and Boardman had used that trust property to his eventual advantage. Although Boardman had acted with complete integrity, his liability to account for the profit he had made did not depend on the presence or absence of good faith.

84   *Westpac Banking Corporation v Savin*
[1985] 2 NZLR 41

Savin and Boyle engaged Aquamarine to sell their boats on their behalf. Savin authorised Aquamarine to sell his boat for not less than $5000 and Aquamarine would receive as commission whatever sale price it could obtain above the $5000 mark. Aquamarine was to remit the $5000 back to Savin. Boyle had a similar agreement. Aquamarine could keep as commission any money over the amount of $3420.

Aquamarine sold both boats: Savin's for $5495 and Boyle's for $3700. It deposited both amounts in its overdrawn account at Westpac. It did not pay either Savin or Boyle and it subsequently went into liquidation. There was no money in the liquidation available to meet ordinary creditors.

The manager of the Westpac Branch at which Aquamarine had an account was familiar with Aquamarine's business. In particular, he knew that Aquamarine often sold boats on other people's behalf, as opposed to out of the company's own stock. The manager knew that the ratio was about three to one of boats sold on other people's behalf to boats sold which were part of the company's stock. Therefore, there were three chances out of four that any cheque in respect of boat sales banked in the overdrawn account was in respect of a sale where Aquamarine was acting as an agent only and accountable to a boat owner.

After everything turned to custard, Savin and Boyle sued both the former director of Aquamarine and Westpac. They alleged against both that there had been a breach of fiduciary duty and conversion. There was an additional claim against Westpac for liability to account for breach of constructive trust. At first instance, the claim for conversion was rejected but Savin and Boyle succeeded on the other causes of action. Westpac appealed.

The Court held that Aquamarine should not have paid the proceeds of the sale into its overdrawn account with Westpac. Aquamarine was Savin and Boyle's agent and was therefore in a fiduciary relationship with them both. In applying the moneys to its overdraft in partial discharge of its indebtedness to Westpac, Aquamarine benefited from this relationship. The important question for Westpac was whether it was liable for participation in the breach of fiduciary duty on the part of its customer.

Richardson J noted the decision in *Thomson v Clydesdale Bank Ltd* [1893] AC 282 to the effect that ordinarily, on the basis of the debtor/creditor relationship between banker and customer, a banker is not required to inquire into the manner in which one of its customers obtained the funds with which it is discharging a debt. Richardson J also noted, however, the principle that any person who acquires property which is subject to an existing trust, becomes a constructive trustee of it himself or herself, if he or she knew of the trust's existence prior to its acquisition.

The essential question was what does it mean to "know" about a trust. Richardson J referred to *Baden, Delvaux and Lecuit v Société Générale pour Favoriser le Développement du Commerce et de l'Industrie en France SA* [1983] BCLC 325, in which five categories of knowledge were identified:

1. actual knowledge;

2. knowledge which is obtainable but for shutting one's eyes to the obvious;

3. knowledge obtainable but for wilfully and recklessly failing to make such inquiries as an honest and reasonable person would make;

4. knowledge of circumstances which would indicate the facts to an honest and reasonable person; and

5. knowledge obtainable from inquiries which an honest and reasonable person would feel obliged to make, being put on inquiry as a result of his or her knowledge of suspicious circumstances.

In principle, Richardson J did not see that there was any justification for excluding categories 4 and 5 as constituting knowledge in the "knowing receipt" class of case such as the present. However it was unnecessary for him to reach a final decision on that question. In the present circumstances the knowledge of the bank about Aquamarine's state of affairs was such that it must have wilfully shut its eyes to the obvious (category 2 knowledge) or, at least, it wilfully and recklessly failed to ascertain and satisfy itself that the receipts were not in respect of "on behalf" sales (category 3 knowledge). As a result of this imputed knowledge Westpac became a constructive trustee of the funds of Savin and Boyle and was liable to account for those funds to them.

See also *Royal Brunei Airlines v Tan* **(86)**.

85   *Lipkin Gorman v Karpnale Ltd*
[1987] 1 WLR 987

Norman Cass was a partner in Lipkin Gorman, a London firm of solicitors, and he was a compulsive gambler to boot. His own income was insufficient to fund his compulsion and he began looting the money in the clients' account of his firm. It was difficult to quantify exactly how much Cass stole, but it was close to £222,000. He lost just about all of it at the Playboy Club of London Ltd.

Cass's plundering of the clients' account was eventually discovered and the other partners sought to recover the money from the Playboy Club and also from the Brook St branch of Lloyds Bank, who were the bankers of both Lipkin Gorman and Cass personally. In order to do so, the other partners pleaded just about everything in the book against the two defendants, the most significant in terms of legal principle being a constructive trust for "knowing receipt" and "knowing assistance".

The critical issue was the question of knowledge of both the club and the bank. In respect of the club, did it know where Cass was getting his money to gamble? In terms of the bank, did it know what was he doing with the money he was withdrawing?

Alliott J found that neither the club nor the bank actually knew that Cass was robbing his clients. Accordingly, the question was whether either of them had constructive knowledge of this fact. If so, they would be liable to account as constructive trustees for the clients' money.

Alliott J referred to the five categories of knowledge described in *Westpac Banking Corporation v Savin* **(84)** but considered that the legal position as to what constituted constructive knowledge in respect of constructive trusts remained unclear. The key aspect in the approach that the Court should take was "want of probity". It was therefore insufficient to show that the defendant was careless or negligent. There had to be an element of wilfulness or recklessness in order for his or her conscience to be affected. Accordingly, Alliott J held (approving the dicta of Megarry V-C in *Re Montagu's Settlement Trusts* [1987] 2 WLR 1192) that only the first three categories of knowledge applied to the question of whether a constructive trust arose, both in knowing receipt and knowing assistance cases.

Applying this standard to the club, knowledge could not be imputed to the club that the money which Cass used to gamble had come from his firm's clients' account. The club's cash desk controller knew that Cass was a man of limited means and as a solicitor he had access to his clients' money. Moreover, Cass was obtaining chips for £1000. Nevertheless, Alliott J was not prepared to draw the inference from those facts that the controller closed his eyes to an obvious fact that the source of Cass's funds was the clients' money held on trust by Lipkin Gorman or that he wilfully and recklessly failed to make the inquiries that a honest and reasonable person would make. Accordingly, the claim that the club was liable for knowingly receiving money obtained in breach of trust failed.

The bank was not so lucky. The manager of the branch was found to have known of Cass's gambling and he even prevented knowledge of that fact from coming to his superior's attention. He also knew that Cass was drawing large amounts of cash from his clients' account. In the circumstances, it could be inferred that the manager had reasonable grounds for believing that Cass was operating the clients' account fraudulently. He did not inquire further because he knew full well what he would find and did not dare look. The manager, and therefore the bank, had constructive knowledge of the breach of trust and was therefore liable to account for the money as a constructive trustee to Lipkin Gorman.

86   *Royal Brunei Airlines v Tan*
[1995] 3 All ER 97

Royal Brunei Airlines appointed Borneo Leisure Travel (BLT) to act as its general travel agent in various South-East Asian locations. As part of this, BLT was to sell passenger and cargo transportation on behalf of the airline. The contract between the two clearly established that money paid to BLT for this was to be held on trust: BLT was required to account to the airline for all money received from sales of tickets, less only its commission.

In practice BLT did not pay the money it received on account for Royal Brunei Airlines into a separate bank account, but into its own current account. Once BLT got into financial difficulties, it was unable to make payments of the money it owed to Royal Brunei Airlines, and the airline sued Mr Tan, BLT's Managing Director and principal shareholder.

At first instance Mr Tan was held liable as a constructive trustee, on the ground that he had knowingly assisted in the breach of trust by BLT. One of the issues to arise was whether it was necessary that both BLT and Mr Tan acted fraudulently or dishonestly for Mr Tan's liability to be established. Eventually the case ended up before the Privy Council.

Lord Nicholls considered that the trustee's state of mind was essentially irrelevant to the question of whether a third party was liable to beneficiaries for knowingly assisting a breach of trust. If the liability of the third party is fault-based, the nature of their fault is what matters, not that of the trustee. His Lordship then went give on to an overview of the accessory liability principle.

Lord Nicholls considered and rejected both the possibility that a third party who assisted in a breach of trust ought never to be liable; and also the strict liability approach. This left the position that a third party may be liable in some circumstances. The next step is to identify those circumstances. The Privy Council were certain that a test of "dishonesty" was applicable. The application of the five categories of knowledge set out in *Baden, Delvaux and Lecuit v Société Générale pour Favoriser le Développement du Commerce et de l'Industrie en France SA* [1983] BCLC 325 (see *Westpac Banking Corporation v Savin* (**84**)) was considered and dismissed.

What then does "honesty" require a third party to do? The House of Lords considered that it is an objective standard, and would expect an individual to attain the standard an honest person placed in their circumstances would observe. The Court will look at all the circumstances known to the third party at the relevant time, and would have regard to their personal attributes, such as their experience and intelligence, and their reasons for acting.

The Privy Council therefore considered that dishonesty was a necessary (and sufficient) ingredient of accessory liability. Further, it is not necessary that both the third party and the trustee were acting dishonestly, although this will usually be the case. In the context of this principle the *Baden* scale of knowledge was best forgotten.

This decision only applies to liability for knowing assistance. The Privy Council made it clear that liability for knowing receipt of trust funds is dealt with under quite separate principles.

In *Equiticorp Industries v The Crown (Judgment No 47)* (reproduced in summary at [1996] 3 NZLR 586) Smellie J considered the level of knowledge required for knowing assistance and knowing receipt liability. The Judge referred to the Privy Council decision in *Royal Brunei Airlines v Tan* as unequivocally laying down the test for accessory liability as one of acting dishonestly. Smellie J noted that the law in relation to knowing receipt liability is not so clear, but used the *Baden* categories of knowledge as a convenient starting point. As in *Westpac v Savin* there was no need to reach the decision about the availability of *Baden* (iv) and (v) knowledge. Smellie J therefore left that issue to be decided on some future occasions when it was squarely before the Court.

87   *Elders Pastoral Ltd v Bank of New Zealand*
[1989] 2 NZLR 180

Elders Pastoral were the stock agents of a farmer named Gunn. Elders persuaded the BNZ to enter into an arrangement with Gunn whereby the bank would advance him some money which would be secured by an instrument by way of security over his stock registered under the Chattels Transfer Act 1924. Under the instrument, Gunn agreed not to sell any of his stock without the prior written consent of the BNZ, unless it was in the ordinary course of business. Gunn also agreed in the instrument that in the absence of any direction to the contrary by BNZ, proceeds of any sale of stock had to be paid to the BNZ.

Elders subsequently conducted a sale of 3081 Corriedale lambs on behalf of Gunn in the ordinary course of his business. From the proceeds of the sale, Elders deducted not only their commission but also the amount which Gunn currently owed them. Only a small balance was deposited in Gunn's cheque account with the BNZ. The BNZ brought proceedings to recover the amount of money which Elders applied in reduction of Gunn's debt to them.

The bank's claim was not for damages for conversion but for the proceeds of sale after the deduction of the expenses for sale. This raised the question as to whether the chattel security had merely contractual force between the parties, or whether it gave the bank an interest in the proceeds of sale or a right to trace the proceeds against a party in the position of Elders. Judgment was entered against Elders in the High Court. Elders appealed to the Court of Appeal.

Cooke P noted that no case precisely or even closely on point had been found. Treating the question as novel he then noted that equitable rights did not arise on the express words of the chattel security, but that this was by no means the only way in which equitable rights could arise. Both Cooke P and Somers J quoted a passage from Gough and Jones, *The Law of Restitution* (3rd ed), 1986, p 77:

> Equity's traditional rules suggest that it is necessary to discover a fiduciary relationship before a plaintiff can trace his property. Now that law and equity are fused this requirement makes little sense, and it has been recently accepted that "the receiving of money which consistently with conscience cannot be retained is, in equity, sufficient to raise a trust in favour of the party for whom or in whose account it was received".

> (The citation is from the judgment of Bingham J in *Neste Oy v Lloyds Bank Plc* [1983] 2 Lloyd's Rep 658, 665-666.)

The constructive trust has come to be used as a device for imposing a liability to account on persons who cannot in good conscience retain a benefit in breach of their legal or equitable obligations. Somers J noted that its evolution or extension as a remedy may not yet have come to an end.

The fact that a transaction is of a commercial nature is not decisive against imposing a fiduciary duty. Thus, in this case it was held that in all the circumstances Elders should be treated as being clearly bound by the obligation in the chattel security. They had actual notice of its existence, and had received the proceeds of sale as the agent for Gunn. They could stand in no better position vis-à-vis the bank than Gunn. As the proceeds of sale in the hands of Gunn must have been held for the bank, so they must be held for the bank by Elders.

88 *Lister & Co v Stubbs*
[1890] 45 Ch D 1

Lister & Co carried on business as silk spinners, dyers and manufacturers. The company employed Mr Stubbs as a foreman. Stubbs regularly dealt with another company, from whom he ordered large quantities of dye and from whom he received large sums by way of commission. Lister & Co did not know that he was receiving these commissions. Over the years the commissions amounted to £5500. Stubbs had invested a large portion of the money he had received, including the purchase of land in York.

When Lister & Co discovered the secret commissions, they sought to recover them from Stubbs. In the process of doing so, they sought an interlocutory injunction to restrain Stubbs from dealing with the land and any other investments he had made with the money or indeed any of the money which was left over.

The Court of Appeal held that Lister & Co could not follow the money in the way which they sought. Stubbs had acted wrongly but the Court was not prepared to hold that the money which Stubbs had obtained by way of bribes was held by Stubbs as a trustee for Lister & Co. The relationship was merely that of debtor and creditor. Lister & Co were therefore not entitled to their interlocutory injunction.

89 *Attorney-General for Hong Kong v Reid*
[1992] 2 NZLR 385

Mr Reid was a New Zealand solicitor who joined the legal service of the Government of Hong Kong. He was eventually promoted to Acting Director of Public Prosecutions. In the course of his career he accepted bribes to obstruct the prosecution of certain criminals.

Reid was eventually caught and pleaded guilty to various offences. He was ordered to pay the Crown the sum of HK$12.4m (about NZ$2.5m). Reid owned three properties in New Zealand, which (it was at least arguable) had been acquired with the moneys received by Reid as bribes. The Attorney-General for Hong Kong intended to issue proceedings against Reid, claiming to be the beneficiary of a constructive trust over the properties. Accordingly the Attorney-General would be able to recover some of the HK$12.4m which Reid was ordered to pay.

To prevent Reid from selling the properties himself in the meantime and hiding the proceeds in a numbered bank account somewhere in the world, the

Attorney-General registered caveats against the title of each of them. Eventually, the Attorney-General had to obtain an order that the caveats should not lapse. The application for the order was opposed by the Reids on the basis that the Attorney-General could have no equitable interest in the properties.

The essential question in this case, therefore, was whether the Crown could have an interest by way of a constructive trust over each of the properties. The New Zealand Court of Appeal felt constrained by *Lister & Co v Stubbs* **(88)**, which was more or less on all fours with the present case. As the Attorney-General could not demonstrate any property interest in the properties, it could not obtain a constructive trust over them. On the authority of *Lister*, the relationship between the Attorney-General and Reid was one of debtor/creditor and not of a fiduciary kind. A constructive trust could not be used in a remedial way.

The Privy Council disagreed. Lord Templeman analysed the law relating to bribery and the law of equity. Lord Templeman pointed out that Reid, as an agent and employee of the Government of Hong Kong, was in a fiduciary relationship with it. In receiving bribes, he breached his fiduciary duty to the government. Although the bribe money belonged in law to him, equity insists that it would be unconscionable for him to retain the money in breach of the duty. The providers of the bribes are obviously not entitled to their money back; instead Reid was liable to account to the government to whom he owed his fiduciary duty. Reid held the bribe money on trust for the Government of Hong Kong.

The Privy Council held that *Lister* was inconsistent with the principles of equity — that a fiduciary cannot benefit from a breach of his or her duty and that he or she is liable to account for any bribe money received. Accordingly, the bribe money or any property representing the bribe money is held on constructive trust by the false fiduciary for the injured party. In the present circumstances, then, if the bribe money was used to purchase the properties in question then the Government of Hong Kong did have an equitable interest in them and the caveats could be renewed until the resolution of that question.

90　　*LAC Minerals Ltd v International Corona Resources Ltd*
　　　　(1989) 61 DLR (4th) 14

Corona was a junior mining company owning mining rights on land. It engaged a geologist, Bell, to undertake an extensive exploration programme on the property. The results of the drilling were encouraging and revealed that the geology of the area had a certain character. This geology led Bell to conclusions about the other properties surrounding that of Corona. He decided that, in particular, an adjacent property owned by a Mr Williams was also likely to carry gold.

The generally encouraging results of the drilling (but not Mr Bell's specific conclusions) were made known. In particular, Corona sought a senior mining company to assist it in exploiting its claims. Representatives of LAC, a senior mining company, read about the encouraging results and approached Corona with a view to forming a partnership or joint venture in order to mine the land.

At the eventual meeting, Corona disclosed its drilling results, its conclusions about the geology of the area and its intention to purchase the Williams' property. LAC found this all very interesting but it did not enter into a joint venture or partnership. Instead, it outbid Corona for the Williams' property and mined it on its own account.

Corona sued. It was held at first instance that industry practice was such that parties negotiating to form a joint venture owed each other an obligation not to act to the detriment of each other. The trial Judge also found that the information was revealed to LAC in confidence for the purposes of a possible joint venture. The trial Judge found that LAC owed a fiduciary duty, was liable for breach of it, and was liable for the tort of breach of confidence. LAC appealed and lost. In particular, the Court of Appeal thought that the industry practice gave rise to a fiduciary duty.

The Supreme Court of Canada was divided on the critical issues. A majority (Sopinka, Lamer and McIntyre JJ) thought that no fiduciary duty arose in these circumstances. Sopinka J did not consider that the industry practice of not acting to the detriment of a possible joint venture party was sufficient to give rise to a fiduciary duty and was not aware of any authority to that effect, although industry practice could potentially give rise to an implied term of a contract.

Sopinka J also thought an important element of a fiduciary duty was that of dependency or vulnerability which was lacking in this case. Furthermore, the mere exchange of confidential information was not sufficient to give rise to a fiduciary duty, although that may be a possible incident of such a duty. If the essence of a complaint is the misuse of confidential information, then the appropriate action and remedy is in the tort of breach of confidence. It is inappropriate to ascribe a fiduciary duty to arm's length negotiations which are alien to the rules of equity. The majority therefore concluded that LAC, although liable for breach of confidence, was not liable for breach of fiduciary duty.

The minority on this issue (La Forest and Wilson JJ), although dissenting on the issue of whether there was a fiduciary duty, agreed that LAC was liable for the tort of breach of confidence.

On the question of the appropriate remedy, a different majority (La Forest, Wilson and Lamer JJ) concluded that there was a constructive trust, notwithstanding that the majority had held that there was no fiduciary duty. La Forest J concluded that a constructive trust over the Williams' land was available as a remedy for the tort of breach of confidence. But for LAC's conduct, Corona would have acquired the Williams' land and the loss suffered by Corona as a result was almost impossible to quantify accurately. La Forest J was not prepared to restrict the remedy of a constructive trust to matters involving the misuse of actual property rights, because that would be to deny its important remedial role.

Wilson J agreed in a brief judgment. Although the majority had found that no fiduciary relationship existed, he thought it would be anomalous if the law of fiduciary obligations would be able to provide more sophisticated forms of relief than those of the law of torts and the in rem remedy was available.

91   *Attorney-General v Blake (Jonathan Cape Ltd, third party)*
[1998] 1 All ER 833

George Blake was a famous spy. He was initially a member of the British Secret Intelligence Service (the SIS), but during his term of employment he also became an agent for the Soviet Union. After being caught in 1960 he pleaded guilty to five counts of unlawfully communicating information, contrary to s 1(1)(c) of the Official Secrets Act 1911. He was sentenced to 42 years' imprisonment but escaped and fled to Moscow, where he now lives. In 1990 his autobiography *No Other Choice* was published, describing his activities on behalf of the KGB, as well as other matters.

The British Government had no idea that the book would be published. As a great deal of its contents related to his activities as a member of the SIS the Crown took the understandable view that it would contain a large amount of information that Blake had learned in confidence, and while under a fiduciary duty to his employer. Perhaps mindful of the lessons learnt in the earlier *Spycatcher* litigation the Crown did not try to prevent the publication of the book. Rather, it sought to prevent Blake from gaining any royalties or financial benefit from his autobiography.

The Attorney-General accepted that as the information in the book was no longer confidential, Blake had not breached his duty of confidence. The action was therefore based on an independent breach of fiduciary duty not to use his position as a former servant of the Crown, or information imparted to him in that capacity, to generate profit for himself. The Attorney-General argued that Blake also owed a duty to give restitution to the Crown of any profit generated in such a manner.

In order to succeed the Crown would have to convince the Court that the fiduciary duty Blake owed to the Crown, his employer, did not cease when his employment ended. Lord Woolf MR, delivering the judgment of the Court of Appeal, could not accept this. The Court does not recognise the concept of a fiduciary obligation which continues despite the determination of the particular relationship which gives rise to it. In this case, the duty of loyalty owed by an employee to his employer lasts only as long as the term of employment. However, a fiduciary relationship of confidentiality can survive the termination of the other relationship as it is independently derived (*A-G v Guardian Newspapers Ltd (No 2)* [1988] 3 All ER 545, [1990] 1 AC 109). But it exists only as long as the information remains confidential. Here, that was no longer the case.

The Court of Appeal was unimpressed with the fiduciary duty claim being remedy-led. Lord Woolf cited Sopinka J's warning in *Norberg v Wynrib, Woman's Legal Education and Action Fund (Intervener)* (1992) 92 DLR (4th) 449 at 481, that equitable doctrines cannot be imported simply to improve the nature and extent of the remedy.

But Blake was not to enjoy his ill-gotten gains. As public policy is to ensure that criminals do not retain profit directly derived from the commission of a crime, so the Court granted an injunction on public law grounds restraining the receipt of payment resulting from the exploitation of the book.

Lord Woolf's views on the possibility of different kinds of fiduciary relationships attracting different kinds of obligations was expressly applied by the New Zealand Court of Appeal in *McLean v Arklow Investments Ltd* [1998] 3 NZLR 680. Again, it was the interaction between the fiduciary duties owed through employment and confidentiality that were under the microscope. The Court of Appeal considered that each particular duty owed is governed by the nature of the particular relationship at issue. Again, it was emphasised that the finding of the fiduciary obligations is not remedy-led.

92   *Korkontzilas v Soulos*
        (1997) 146 DLR (4th) 214

Mr Korkontzilas was a real estate agent in Ontario. One of his clients was Mr Soulos, who was interested in purchasing a commercial building. One particular building was attractive to Mr Soulos as it included among its tenants a branch of his own bank. Being your banker's landlord was a source of prestige in the Greek community of which Mr Soulos was a member. He accordingly was very interested in purchasing that building.

Mr Korkontzilas made an offer of $250,000 on behalf of Mr Soulos. The vendor rejected the offer, and counter-offered $275,000. In turn Mr Soulos rejected the counter-offer but indicated he would be prepared to pay $260,000 or $265,000. The vendor advised Mr Korkontzilas it would accept $265,000. Instead of letting Mr Soulos know this, Mr Korkontzilas arranged for his wife to purchase the property. When Mr Soulos asked him what happened to the property he was told to forget about it as the vendor no longer wanted to sell.

Some years later when Mr Soulos learned that his real estate agent had arranged for his wife to purchase the property he brought proceedings against him alleging breach of fiduciary duty. There was a difficulty with the claim however: the property had actually diminished in value between the time it was purchased by Mr Korkontzilas' wife, and the suit brought by Mr Soulos. Mr Soulos, therefore, did not seek damages as a remedy (he had suffered no loss). He did, however, seek an order declaring the building was held by his real estate agent on constructive trust for him.

The issue before the Supreme Court of Canada was whether the remedy of a constructive trust could be imposed where a defendant had not been unjustly enriched by their wrongful act. The lower Courts held it would be anomalous to declare a constructive trust, in effect, because a remedy in damages was unsatisfactory. The Court of Appeal and the Supreme Court did not share this view.

The majority judgment was given by McLachlin J. She noted that the appeal presented two different views of the function and ambit of the constructive trust. One saw it as exclusively a remedy for clearly established loss, when the defendant has been enriched and the plaintiff correspondingly deprived. The other view considers that a constructive trust may apply in the absence of established loss to condemn a wrongful act. It was the majority view that the second, broader approach should prevail.

McLachlin J considered that although the majority of Canadian cases considered an unjust enrichment to be a necessary ingredient, such decisions should not be taken as expunging from Canadian law the constructive trust in other circumstances. The Judge cited Canadian authorities she considered supported this thesis, and also looked at principles set out in various international scholarly writings and authorities. Her conclusion was that a constructive trust may be imposed where good conscience so requires. This can fall into two general categories. The first concerns property obtained by a wrongful act of the defendant, notably breach of fiduciary obligation, or breach of a duty of loyalty. The second category arises where the defendant has not acted wrongfully in obtaining the property, but would be unjustly enriched at the plaintiff's expense by being permitted to keep it. These categories are not necessarily mutually exclusive, and either may be sufficient to justify the imposition of a constructive trust.

Her Honor then decided that in this particular case the prerequisites for a constructive trust had been fulfilled. Mr Korkontzilas was under an equitable obligation in relation to the property at issue, and was clearly in breach of that in thwarting Mr Soulos' wish to purchase the property. While he was not materially enriched by his wrongful acquisition of the property, there were ample reasons for the imposition of a constructive trust. One of these was the desirability of deterring other fiduciaries from acting in a like manner.

Sopinka and Iacobucci JJ both dissented. They considered that it was basic that a constructive trust is not available as a remedy where there has been no unjust enrichment. They did not consider that the plaintiff would be left without a remedy if no constructive trust were available in the present case. Mr Soulos had a right to have his fiduciary adhere to his duties, and, if damages were suffered, he then had a corresponding right to a remedy. But here, where there was no damage, this remedy was not available. It was, however, open to Mr Soulos to pursue exemplary damages from Mr Korkontzilas' breach of trust. Also, in the views of the minority deterrence was not a factor that required modifying the law and permitting the constructive trust.

93   *Fortex Group Ltd (In Receivership and Liquidation) v MacIntosh*
[1998] 3 NZLR 171 (CA)

Fortex was a large New Zealand meat processing company that went into receivership and liquidation in 1994. A number of Fortex's employees were members of a superannuation scheme under which they made contributions to a superannuation fund. Their contributions were supplemented by Fortex, as both participating employer and trustee of the fund. The employees' contributions were deducted directly from their salary or wages. Pursuant to the trust deed Fortex was supposed to pay those contributions, plus its own supplements, to the scheme manager on a monthly basis. Fortex had, however, developed the practice of paying the contributions to the scheme manager on an annual basis. While Fortex intended to make its annual payments for the 1993/1994 year, receivers were appointed on 23 March 1994 before this was done. At all times Fortex's bank accounts were overdrawn. No separate fund had been set up in respect of the unpaid contributions, and therefore they had "disappeared" into Fortex's overdraft.

Fortex's employees bought a claim against the company, relying on three causes of action. The first two were claims for damages for breach of trust and breach of contract. While there was no doubt at all that the company was liable in respect of these claims, this would have merely given the employees an unsecured creditor's claim which was likely to yield them nothing in the company's liquidation. Accordingly they were relying upon their third cause of action: a declaration that Fortex held the contributions on an express or constructive trust, or that the employees were entitled to a remedial constructive trust.

In the High Court the claims based on the express and institutional constructive trusts were rejected, but the remedial constructive trust was upheld. The decision was appealed to the Court of Appeal.

Tipping J started by categorising the three types of trusts contended for. These are:

1.   an express trust — one which is deliberately established and which the trustee deliberately accepts;

2.   an institutional constructive trust — one which arises by operation of the principles of equity and whose existence the Court simply recognises in a declaratory way; and

3.   a remedial constructive trust — one which is imposed by the Court as a remedy in circumstances where, before the Court order, no trust of any kind existed.

Tipping J noted that the difference between the latter two types of constructive trusts is that an institutional constructive trust arises upon the happening of the events which bring it into being. Its existence is not dependent on any order of the Court. However a remedial constructive trust depends for its very existence on the order of the Court.

Following this, Tipping J stated that he agreed with the High Court that there was no express or institutional constructive trust in this case. The primary difficulty was the non-existence of any subject-matter for the trust. The moneys Fortex held were paid into an overdrawn bank account. They never had, or ceased to have any separate identity, thus there was never any identifiable subject-matter for the alleged trust.

On the question of a remedial constructive trust, Tipping J noted that before the Court could contemplate declaring any such remedial trust, there must be some principled basis for doing so. In general, equity will intervene to protect those with rights at law from enforcing them when in the eyes of equity it would be unconscionable for them to do so. The question in this case was whose conscience should be affected so as to prevent them from exercising their legal rights. In this situation Tipping J was clear that it must be the debenture holders and secured creditors whose conscience was at issue, not Fortex. If they exercised their rights under their securities, the employees would be left with nothing.

The evidence showed that there was nothing which ought to have put the secured creditors on inquiry, and they certainly had no actual knowledge of Fortex's default. Therefore there was nothing shown which meant the secured creditors should be deprived of their contractual rights to realise their security for their own benefit. Tipping J concluded that the High Court's conclusion must have been derived from focusing on the conscience of the wrong party, that is, Fortex as opposed to the unsecured creditors. For these reasons, the employees' appeal was dismissed.

Henry and Blanchard JJ also gave judgments in the matter. While they agreed with the majority's analysis of trusts, each had comments to make on other difficulties involved in imposing a remedial constructive trust. Henry J drew attention to the lack of any identifiable fund; the lack of any unjust enrichment to the debenture holders; and the difficulty of moneys ceasing to exist after they are paid into an overdrawn bank account. Both Henry and Blanchard JJ considered the problem of imposing the duties of a trustee or fiduciary upon Fortex simply because of its contractual obligation to pay contributions from its general bank account into the Scheme Managers' Fund. Both cautioned against assuming that a fiduciary duty, rather than a mere contractual duty, results from such a relationship.

94   *Smith v Hugh Watt Society Inc*
        [2004] 1 NZLR 537 (HC)

In 1973 a hall was acquired in Onehunga for the Labour Party, and this was transferred to the Hugh Watt Society Inc in 1985 (Hugh Watt was the long-serving Onehunga MP). The hall was sold again in 1988 and a unit purchased in its place. It was claimed by the plaintiffs (members of the Labour Party) that the unit was held in trust for them.

The plaintiffs claimed that funds for the hall had been raised by Labour Party members in Onehunga for the benefit of those Labour Party members in Onehunga and, once that electorate ceased to exist with the advent of MMP in 1996, the hall was held on trust for the Labour Party as a whole. It was undisputed that until 1985, the hall was held on trust for those members, though there was no express trust deed. There were also issues with the rules of the society being amended in 1992 to exclude references to the benefit of the Labour Party.

The Court found that when the hall was transferred to the society in 1985, not all the beneficiaries of the trust gave consent, and the Court did not sanction the change. This transfer therefore constituted a breach of trust. In addition, the society, as trustee, received the property with notice that it was subject to a constructive trust, and was therefore liable as constructive trustee to account for the trust property. The hall was transferred subject to the understanding and expectation that the society would remain connected to and responsible to the Labour Party in the Onehunga electorate. It was never intended that the beneficial interest in the property might alter. The unit was also trust property and was subject to the same trust.

De facto property

95   *Oliver v Bradley*
        [1987] 1 NZLR 586

In 1980 Mr Oliver (a single man) and Ms Bradley (a separated married woman with dependent children) became engaged. Shortly after, they purchased a house for $27,500 with the intention that this would become the matrimonial home. Oliver paid the deposit of $2006 and the balance was financed by a Housing Corporation loan of $20,000; Bradley's family benefit capitalisation of $2532; and a suspensory loan of $2500 from the Corporation for which Bradley was eligible. Title was taken in the sole name of Bradley.

The parties lived together in the house for almost four years. During that time Oliver earned a total gross income of $113,000 while Bradley earned a total gross income from part-time work of $24,000. She used her income to pay for clothes for herself and the children and for some personal expenses. Oliver paid her a weekly allowance of $100. Oliver paid all the mortgage repayments, insurance, rates and other outgoings. He did work to improve and maintain the property and paid for those improvements.

In February 1984 Bradley broke off the engagement and the de facto relationship. She left with the children. Oliver stayed on in the house until August 1984 when Bradley returned to it with another man.

In May 1985 Oliver began an action based on resulting, implied or constructive trust. In the High Court Bisson J found that this case was "one which cries out for the Court to hold that there is a constructive trust in the interests of justice and good conscience". However, in finding for Oliver he also held that the Domestic Actions Act 1975 applied and made his order under that legislation. He ordered Bradley to pay $19,500 to Oliver, being about half of the current equity of the property. Oliver appealed.

By the time the case came before the Court of Appeal the house had been sold for $67,500. The Court decided that now that Bradley and her children had moved out, the appropriate course of action was to award Oliver a proportion of the proceeds of sale, whether under constructive trust or the statute. Cooke P stated that he felt that it was immaterial whether the Court exercised its jurisdiction under the Act or under the law of constructive trusts. The central issue was what Oliver's share should be.

The parties intended an equal sharing if the marriage eventuated but did not expressly address their minds to their rights if it did not. However, a reasonable person in Oliver's shoes would undoubtedly have understood that his contribution and efforts would result in an interest in the property. Likewise a reasonable person in the shoes of Bradley would have had to acknowledge such a legitimate expectation. When the comparative contributions of the parties were weighed, Bradley was entitled to no more than 30 per cent of the equity in the property. The appeal was allowed and an order made that the net proceeds of the sale be divided in proportions of seven to Oliver and three to Bradley.

96   *Gillies v Keogh*
       [1989] 2 NZLR 327

The plaintiff and defendant met in 1981. He was a single man and she was recently separated from her husband. The defendant's matrimonial home was retained by her husband. She intended to use the $15,000 which she received for her interest to put towards a new home. Shortly after they met the parties left together for Australia on a working holiday. On returning to New Zealand in December 1982, they bought a house. The agreement and the title were in the defendant's sole name. Both parties found work and the bulk of their earnings was paid into a joint account which was used for household expenses and outgoings in connection with the house. Improvements were made to the house, principally by the plaintiff.

In mid-1984 the house was sold and a new property was purchased by the defendant in her name alone. The house and grounds required a substantial amount of work. The plaintiff contributed to this as did the father and brother of the defendant and the defendant herself.

A comparatively short time later the relationship ended. The defendant retained the house property and the plaintiff initiated proceedings. He claimed a 40 per cent share in the net equity of the second property or judgment for $20,000. The claim was based on an express or implied agreement or a constructive trust. The Judge did not find any express or implied agreement but found a constructive trust on the basis of unjust enrichment and awarded the plaintiff $10,000 being approximately half of the capital gain in respect of the first property. The defendant appealed.

The appeal was allowed on the basis that the defendant had, at all times, made it clear to the plaintiff that she was asserting that the house was hers and hers alone. One cannot say that a reasonable person in his shoes would have understood that he was acquiring an interest. Therefore no constructive trust could arise.

Cooke P stressed that facts are very important in cases arising out of the end of matrimonial or de facto unions. This is so whether the jurisdiction being exercised is statutory or derived from common law or equity. Normally it makes no practical difference whether one talks of constructive trust, unjust enrichment, imputed common intention or estoppel. In deciding whether any of these are established it is necessary to take into account the same factors:

    1.   the degree of sacrifice by the claimant;

2. the value of the contributions of the claimant compared to the value of the benefits received; and

3. any property arrangements the parties may have made themselves.

Whatever legal label cases in this field are placed under, reasonable expectations in the light of the conduct of the parties are at the heart of the matter. As well as taking title and making the contractual and financial arrangements in her own name, the appellant made it clear to the respondent at all times that she was asserting that the house was hers and hers alone. One cannot say that a reasonable person in his shoes would have understood that he was acquiring an interest.

Richardson J preferred to apply a two-part test to such cases:

1. Has there been a direct or indirect contribution by the claimant in respect to the property in circumstances such that it should be inferred that the claimant should have understood that the efforts would naturally result in an interest in the property?

2. Do the settled principles of estoppel preclude the legal owner from denying the existence of an equitable interest in the property?

97   *Cossey v Bach*
[1992] 3 NZLR 612

Mr Cossey and Ms Bach had a somewhat complicated relationship. They married each other and subsequently divorced, without resolving their matrimonial property rights. They then married other people and divorced them, before Mr Cossey won $666,660 in Lotto. They then entered into a de facto relationship with each other before finally separating when the money ran out. Ms Bach was also prosecuted for benefit fraud, just for good measure. As Fisher J noted, their relationship spawned novel questions beyond the wildest imaginings of the draftsperson of the Matrimonial Property Act 1976.

After a detailed analysis of the provisions of the Matrimonial Property Act 1976, Fisher J held that the provisions of the Act did not apply and that the determination of the former couple's property rights should be made as if they had never been legally married.

Fisher J, as often is his wont, summarised the principles for the common law division of de facto marriage property, which were:

1. Legal title is always the starting point. It will be taken to reflect the beneficial interests in the absence of proof to the contrary.

2. The express intentions of the parties will usually be determinative if: (a) unequivocally expressed; (b) common to both parties or expressed by the party or parties with the then disposing power in the property in question; and (c) still pertinent to the circumstances currently before the Court.

3. A unilaterally expressed intention can still affirm or override distribution in accordance with the legal title if expressed by the party with the then disposing power in the property. If one party clearly expresses his or her intention to retain exclusive ownership of property in advance, then that may negate any suggested division based upon subsequent contributions, sacrifices or expectations. Conversely, if the legal owner gifts something or settles the beneficial interest in it to the other, then the transfer is binding and irrevocable.

4. However, the Courts will no longer strain to create inferred intentions from equivocal conduct. The way in which the parties had arranged their legal title will often be a poor indicator of proprietary intentions, particularly if to the knowledge of both, the party or parties who had provided the original purchase price had not intended that division would follow the legal title in the events which have since occurred.

5. If there is no governing expression of intention, a convenient starting point may be to ascertain ownership according to traditional proprietary principles before turning to reasonable expectations. Traditional proprietary principles include the presumption of resulting trusts.

6. Ownership determined provisionally in that manner will then be subject to any reasonable expectation by the claimant that he or she would receive an interest or greater interest in the property of the other party based upon the defendant's active or tacit encouragement of a belief that by taking certain steps the claimant would acquire such an interest and steps were taken by the claimant to his or her detriment in reliance on his or her belief.

7. In a stable and enduring de facto relationship, and in the absence of any expressed intention to the contrary, it will readily be accepted as reasonable for the claimant to expect that, following those contributions and sacrifices normally associated with de facto marriage, family assets would be shared. For this purpose

contributions may be of an intangible nature, need not be traceable to the property in dispute, and may have little measurable value.

8.   Once a successful claim has been demonstrated, its quantum will be determined by: (a) giving priority to any overriding expression of intention; (b) by reference to the value of the parties' respective proprietary contributions to the property; and (c) by reference to any reasonable expectation.

The last will turn principally upon the net value to the owner of assistance and contributions provided by the claimant while acting in reliance upon the expectation after deducting the value of the benefits which the claimant had enjoyed during the same period, but it will also be affected by such matters as the terms and nature of the defendant's encouragement, the extent of the claimant's sacrifice, the value of the property and the duration and nature of the relationship.

In the context of reasonable expectations, as distinct from provisional interests based upon traditional proprietary principles, "contributions" can be broadly equated with those applicable under the Matrimonial Property Act 1976.

9.   When the quantum of the claim has been determined in that manner, the remedy may take the form of an interest in the property in dispute or a monetary award in lieu of it.

10.   The result of applying those principles to jointly owned property paid for exclusively by one party is that his or her act of deliberately placing his or her property in joint names will, without more, be taken to indicate an intention that the joint interests were to be beneficial, permanent and irrevocable. However, that inference may be rebutted by showing that on an objective appraisal of the words and conduct in their full context at the time, there was no unequivocal expression of an intention that joint interests would prevail in the events which have since occurred.

The assets which were the subject of dispute were a house bought in Howick, a Ford panel van, a ring, household chattels, RJI shares and a fixed term deposit with Tower Corporation. Fisher J held that Bach should be allocated a 15 per cent interest in the house; the van and the household chattels on the basis of her domestic contribution. These were part of the domestic environment and Bach had some sort of reasonable expectation in relation to them.

The ring, which Cossey had given to Bach at her insistence, was a perfected gift and she could keep it. She was not, however, entitled to any of the shares or the money on term deposit. Although they were held in their joint names, this occurred in express contemplation of marriage. Since that condition was not fulfilled, on ordinary resulting trust principles, Mr Cossey held the entire beneficial interest.

Fisher J identified Ms Bach's 15 per cent interest in the house, the van and the chattels as being worth about $56,250.

98   *Lankow v Rose*
[1995] 1 NZLR 277

Terence Lankow and Suzanne Rose began living together in a de facto relationship in 1980. After ten years things soured to the point where they broke up and began squabbling about their assets. During the ten-year period, Lankow's financial situation had improved quite remarkably. When the relationship began, Lankow owned two flats, a vacant adjoining section, two vehicles, some furniture and two-thirds of a company called Concrete Placements Ltd. Apart from a life insurance policy, his indebtedness more or less equalled the value of his assets. In 1990, Lankow's net worth was something in the vicinity of $650,000.

Rose initially brought to the relationship about $2300 cash, a car worth $3000 and some furniture and other personal effects. At the end of the relationship, she had a car worth about $22,000, $5000 in savings and some furniture and other personal effects. Her net worth in 1990 totalled about $30,000.

Rose claimed that she had a beneficial interest in the Lankow's assets by virtue of a constructive trust. Lankow claimed that she was entitled to nothing; and he also wanted the return of $7500 which he had paid her earlier.

Rose had contributed to Lankow's general financial well-being in a number of ways over the course of their relationship. Her financial outlay during the relationship was $180,000 and she left it with $30,000. Accordingly, approximately $150,000 had been used for joint purposes.

In particular, Rose paid for all household expenses throughout the relationship. When the relationship began, Lankow had recently divorced and Rose provided him with $3500 to help in his matrimonial property settlement. Rose had also recently divorced and she applied everything she received from her settlement to the joint benefit of herself and Lankow. Lankow's company was in a state of crisis in the early years of the relationship and the couple had lived off Rose's income. In 1986 the couple built a new house on the vacant section owned by Lankow, and Rose contributed about $29,000 to the cost of building, which totalled $150,000. Rose had also provided free secretarial services for Lankow's company and she administered the tenancies of both his flats.

In the High Court, Ellis J found that Rose's commitment to the relationship was total. His Honour imposed a constructive trust on their house and certain other chattels. Lankow appealed to the Court of Appeal and Rose cross-appealed in respect of Lankow's assets, in case the Court of Appeal made an adverse finding in relation on Lankow's appeal.

Counsel for Lankow launched a somewhat intemperate attack on the line of cases which had developed since *Gillies v Keogh* **(96)** and appeared to invite the Court to reject the de facto constructive trust jurisprudence which had arisen both in this jurisdiction and in the Commonwealth generally. He ranted about "meaningless leguleian judicial activism" and "self-serving feminist assumptions".

In response to counsel's tirade, Cooke P noted that some of counsel's submissions had "an entertainment quality which robs them of all sting". Similarly, in respect of counsel's submission that "reasonable expectations" were not a principle of equity and that the concept enjoyed the same lack of substance as proved to be the case in Charles Dickens' *Great Expectations*, Tipping J said that the only relevance of that work to the case was that it was written at a time when counsel's reactionary submissions may have found greater favour.

Needless to say, the Court of Appeal did not reject the de facto constructive trust jurisprudence which has developed in this country and elsewhere. Hardie Boys J thought that it was important that there were clear criteria for the imposition of constructive trusts in the area of de facto relationships. He thought that there were two essential requirements:

1. the plaintiff must have contributed in a more than minor way to the acquisition, preservation or enhancement of the defendant's assets, whether directly or indirectly; and

2. in all the circumstances the parties must be taken to have reasonably expected that the plaintiff would share in the defendant's assets as a result of his or her contribution.

In respect of the first limb, Hardie Boys J stated that contributions to assets did not include those contributions to a common household that are adequately compensated by the benefits the relationship itself confers. The contribution must manifestly exceed the benefits. In terms of estoppel, Rose's contributions must have been to her detriment. In terms of unjust enrichment (the Canadian approach) the contributions must have resulted by the end of the relationship in the enrichment of one to the juristically unjustified deprivation of the other. Contributions need not be in money; they may be in services or in any other respect.

There must also be a causal relationship between the contributions and the acquisition, preservation or enhancement of Lankow's assets. The reason for this is that a claim to a constructive trust is a proprietary claim and the contributions must have been made to assets, not necessarily to particular assets, but certainly to assets in general.

Tipping J, with whom McKay J agreed, thought that the de facto claimant must show:

1.   contributions, direct or indirect, to the property in question;

2.   the expectation of an interest therein;

3.   that such expectation is a reasonable one; and

4.   that the defendant should reasonably expect to yield the claimant an interest.

If the claimant can fulfil each of these requirements, then the Court would not allow the defendant to assert his or her strict legal rights. A constructive trust will be imposed. Tipping J expanded on the nature of "contributions". He stated that although direct financial contributions to the acquisition of property will certainly qualify, indirect contributions qualify as well. There might be difficulties with proof and assessment but once they are established such contributions are as real as direct contributions. Tipping J defined contribution as any payment or service by the claimant which either:

1.   of itself assists in the acquisition, improvement or maintenance of the property or its value; or

2.   by its provision helps the other party acquire, improve or maintain the property or its value.

The Court of Appeal as a whole agreed that Ellis J had been correct in finding a constructive trust and that Rose was entitled to a half-share in her former home and in the shared chattels. The contributions made by Rose were such that they reasonably led to an expectation in the property.

99 *Gormack v Scott*
[1995] NZFLR 289

Mr Gormack and Mrs Scott had been involved in a turbulent relationship since 1979. In 1981 they had purchased a house together. They signed a property agreement which provided that if the house was to be sold, the proceeds would be unequally divided. This was in recognition of the fact that Gormack had contributed more in dollar terms to the property. In 1983, Scott left Gormack, but he pleaded with her to return, offering to find a new place, and make "a new start together with a new house in equal shares". Scott was persuaded, and in 1983 they purchased a new house. It was registered in both their names as tenants in common in equal shares.

Following another departure from the relationship in 1985 Scott was again induced to return after Gormack presented her with the following agreement:

> I, the said David John Gormack, agrees that if Barbara May Scott returns to live with the said David John Gormack and if he should subject himself to drinking gin or whiskey or other spirit he will leave and let Barbara May Scott in the above address (or any such address we may share) and will continue to keep up payments on the above address until sold. When sold Barbara May Scott is entitled to 50/50 arrangement on the above address or any other we may share.

The relationship was doomed and the two irrevocably parted in May 1990.

In September 1990 Scott commenced proceedings seeking partition or sale of their property. The real issue soon became whether Gormack had a beneficial interest in her registered half-share. He initially contended that the earlier agreement that had provided for unequal division was intended to apply also to their second house.

In the High Court Holland J considered with the reasoning in *Gillies v Keogh* **(96)** and *Cossey v Bach* **(97)** in relation to reasonable expectations before reaching a finding in favour of Scott. The basis for this was that the property was purchased by the two jointly, with legal ownership in each equally, and there was no common intention for other than equal ownership. Holland J noted that in such cases it would be rare for a Court to find that the parties' reasonable expectations were for other than equal ownership.

The Judge noted that this case differed substantially from the earlier reported cases. In the earlier cases, disputes had arisen over property legally owned by one party, and in which the other party claimed an equitable interest arising from their contributions. Here legal ownership was shared, and all indications were that reasonable persons in the shoes of the parties would expect that they would be bound by that. While the evidence was a little too vague to be an express common intention, it did define the parties' reasonable expectations.

Gormack took his case to the Court of Appeal claiming a constructive trust over Scott's half-share to reflect his contributions to the property.

This argument did not find favour with Cooke P, Hardie Boys or Gault JJ. Cooke P considered that Holland J had correctly applied the relevant legal principles, but did go on to make some further observations. He felt that this case came very close to one of express common intention, and if there was such common intention it would be unnecessary to fall back on reasonable expectations. However, if, as in this case, the common intention was too vaguely expressed to be implemented as such, it could still be relevant in assessing the reasonable expectations of the parties.

A point made by both Cooke P and Hardie Boys J was that in determining the parties' reasonable expectations the Court cannot simply look at a snapshot of a particular stage of the relationship. Expectations will inevitably change with the passage of time and changing circumstances.

In this case the Court was satisfied that Holland J had made a correct finding of fact on the issue of reasonable expectations, and Gormack's appeal was dismissed.

See also *Nation v Nation* [2005] 3 NZLR 46

TRUSTEES

100 *Letterstedt v Broers*
[1881-5] All ER Rep 882

This Privy Council decision deals with the difficult question of when a trustee can be removed from his or her position.

Miss Letterstedt was the beneficiary of a vast estate left to her by her father — "her father owned a brewery" — to coin a phrase. In his will, Mr Letterstedt left his business empire to his three trustees and executors to administer on trust for the benefit of his daughter.

Two of the trustees were individuals, and the third was an incorporated body (the Board of Executors of Capetown), which specialised in the administration of estates and trusts (somewhat similar to modern trustee companies). The two individual trustees and executors died leaving the Board to administer the trust.

Miss Letterstedt became concerned with some of the activities of the Board. In particular, she became concerned with the relatively large payments which the Board had taken by way of commission. As a result, the relationship between herself as beneficiary, and the Board as trustees, broke down completely.

Miss Letterstedt issued proceedings against the Board seeking, among other things, an order removing the Board as trustee.

In the Privy Council (on appeal from the Supreme Court in South Africa) Lord Blackburn first concluded that there had been no impropriety, or actual dishonesty on the part of the Board in its activities as administrator of the trust.

The Court always retained a jurisdiction to remove a trustee where the need arose. Removal would arise in the clearest of cases such as those involving positive misconduct, where the Courts of equity have no difficulty in intervening to remove trustees who have abused the trust. His Lordship found that any misconduct, or serious neglect or mistakes, must be of such a degree as to endanger the trust property, or show a want of honesty, or a lack of proper capacity to execute the duties imposed upon the trustees.

But all of those circumstances were really ancillary to the principal duty of a trustee — to see that the trusts are properly executed. Lord Blackburn stated:

> It must always be borne in mind that trustees exist for the benefit of those to whom the creator of the trust has given the trust estate.

The Judicial Committee did not wish to lay down any general rule, beyond the very broad principle that the main guide for the Court must be the welfare of the beneficiary. Each case would turn upon its own particular circumstances. In this particular case there were several factors which were a cause for concern. First, the Board had become the sole trustee and executor, although under his will Mr Letterstedt had appointed three executors. It was also of concern that the Board had become a manager of one branch of the business through its own directors, and only appointed auditors connected with the Board itself. Third, there was concern over the commission charged by the Board for its work as a professional trustee (although this did not amount to bad faith or dishonesty). The charges were "naturally offensive to [Miss Letterstedt] and unfair towards the trust estate".

Based upon the findings outlined above, Lord Blackburn stated:

> It is quite true that friction or hostility between trustees and the immediate possessor of the trust estate is not of itself a reason for the removal of the trustees. But where the hostility is grounded on the mode in which the trust has been administered, where it has been caused wholly or partially by substantial overcharges against the trust estate, it is certainly not to be disregarded.

> Looking therefore at the whole circumstances of this very peculiar case, the complete change of position, the unfortunate hostility that has arisen, and the difficult and delicate duties that may yet have to be performed, their Lordships can come to no other conclusion than that it is necessary, for the welfare of the beneficiaries, that the Board should no longer be trustees.

101   *Hunter v Hunter*
[1938] NZLR 520

When Sir George Hunter died, he left the majority of his estate in trust for the benefit of his wife, Lady Hunter. Cyril Hunter was appointed as an executor and trustee under Sir George's will. Cyril Hunter appointed a co-trustee — Thomas Hunter.

Lady Hunter alleged gross mismanagement of the trust property, misconduct and maladministration of the trust and sought an order removing the trustees.

Smith J made an order removing the defendants as trustees and appointing a trustee company in their place. Messrs Hunter appealed.

Myers CJ, in the Court of Appeal, felt that the trustees were seeking to have their case dealt with as if it depended upon a question of whether or not the various grounds advanced for removal amounted to breaches of trust. That however, was not the true position in law. The principles to be applied were clearly laid down in *Letterstedt v Broers* **(100)**. The jurisdiction to remove trustees was ancillary to the principal duty of the Court to see that the trusts were properly executed by the trustees. Whether or not charges of misconduct were made out was irrelevant.

The real issue was whether the continuation of the trustees in office would prevent the trusts from being properly executed. Myers CJ reiterated that "it must always be borne in mind that trustees exist for the benefit of those to whom the creator of the trust has given the trust estate". It was sufficient for the purposes of removal of trustees if the evidence showed:

1. That there was a conflict between interest and duty on the part of the trustees; or

2. That the trustees had failed to recognise a conflict and to take steps to ensure that their interest would not prevail against their duty, and had disregarded the interest of the beneficiaries; or

3. That a state of hostility existed between the trustees and the beneficiary which would work against the true interests of the estate.

The evidence indicated clearly that a state of hostility existed between Lady Hunter and the trustees. *Letterstedt v Broers* indicated that that factor, of itself, would not amount to a ground for removal. Where hostility was one-sided or deliberately induced by a beneficiary the Court could probably refuse to order a removal of the trustees. However, the evidence in this case clearly indicated that the hostility was not one-sided. The "aggro" was mutual. There was a proven conflict of interest between the trustees and the trust.

In light of those findings, the Court of Appeal had no difficulty in upholding Smith J's decision that:

> The welfare of the beneficiaries and of the trust estate will be best secured by removing the defendants as trustees and appointing some independent person or persons or corporation in their place.

102   *Re Anne Myfanwy Fulton Trust*
High Court, Auckland M706/88, 4 December 1989, Eichelbaum CJ

This case epitomises the exercise of the Court's inherent jurisdiction to remove a trustee when the need arises.

Mark Fulton was the sole surviving beneficiary under a trust known as the Anne Myfanwy Fulton Trust. David Coxhead was Anne Fulton's brother (and Mark Fulton's uncle), and was also the trustee of the trust. The assets of the trust were mostly in the form of substantial shareholdings, debentures and various other securities over a related number of companies. Collectively, the companies were referred to as the "Mutual Group" (which carries on business today as Avis Rental Cars).

Mr Coxhead was the governing director and/or director of the various companies making up the Mutual Group. He was also either personally interested in the various companies in Mutual Group, or was interested by means of companies in which he had a controlling interest. He had an interest as trustee of the various trusts, and held shares in the same companies as trustee.

For three years in the early 1980s Mark Fulton was employed by Mutual Group. He left this job to go overseas. By 1986 relations between Mark Fulton and David Coxhead had deteriorated to the point where no personal communication of "any effective nature" existed between them.

Mark Fulton brought an action in the High Court for the removal of David Coxhead as trustee. He did so by relying upon the inherent jurisdiction of the Court to remove trustees.

Eichelbaum CJ stated the legal principles. The power of removal of trustees is ancillary to the Court's principal duty to see that the trusts are properly executed (referring to *Letterstedt v Broers* **(100)**). The two factors which gave rise to the potential exercise of the Court's jurisdiction are:

1.   a situation of hostility between the trustee and the beneficiary; and

2.   the existence of an actual or potential conflict of interest.

First, Eichelbaum CJ found that the situation had deteriorated to an extent which warranted the intervention of the Court. There was evidence of specific instances of personal abuse and "belittlement" of Mark Fulton by Mr Coxhead. Mr Coxhead had previously rejected what appeared to be a reasonable attempt at reconciliation. There was also evidence of a similar breakdown in the relationship between Mr Coxhead and his two sisters.

Secondly, the Court found that there was not only a potential conflict, but an actual conflict of duty and interest between Mr Coxhead as governing director or director of the various companies in the Mutual Group, and as trustee for the benefit of Mark Fulton. There were two instances which gave rise to the conflict of interest:

1. A guarantee given by a company, to a "Nathan Group" gave rise to a considerable risk of exposure for the guarantor company (part of the trust property being shares in the company). However Mr Coxhead stood to gain under the guarantee.

2. The acquisition by Mr Coxhead of shares in another company which constituted part of Mutual Group.

In the case of the Nathan loan and guarantee, there was sufficient material before the Court to enable it to draw the inference that one of the companies in Mutual Group had been exposed to the risk of a guarantee without any or any sufficient counter-balancing gain.

In the circumstances, Eichelbaum CJ was not inclined to accept the defendant's case that it was a coincidence rather than a conflict of interest that had evolved. That factor, combined with the deterioration in the relationship between the parties justified the removal of Mr Coxhead as trustee.

103   *Mendelssohn and Schmid v Centrepoint Community Growth Trust*
[1999] 2 NZLR 88 (CA)

In June 1996 the Solicitor-General appointed a committee of inquiry to investigate the Centrepoint Community Group Trust. The trust was incorporated in 1977 under the Charitable Trusts Act 1957 (see *Centrepoint Community Growth Trust* **(63)**). That committee of inquiry's report stated, among other things, that there was doubt about the identity and validity of the appointment of the existing trustees; the trust was beset by dissension, and there was doubt as to whether it continued to be charitable in purpose. The Attorney-General accordingly applied to the High Court for the appointment of new trustees. It was not disputed that new trustees were necessary. The issue, however, was who those new trustees should be. As no consensus could be reached, Robertson J appointed the Public Trustee to act in a neutral and caretaker role. Two members of the Centrepoint community, Messrs Mendelssohn and Schmid, challenged this decision.

Mendelssohn and Schmid were supporters of the trust's spiritual leader, Herbert Potter. Both the appellants and Mr Potter believed it was imperative that the new trustees be adherents of Mr Potter and committed believers in his faith and teachings. They challenged the appointment of the Public Trustee on the grounds that he was disqualified from appointment; and also that Robertson J was wrong to exercise his discretion in favour of the Public Trustee.

The appellants considered that the Public Trustee was disqualified from appointment as he was not an adherent of the religion nurtured by the trust. The Court of Appeal considered the Trust Deed of 22 December 1997 when reaching a decision as to whether or not this was a necessary requirement. They did not accept that a mandatory criterion for trusteeship was an acknowledgment of the primacy of the teachings of the spiritual leader. No such requirement was part of the Trust Deed. The structure of the trust also did not support this; the trustees were to deal with matters temporal, and the spiritual leader deals with matters spiritual.

The second basis on which it was said the Public Trustee was disqualified was that his appointment would be a breach of the appellants' right to freedom of religion under the New Zealand Bill of Rights Act 1990. The Court of Appeal's difficulty with this argument was that there was no evidence supporting the contention. The Court of Appeal, therefore, did not consider that the Public Trustee was disqualified from appointment.

The appellants further argued that the Judge was wrong to exercise his discretion in favour of the Public Trustee. This was on the basis that he had not given enough weight to the underlying purpose of the Trust Deed, namely the founding and practising of a religion centred on the teachings of Mr Potter. It was argued that this made it overwhelmingly desirable to appoint as trustees persons who were adherents of that religion.

The Court of Appeal considered a number of authorities dealing with the administration of charitable trusts with religious components. They noted that if there was a general principle, it was that the Court's task is to appoint the person or persons best suited to administer the trust in the circumstances prevailing. In these circumstances, there was ample evidence before the Judge justifying his conclusion that an independent trustee was desirable and indeed necessary. The point about freedom of religion was also raised, and again dismissed because of lack of evidence. As a third point, the appellants suggested that the Judge had not properly applied settled principles in relation to the appointment of new trustees by the Court. In short, these principles are: consideration of the settlors' intentions; neutrality between beneficiaries; and promotion of the purposes of the trust (*Re Tempest* (1866) 1 Ch App 485). The Court did not believe that Robertson J could be said to have failed to follow this approach, and the appointment was entirely appropriate.

Accordingly the Court of Appeal refused to vary the appointment made of the Public Trustee as a caretaker for the Centrepoint Trust.

104   *Speight v Gaunt*
            (1883) 9 App Cas 1

Mr Gaunt had an unfortunate run of luck. He was the trustee of Mr Speight's will, and the beneficiary of that will was Speight junior. In 1881 Gaunt had £15,275 as trust property, which he decided to invest in shares in three municipal corporations. Gaunt employed Richard Cook, a stock and sharebroker to undertake the investment. At that time Gaunt had no reason to distrust the professional capacity, solvency, or integrity of Richard Cook. That situation however quickly changed. After giving Richard Cook the trust moneys to invest, Cook gave Mr Gaunt a "bought-note" which indicated that, £15,275 worth of shares had been purchased in the three municipal corporations. Cook had in fact had a good time using the money for his own purposes, and no shares in any of the Corporations had been purchased. Cook then became insolvent, and the moneys were lost.

Speight junior brought an action against Gaunt alleging that he had failed in the exercise of his duties as a trustee.

In the House of Lords there were two questions to be determined:

1.   whether it was proper for Gaunt, as trustee, to use a broker for the purpose of investing the moneys; and

2.   whether (if so) the actual payment or passing of the money to the broker in the circumstances of the case was justified.

In answer to the first question, the Lord Chancellor held that a trustee is not bound himself or herself to undertake the business ("for which he may be very ill qualified") of investing the trust moneys. Gaunt was entitled to give instructions to a competent broker to give the instructions which he had given to invest the moneys.

In answer to the second question, the Lord Chancellor held that it was a common practice, or "custom and usage" in the London Stock Exchange for moneys to pass directly to the broker from the investor.

Lord Blackburn's decision clearly articulates that the "ordinary prudent man of business" test applies to the investment of funds by trustees. When making investments of trust funds (which must of course be authorised by the trust deed), the usual test to determine whether the trustee has fulfilled his or her duty to invest funds adequately, is whether an ordinary prudent man or woman of business would have made the investment in managing his or her own affairs:

> The authorities cited by the late Master of the Rolls, I think show that as a general rule a trustee sufficiently discharges his duty if he takes in managing trust affairs all those precautions which an ordinary prudent man of business would take in managing similar affairs of his own. There is one exception to this: a trustee must not choose investments other than those which the terms of his trust permit, though they may be such as an ordinary prudent man of business would select for his own money; and it may that however usual it may be for a person who wishes to invest his money, and instructs an agent, such as an attorney, or a stock broker, to seek an investment, to deposit the money at interest with the agent until the investment is found, that is in effect lending it on the agent's own personal security, and is a breach of trust. No question as to this arises here, for Mr Gaunt did nothing of that kind. Subject to this exception, as to which it is unnecessary to consider further, I think the case of *Ex Parte Belchier* establishes the principle that where there is a usual course of business the trustee is justified in filing it, though it may be such that there is some risk that the property may be lost by the dishonesty or insolvency of an agent employed.

The duties of a trustee could not be carried on without some confidence being bestowed in others (such as stockbrokers). In this case, Gaunt had been deliberately deceived by Cook. The fact that the shares had not been purchased, as a consequence of Cook's dishonesty, was not something for which Gaunt could be held accountable. The usual and regular course of business had been adopted and there was nothing to call into question Gaunt's actions.

105   *Re Mulligan (Deceased)*
[1998] 1 NZLR 481

Mr Mulligan was an Ashburton farmer, who died in 1949. His widow, Mrs Mulligan was some ten years younger than he was, and was to live another 40 years, dying at the age of 90 in 1990. Mr Mulligan's will left his widow a substantial legacy, and gave her a life interest in the income of his estate. The residual beneficiaries of the estate were his nieces and nephews, as the Mulligans had no children. The trustees of his estate were his widow, and Pyne Gould Guinness, a professional trustee company.

After a few years, the trustees made the decision to sell the Mulligans' farm. This achieved a sum of approximately $108,000 — a considerable sum of money at the time. For the next 25 years the trust's capital was placed in fixed interest investments, usually local body stock and first mortgages. This provided the widow with a very healthy income on the capital, but did not result in any capital growth. Pyne Gould Guinness's representatives regularly tried to persuade Mrs Mulligan to diversify the trust's capital, and invest in equities and shares, but the widow remained adamant that she would have none of it. She regarded investments in companies as entirely speculative, and was preoccupied with maximising her own income from the estate.

In addition, Mrs Mulligan was not happy for Pyne Gould Guinness to have any contact with the residual beneficiaries of her husband's estate. She regarded herself as the main link to the rest of the family, and insisted that all correspondence be through her. She forcibly resisted any suggestion that they be provided with full copies of the will, or yearly accounts, and accordingly the beneficiaries remained in ignorance of what was going on until after Mrs Mulligan's death.

On her death in 1990, it was discovered that the capital of the trust was still only around $108,000. Obviously, in real terms the value of that money had depreciated considerably in the intervening period. Accordingly, the beneficiaries sought to have Pyne Gould Guinness and Mrs Mulligan's estate held jointly and severally accountable for breach of trust. The case was founded upon two central propositions: namely that had a percentage of the estate been invested in equities the real capital balance available in 1990 would have been much greater, and that it was a breach of trust for the trustees not to have achieved that result.

Panckhurst J first noted that trustees have a duty to act with due diligence and prudence. In judging the past performance of trustees, the standards of the relevant period have to be applied, with no allowance for hindsight or modern day standards. Secondly, a general principle of relevance was a duty of impartiality. A trustee must act with strict impartiality and endeavour to maintain a balance between the interests of a life tenant and residual beneficiaries. Thirdly, there is separate responsibility of each trustee where there are co-trustees. The Judge felt that upon entering the office of trustee each individual has a separate responsibility to ensure that the terms of the trust are carried out. It is not open for one to defer to the wishes of another trustee in the absence of proper reasons for doing so. This was even more so in the particular case where one trustee was a professional trust company, and the other an individual plainly affected by a conflict of interest arising from her entitlement to the income of the trust during her life.

When considered against those standards, the Judge had no doubt that a breach of trust had been established. Over the 20 years the Pyne Gould Guinness trust officers had all separately recognised the risk posed by inflation and all had recommended diversification. The Judge saw this not just as significant, but decisive. In the circumstances, he found that it was not reasonable for them to have deferred to Mrs Mulligan's stubbornness on this point, and Pyne Gould Guinness had failed to take adequate steps to respond to the problem. There were no reasonable grounds for them not to have applied to the Court for directions on this issue. The Judge also found that Mrs Mulligan had been in breach of trust. She was clearly affected by a conflict of interest, and had prevented the residual beneficiaries from receiving any information on what was happening with her husband's estate.

Both Pyne Gould Guinness and Mrs Mulligan's estate had contended that the Court should exercise its discretion under s 73 of the Trustee Act 1956 to relieve the trustees from personal liability. That section allows the Court to exercise its discretion if it appears that a trustee has acted honestly and reasonably and can fairly be excused for the breach of trust. The Court refused to exercise its discretion in this case. It did not believe that either the professional trustees, or Mrs Mulligan had acted reasonably.

Once the breach of trust had been established, a further question was the measure of damages. The Court adopted a complicated formula whereby the predicted returns to the trust's estate had 40 per cent of the estate been invested in shares from 1972 to 1990 was calculated and ordered to be paid to the trust.

106   *Bank of New Zealand v New Zealand Guardian Trust Company Ltd*
[1999] 1 NZLR 664 (CA)

Commercial Securities Limited (ComSec) was a property investment company, which needed to raise $40m required for investments overseas. It accordingly arranged to raise the finance by enticing the National Australia Bank (NZ) Limited (NAB), and three other banks to form a syndicate to subscribe for debenture stock issued by Comsec. NAB and BNZ were originally separate lenders. In the early nineties NAB bought BNZ. Accordingly BNZ is the plaintiff, although its claim relates to events happening to NAB.

The New Zealand Guardian Trust Company Limited (NZGT) was appointed trustee to hold the securities and act for the benefit of the banks. The trust deed provided for ComSec to issue the stock as security for the loans, and give charges in favour of NZGT over all its undertakings and assets. Certain of Comsec's subsidiaries were also to provide security. Under the deed ComSec specifically agreed that it would not lend money to any subsidiary that had not provided security (a "non-charging" subsidiary) unless any such loan was secured to the satisfaction of NZGT.

On 1 July 1987 ComSec sent NZGT and the syndicate of banks its financial statements for the year ended 31 March 1987. Included in those financial statements was a note stating that there had been a \$19m loan by ComSec to certain of its non-charging subsidiaries. This note ought to have alerted NZGT to the fact there had been a breach of the trust deed, but NZGT did not make that connection.

During 1988 ComSec's financial position increasingly deteriorated. Eventually, in February 1989 NZGT appointed receivers of ComSec and its charging subsidiaries.

After all of the assets were realised and distributed, NAB recovered approximately 10 per cent of the money it was owed as at February 1989. On discovering that ComSec had made loans to non-charging subsidiaries, and that NZGT had taken no action, NAB sued NZGT for breach of trust. The claim was for the loss of opportunity for NAB to withdraw from the loan facility. That loss of opportunity, it was alleged, arose because of NZGT's failure both to discover the loans; and to notify NAB. If NAB had known ComSec was in breach, it could have exercised its rights under the trust deed, or loan facility agreement and withdrawn. NAB argued that if it had done so in 1987 it would have recovered all of its advances to ComSec.

In the High Court, Fisher J accepted that NAB was, throughout 1987, looking for an excuse to withdraw from the facility. He accepted the evidence of NAB that had they known of the non-charging advances in July 1987 they would have taken steps to withdraw. Further, the Judge found the fact that had it exited the loan facility in 1987 it would have been repaid in full. Having held this, however, Fisher J then determined that NAB's claim must fail because of problems with causation.

The Judge considered that while a trustee must restore to the trust assets losses which would not have occurred "but for" their breach of trust, liability of a trustee for indirect losses of the beneficiary's own property is to be tested by a "close nexus approach". This is a similar test to causation and remoteness such as applies to claims in contract and tort. In these circumstances, he held that it was not reasonably foreseeable to NZGT that a failure to detect the non-charging advances would lead to NAB losing the opportunity to exit the loan facility. NZGT had no reason to know that NAB wanted to exit the facility before the end of the term, or that NAB was looking for a breach which would give it this opportunity. Therefore, while it had been demonstrated that NAB's loss would not have occurred but for NZGT's breach, it did not follow that the breach was a substantial cause of the loss. The most immediate cause was ComSec's business failure.

NAB appealed the Judge's finding on causation, while NZGT appealed the factual finding that if NAB had been informed of the loans to non-charging subsidiaries it would have opted out of the facility early and been repaid in full. The Court of Appeal was not able to support that finding of fact. In any event, they also upheld Fisher J's view of causation.

The Court considered the issue was whether the breach of duty by a trustee to act with reasonable diligence attracts liability on the same basis as a breach of trust causing loss to the trust estate, or breaches of the fiduciary duties of loyalty and fidelity. They noted that where a person, though under some fiduciary obligations as trustee, merely fails to exercise reasonable skill and care, there is no reason in principle to treat that person any differently from those who breached duties of care imposed by contract or tort. There is no difficulty with the view that a fiduciary, who breaches their duties of loyalty and fidelity held in that capacity, is subject to the strict "but for" test of causation. However that was not the case here. Absent any fraud, impropriety, or breach of duty of fidelity on the part of NZGT, there was no reason to approach its breach of duty to act diligently any differently than if the cause of action were in contract or tort rather than equity. Therefore, the test for causation was more akin to what was reasonably foreseeable to NZGT.

The scope and purpose of the duty NZGT owed was derived from the trust deed. Their duty was to notify stockholders of any breach by ComSec in order to protect them from losses caused by that breach. In this context NAB's desire to withdraw as a stockholder early in the term of the facility was not reasonably foreseeable. As the Court of Appeal reached a different view from Fisher J on the issue of whether NAB could have successfully withdrawn from the facility due to the breach, the type of loss claimed was rendered even less foreseeable.

Accordingly, the Court of Appeal was satisfied that the scope and purpose of NZGT's duty did not extend to protecting NAB from the losses it suffered from ComSec's failure through causes unconnected with the unsecured advances that NZGT failed to detect and report. NAB's appeal was dismissed.

107   ***Foster v Spencer***
[1996] 2 All ER 672

The village of Beckenham had a cricket and tennis club since 1921, which held the sports grounds on trust. In 1969 three young former players of the club were persuaded to become trustees of the club. Unfortunately, as they soon discovered, all was not well. Membership was declining, the tennis court and cricket field were badly maintained, and the pavilion had degenerated into an undesirable drinking den. The trustees fairly soon came to the conclusion that the best chance of obtaining funds to continue the club was to sell the grounds for development and look for another site.

Formidable obstacles to this course of action existed. There was a proposal to route a new road through the cricket field, and even once this plan was abandoned the land remained zoned as open space. Also, it was not clear from the trust documents whether in fact the trustees had a power to sell the land, or who the beneficiaries of the trust were. Applications to Court were necessary to sort out these two points. Following this a number of gypsies moved onto the field and refused to leave without formal eviction.

In all, it took the persistent trustees some 20 years before the land was sold. Luckily, it was sold for a substantial profit. The trustees then made an application to the Court seeking payment of remuneration and the considerable expenses they had incurred in acting on behalf of the trust.

All three trustees were professionals, one who lived nearby and who had borne the brunt of the work over the 20 years; one based in England and Brussels, and the third who was for most of the relevant time based in Malaysia. The Judge had no hesitation in accepting that their various specialist skills had contributed immensely to the success of their sale project, nor did he doubt that they had incurred considerable personal expense to achieve the sale, while not knowing whether they would be reimbursed.

The right of trustees to be reimbursed their expenses out of the trust estate has long been established, and once the Judge was satisfied that the expenses claimed were reasonable (a somewhat difficult exercise as, owing to the passage of time, it was impossible to provide receipts) a sum was ordered to be paid to the trustees to represent their expenses. No interest, however, was able to be claimed on this sum.

The question of remuneration was a little more difficult. There were two claims: two trustees sought remuneration for their past services; and all three sought remuneration for tasks which they had yet to perform. As the Judge noted it was clear that a trustee is not entitled to an allowance for time and trouble unless it is expressly authorised by the trust instrument. However, the Court does have power under its inherent jurisdiction to allow a trustee to receive remuneration. The jurisdiction had been described as highly exceptional, and to be exercised sparingly. To balance against this is the desire for trusts to be well administered, which may require remuneration in some cases.

The Judge found that the services rendered by the trustees here were completely outside their contemplation when appointed. Their task was far more difficult than they would ever have expected, and made great demands on their time and expertise. The Judge had no doubt that if they had realised what they were in for, they would never have taken on the role of trustees unless they were to be paid in some way. For these reasons, the Judge ordered that the two trustees were allowed to be paid remuneration for their past services, one on the basis of a 5 per cent commission on the purchase price achieved; the other on the basis of an annual fee of £5000. The difference represented their varying contributions. However, the Court would not award any of them remuneration for services yet to be performed. It was not satisfied that there was any need for particular skills in finalising the sale, and there was no evidence that, if these trustees resigned, other trustees could not be found who would be able to complete the sale.

108   *Niak v Macdonald*
[2001] 3 NZLR 334 (CA)

Mr Macdonald and Ms Somerville were married in 1971 and separated in 1994. They were both trustees of a family trust, along with a solicitor. In 1994, Mr Macdonald purchased a yacht for around $83,000 using trust funds. A chattel security was given to the BNZ over the yacht and a motor vehicle in 1997.

The solicitor for the BNZ was also Mr Macdonald's personal solicitor and was aware in 1996 that the trustees and Mr Macdonald were disputing ownership of the yacht, but did not advise the BNZ of the trust's claimed interest.

Mr Macdonald was removed as trustee shortly after the chattel security was given. The remaining trustees took possession of the yacht and sold it, but the proceeds were only around $54,000 and were insufficient to repay the BNZ's debt and obtain release of the security. Somerville and the other trustee then brought proceedings to argue that the purchase of the yacht was an unauthorised use of trust funds, and that the BNZ had imputed knowledge of the trustees' claim to the yacht, which therefore meant that the trustees' claim should have priority over the BNZ's claim.

The Court noted the general rule that trustees must not delegate their duties or powers, even to co-trustees, unless specifically permitted by the trust instrument or statute, or in the ordinary course of business of the trust where such delegation was "practically unavoidable". Trustees could appoint agents to implement decisions already made, but not to make actual decisions on the trustees' behalf. The Court found that the trustees had not unanimously approved an advance from the trust to Mr Macdonald to purchase the yacht, and that Mr Macdonald's use of the trust funds in this manner was an unauthorised use of those funds.

The Court also found that Mr Macdonald's solicitor (also the solicitor for the BNZ) knew of the trust's claim to the yacht at the time the BNZ instructions were received. Keeping in mind the solicitor's duty of confidentiality to Mr Macdonald, however, the solicitor's knowledge could not be imputed to the BNZ. The BNZ's legal interest therefore took priority over the trustees' equitable interest.

109 *Manukau City Council v Lawson*
[2001] 1 NZLR 599 (HC)

As part of the government's restructuring of the electricity industry in the early 1990s, Vector Limited acquired the electricity undertaking formerly operated by the Auckland Electric Power Board in 1993. Shares in Vector were held by the Auckland Energy Consumer Trust (AECT). The Manukau, Auckland City, and Papakura Councils, were the residuary beneficiaries of the trust fund capital after 80 years, and sought orders to prevent Vector authorising any dividends of capital. (These would go to AECT who would essentially pass them on to electricity consumers.)

The Court took the view that the AECT trust deed did not mean that the trustees were required to prevent payment of a dividend by Vector. The councils' only interest in the trust's capital was at the end of the 80-year perpetuity period, and no payment to the councils was permitted under the trust deed before this time. The usual rule was that a payment by a company to a shareholder was a distribution of income, and nothing in the trust deed altered this.

Further, the *power* in the trust deed for the trustees to determine whether assets were income or capital did not impose a *duty* on trustees to consider the nature of each dividend to consumers. The Court also discussed s 64B of the

Trustee Act 1956, which gave the Court the power to declare any capital dividend by a company to a trustee to be treated as capital of the trust. This would have had the effect of increasing the amount of AECT capital eventually payable to the councils. After noting that the application of this provision depended on what was fair and just in the circumstances, the Court declined to exercise its discretion.

110   *Neagle v Rimmington*
         [2002] 3 NZLR 826 (HC)

This is another case arising out of the government's energy reforms in the early 1990s. Ms Neagle was an elected trustee of the WEL Energy Trust, which owned all of the shares in WEL Networks Limited.

Ms Neagle was censured by the trust on a number of occasions for activities such as picketing a function held by the trust, and disclosing certain information to the media that the other trustees deemed confidential — in one case, information concerning the proposed acquisition of another electricity lines business by WEL Networks Limited. After this, Ms Neagle was excluded from all trust meetings and matters relating to confidential and commercially sensitive information.

Ms Neagle sought a number of orders and directions from the Court under s 66 of the Trustee Act 1956: directions as to trustees' entitlement to receive information; whether the trustees had the right to impose a media embargo; whether a trustee could seek independent legal advice at the expense of the trust; and whether the other trustees had the right to exclude Ms Neagle. After issuing proceedings, Ms Neagle failed to be re-elected as trustee, and the remaining trustees argued that since Ms Neagle had ceased to be a trustee, she had no standing to bring a s 66 claim.

The Court observed that many of the directions sought by Ms Neagle were no longer current or practical issues, and that the Court was not interested in giving unspecified directions. Directions under s 66 could not assist Ms Neagle as all the relevant matters were now historical. Section 66 was "designed to remove doubts about the propriety of any contemplated course of action". As Ms Neagle was no longer a trustee, there was no contemplated course of action by her as trustee and the provision could not apply. There was also no real basis on which to apply the Court's inherent jurisdiction to the matter.

111 *Collinge v Kyd*
[2005] 1 NZLR 847 (HC)

This was another electricity industry restructuring case. Collinge was an elected trustee of the Auckland Energy Consumer Trust (AECT), which held all of the shares in Vector Limited. Vector issued capital bonds, and Collinge obtained 200,000 shares as trustee of two trusts. The trust deed for AECT prohibited any trustee of AECT from voting on any decision where that trustee had any material interest in any matter (other than as an energy consumer). Vector proposed a merger with another company which had potential implications for the value of the bonds. Kyd, as the chairperson of AECT, ruled that Collinge could not vote on the matter, and Collinge applied to Court for a declaration that he was not prohibited from voting.

The Court noted that the trustees' duties were those imposed by the trust deed and the general rules of law and equity. Even though trustees might be elected, their political platforms could not be allowed to interfere with their duties as trustees on the terms of the trust. The test of whether a trustee's interest was material was objective, and the subjective views of the trustee could not be taken into account. Ultimately, the chairperson's ruling was final under the trust deed, and the declaration sought by Collinge was not granted.

112 *Re Gerbich*
[2002] 2 NZLR 791(HC)

A de facto couple had lived together for ten years and had a new baby (Charlie); then, unfortunately, Charlie's father was killed in an accident. The father had no will and letters of administration were granted to the mother, who obtained the father's half-interest in their previously shared house and some money. The mother paid money from the estate to her own mother (who was mortgagee of the previously-shared house) to enable the purchase of a new house for herself and Charlie. The mother then applied to the Court to validate these actions under s 41 of the Trustee Act 1956 as an advancement for the maintenance, education and advancement of Charlie — as this would enable discharge of the mortgage and would also mean that the mother could avoid working full-time and could spend more time looking after Charlie. During the litigation, it was agreed that the house would be mortgaged back to the mother as trustee for Charlie.

The Court found that an "advancement" under s 41 was the payment to a beneficiary of part of the capital of a bequest before the time that capital came into the beneficiary's hands and was generally for the setting up in life of a young person. The provision of housing was an acceptable benefit for Charlie under s 41, as Charlie would have the benefit of full care without pressure on the mother to service a usual mortgage loan. The loan would be repaid when Charlie turned 20, as this was the age at which Charlie would have received moneys under the intestacy. The mortgage was not transferable.

Hammond J described this case as being "at the farthest shores of s 41" — a testament, perhaps, to the uniqueness of the circumstances.

113   *Re Schroder's Wills Trusts*
[2004] 1 NZLR 695 (HC)

Eric Schroder must have lived a full life, for he left assets of $3.5m, including assets held by two trusts he had established. There were gifts to his two children and his second wife, Mrs Schroder, who, along with his grandchildren, were also discretionary beneficiaries of his trusts.

Eric also left behind a memorandum of his wishes, requesting the trustees of his estate to provide accommodation to Mrs Schroder in the range of $250,000-$350,000. Mrs Schroder wished to purchase a property for $331,000, but the trustees declined to approve this purchase. Mrs Schroder issued proceedings in the Family Court, which ordered that the estate pay her $400,000 for future income needs and lend her a further $400,000 to enable her to purchase a home. This loan was to be interest free for her lifetime, and to be secured by a mortgage over the home back to the estate.

After some unsuccessful proceedings by Eric's son and the trustees against this decision, the trustees applied to the High Court for directions as to whether their duty to the beneficiaries (including the grandchildren and other descendants) required them to appeal or support an appeal by Eric's son against the son being refused leave to appeal.

The Court observed that a trustee has a duty to act impartially, particularly when the beneficiaries are in a scrap. There was clearly no overriding duty to act in the interests of the grandchildren or more remote descendants which might require the trustees to support this kind of appeal. Given a lack of trustee neutrality and the presence of anti-Mrs Schroder motivation, the trustees were directed not to take any further steps to challenge the existing Court orders.

114   *Kain v Hutton*
[2004] 2 NZLR 318 (HC)

The Brookfields Trust was settled in 1978 by Mrs Kain. Her husband and brother were also trustees. The beneficiaries were the children of Mrs Kain born before 7 August 1998, the date of distribution. There were six children. The trust fund was to be distributed by the trustees to any of the children in such shares and proportions or in such manner as the trustees saw fit "in their absolute discretion", or, if no decisions were made, among the children equally.

Shortly before the distribution date there were communications between the surviving trustees, Couper and Kain. Kain wished to distribute the trust property equally between the children, but Couper believed that the whole of the trust property should be distributed only to the Kains' two daughters, with the four sons to get nothing.

Agreement was allegedly reached by telephone two days before the distribution date to distribute the whole fund to only one of the daughters, although there were some differences on the details. Formal documentation prepared by Couper provided for payment to the two daughters, and Kain refused to sign this documentation. Following the passing of the distribution date, Kain, the four sons and one daughter brought proceedings against Couper and the remaining daughter.

The Court determined from the circumstances that the trustees did not intend any agreement to be binding until it was in writing and signed. The trust's main asset was valuable land, and a distribution to some beneficiaries to the exclusion of others was a major decision. The steps taken by Couper in preparing the deed, signing it, and then sending it to Kain also suggested that they did not intend the distribution to be binding until the deed was signed. The informal telephone conversations were insufficient to constitute agreement by the trustees as to distribution.

This did not bring an end to the parties' dispute. An appeal was brought, covering a range of issues between the parties. All appeals were dismissed by the Court of Appeal (see [2007] NZCA 199).

115   *Wong v Burt*
[2005] 1 NZLR 91 (CA)

William Wong and his wife Estelle had three trusts. William died in 1984, with Estelle the sole trustee of his estate from 1990 onwards. Estelle died in 1999. William and Estelle had three children, William Jr, Phillipa and Liu, although both William Jr and Phillipa were deceased by the time of the case.

Clause 5 of William's will provided that his residual estate would be held in trust, with the net income to go to Estelle. After her death, the income was to go to those of their two daughters who were still alive (with no gift over to any grandchildren). If both were dead, then Phillipa's descendants were to inherit.

Clause 6 granted the trustees of the estate the discretion to pay Estelle such sums from the trust's capital as they saw fit. After Phillipa's death in 1995, Estelle was concerned that Phillipa's children would not take Phillipa's share if Liu was alive at the time of Estelle's death. To overcome these concerns, $250,000 of the capital from William's estate was distributed to Estelle in 1996 (using cl 6), and this was lent to one of the trusts for the benefit of Phillipa's children, being periodically forgiven over a number of years.

Liu brought proceedings against the trustees of William's estate, claiming that the trustees had acted beyond the powers of the trust, they had not exercised their powers for a proper purpose, and they had breached their duty to act impartially and even-handedly between the beneficiaries. The High Court dismissed the claim, noting that the Courts could review trustees' decisions on administrative grounds, but could not hear appeals on them; that the payment was within the powers of the trustees; and that the payment to Estelle was for her "benefit" in terms of cl 6, even though it was not to be immediately used by her.

In allowing the appeal, the Court of Appeal noted that a power under any form of authority may only be exercised for the purposes conferred under that authority. An "improper" exercise of power depended on the improper intention of the person exercising it, rather than whom the exercise of the power actually benefited, and this led to the expression "a fraud on a power".

The use of cl 6 of the will to get around the express provisions of cl 5 was, in the Court's view, a deliberate and preconceived fraud. The money had not just been advanced to Estelle and then, in her discretion, advanced to the grandchildren's trust. Rather, there had been a deliberate and impermissible attempt to subvert the terms of the will.

The Court also noted that a clause in an instrument exempting a trustee against liability was to be construed narrowly against the trustee seeking to rely on it, and the trustees' actions were not protected under the terms of the trust deed or under s 73 of the Trustee Act 1956. In addition, the fact that they had relied on legal advice was no defence, and, in the event of uncertainty, the proper course of action would have been to apply to the Court for directions under s 66 of the Trustee Act. The trustees of William's estate were found to be personally liable for repayment of the $250,000.

116   *Banicevich v Gunson*
        [2006] 2 NZLR 11 (CA)

Ivan Banicevich died in 1999, having made a will the previous year. He had four children, and his company, Sail Point Farms Limited, owned a farm in Northland (which had been in the family since 1941) from 1971. The will sought to keep the farm in the family.

Ivan's son Lloyd had been heavily involved in the farming of the land in the 1970s and 1980s, but Lloyd died suddenly in 1990 leaving two sons (Cameron and Dene). They were to be given the chance to buy the farm when the youngest turned 25 in 2003. This objective was to be achieved by Ivan's executors keeping control of Sail Point and giving Cameron and Dene the opportunity to buy the controlling "A" shares in Sail Point. The will also sought to permit Ivan's three daughters to continue using two old baches on the water's edge at the farm land, and Cameron and Dene's rights were subject to them recognising their aunts' rights of occupation of these baches.

A dispute arose between Cameron, Dene and their mother, and Ivan's three daughters, over the recognition of these occupation rights. Jocelyn, one of Ivan's daughters and executors, brought a claim under the Family Protection Act 1955 for all the shares in Sail Point to go her, and the baches to be given to her sisters. Jocelyn also wanted to subdivide the land so that the baches could have their own titles separate from the farmland title. Cameron and Dene opposed subdivision.

Ultimately, the executors/trustees applied to the High Court under s 64 of the Trustee Act 1956 for directions as to the validity of the will and whether or not the land should be subdivided. In the High Court, the Family Protection Act claim failed and the will was declared valid. The trustees were also authorised to subdivide the land, with any sale by the daughters to be subject to pre-emptive rights by Cameron and Dene and with covenants to protect the farming activities. Cameron and Dene then appealed.

The key issue of the appeal was whether the High Court's jurisdiction under s 64 of the Trustee Act 1956 allowed an order that fundamentally altered the provisions of the will and the entitlements of the beneficiaries under it.

The Court noted that this power could only be exercised if it was in the best interests of the beneficiaries and the trust as a whole. Section 64 did not permit action expedient for one beneficiary but not for another. It was also noted that while under the will Cameron and Dene would obtain the baches automatically when the daughters died, under the High Court's order they would have to buy the baches back at cost when the daughters wished to sell.

In addition, Cameron and Dene should not have had to wait to exercise the option for the shares in Sail Point. The option had been held back in 2003 because of Jocelyn's Family Protection Act claim, but this was now resolved. Waiting for subdivisional approval would mean further delay for them. Ultimately, s 64 of the Trustee Act did not permit the kind of order made by the High Court and the will was found to be workable as it stood. The board of Sail Point was also found to be bound by the terms of the will.

117 *Youyang Pty Ltd v Minter Ellison Morris Fletcher*
[2003] HCA 15, 212 CLR 484, 196 ALR 482, 77 ALJR 895 (3 April 2003)

Youyang was trustee of a discretionary trust formed in 1974. Bill Hayward and his wife Alison were directors of Youyang, and Fowler, the Haywards' accountant and investment adviser, was Youyang's secretary. The Haywards controlled assets of around $25m and consulted Fowler regularly about investment decisions.

In 1993, the Haywards were invited to invest $500,000 or more in ECCCL (via Fowler), with the investment to mature in 2003. This money was to be paid to Minter Ellison and held in trust pending satisfaction of certain conditions stated in the offer. Under the relevant subscription agreement, Youyang was to obtain a tradable Deposit Certificate, which provided some security to Youyang. Youyang proceeded with an investment of $500,000 which Minter Ellison received as trustee. However, Minter Ellison paid the subscription moneys to ECCCL without obtaining a Deposit Certificate for Youyang, and Youyang was left without security.

ECCCL became insolvent and was wound up in 1997. There was no money remaining to pay unsecured creditors and Youyang recouped none of its $500,000 investment. While Minter Ellison's client was ECCCL rather than Youyang, the Court found that Minter Ellison had breached its trustee obligations to Youyang by paying (or "misapplying") the subscription money to ECCCL without having obtained a Deposit Certificate for Youyang. This case provides a salutary lesson on the competing duties of solicitors that can arise in practice.

NATURE OF A BENEFICIARY'S INTEREST

118   *Saunders v Vautier*
(1841) 4 Beav 115

Mr Vautier received both good and bad news from a will read in 1841. The good news was that he had been left a substantial amount of stock, and its associated dividends. The bad news was that both stock and dividends were to be held on trust for him until he reached the age of 25. By the time Vautier turned 21 he had tired of this arrangement and, presumably, needed the cash. He applied to have the bequest transferred to him absolutely on the grounds that the stock and accumulated dividends were for his sole benefit, and that he should be entitled to waive the remaining period of the trust.

The Court of Appeal agreed. It held that the fund was intended wholly for the benefit of Vautier, and although his enjoyment of it was postponed by the terms of the trust, his interest in it had vested. Vautier was not bound to wait until the expiration of the trust period, but could require the trustees to transfer the trust property to him the moment he was competent to give a valid discharge. In this case, as he was 21, he could require it immediately, and the trust would be at an end.

The rule in *Saunders v Vautier* applies when all beneficiaries agree to end a trust, and all are competent to so agree (that is, are sui juris). However it will not apply when others have an interest in the trust property, or the beneficiary or beneficiaries are not, individually or collectively, absolutely entitled to the trust property.

119   *Stephenson (Inspector of Taxes) v Barclays Bank Trust Co Ltd*
[1975] 1 WLR 882, [1975] All ER 625

Sir Richard Winfrey appointed Barclays Bank Trust Co Ltd to be the executor and trustee of his will. He left sums of money to his wife, and three daughters, and the remaining capital fell into a residuary estate which was to be divided among his grandchildren.

Sir Richard's wife and daughters entered into a Deed of Family Arrangement whereby a fund was set aside for the daughters' annuities, and the balance was given to Sir Richard's grandchildren.

The question arose whether, as a result of the deed, capital gains tax became payable by Barclays Bank Trust Co Ltd, on the basis that there was a disposal of the whole of the remaining residuary estate.

The case is only relevant here for the determination of the beneficiaries' interest. As Walton J framed the issue — "at what point of time did or will the two grandchildren become absolutely entitled as against their trustees to the residuary estate?"

1.   when the younger of the two grandchildren attained the age of 21; or

2.   when the Deed of Family Arrangement was executed; or

3.   the date or dates upon which there was, or will be, an actual distribution of the residuary estate to the two grandchildren.

As to point 1, it was held that the grandchildren (or annuitants), did not have a "charge, lien or other right", within the meaning of the Finance Act (UK) 1969. As such, the grandchildren were not "absolutely entitled as against the trustees", and therefore the first date was not a date upon which the grandchildren became beneficially entitled to their future interest.

As to point 2, Walton J considered the effect of the Finance Act 1965. The issue turned upon consideration of the phrase "absolutely entitled as against the trustee" used within that Act. That term had been defined as the person having an exclusive right, to an asset for payment of duty, taxes, costs or other outgoings, and the power to direct how that asset would be dealt with. In determining the meaning of the expression, there were four elementary principles:

1.   Where persons hold between them a beneficial interest in a particular trust fund, and are all sui juris, they are entitled to direct the trustees how the trust fund should be dealt with.

2.   The first principle did not mean that the beneficiaries can at one and the same time override the pre-existing trusts and keep them in existence.

3.   The beneficial interest holders are not entitled to direct the trustees as to the particular investment which they should make of the trust fund. Moreover, once the beneficial interest holders had determined to end the trust, they are not entitled to further services from the trustees. The trustees can be compelled to hand over the trust assets to any person selected by the beneficiaries, but cannot be compelled

to do anything else with the trust fund which they are not willing to do.

4. The rights of the beneficial interest holders will always be subject to the right of the trustees to be fully protected against any duties, taxes, costs or other outgoings (for example, for rent under a lease), which the trustees had properly accepted as part of the trust property.

It followed that the third time frame (the date of distribution of the assets), must be rejected as the date upon which liability for tax accrued.

In conclusion, it was held that upon the execution of the Deed of Family Arrangement the two grandchildren became absolutely entitled as against the trustees to the whole of the remaining assets for the residuary estate. As a result, the Finance Act 1965 came into play, and tax accrued from the date of execution of the deed.

120 *Gartside v IRC*
[1968] AC 553, [1968] 1 All ER 121

This riveting and very interesting tax case is relevant because it deals with the issue of a beneficiary's interest in trust property.

Thomas Gartside, by his will, gave to trustees a residuary trust fund to be divided into four equal parts. One part was left on a discretionary trust for the support of Mr Gartside's son, his wife and any of his children. There was also a power for the trustees to advance directly to any grandchild up to half of the share of that child. Gartside's son had twin sons. When the twins were aged 17 the trustees exercised their power of advancement to the twins. In two deeds, the trustees declared that they held the balance of the trust property on trust for the twins until they attained 21 years of age.

Gartside's own son died in 1963 when the value of the fund comprising each of the deeds was about £23,500.

The Commissioners claimed estate duty on the two funds of £23,500. Estate duty is a claim made where a gift is made by a dead person to a living person, where the value of the gift exceeds a set value. In this case, the total duty claimed amounted to £32,000.

The case came before the House of Lords.

It was argued for the Commissioners that by making the advances, the twin sons had gained an interest in possession. Until the trustees had advanced the funds, they were bound under Mr Gartside's will to decide from time to time whether and to what extent income would be applied to the benefit of Mr Gartside's son, his wife, or the twins. Once the advances had been made, they were no longer entitled to deal with the income from the advanced funds in that way. The argument was that it was immaterial whether or not the trustees did in fact give to any of the beneficiaries any sum or other benefit; they each had an interest in possession of the whole fund once the grants to the twins were made.

The twins argued that a person's right to require a trustee of a discretionary trust to consider from time to time whether or not to apply some of the income for his or her benefit was not an interest, and in any event, was not an interest in possession in *the whole fund* for the purposes of the relevant English tax legislation.

The whole issue for determination before the House of Lords was the meaning to be ascribed to the word "interest" of a beneficiary in the relevant English tax law.

First, the Court held that "interest" included the right of a son to prevent a father dissipating his property.

It followed from that principle that a person who had a contingent right to some benefit from a trust fund upon the occurrence of some future event had a present right to prevent the trustees from dissipating the fund. But that right was not an interest in possession separate from, and in addition to, a contingent interest. There was a distinction between the right to control the actions of the trustees in dissipating a fund on the one hand, and a right to require trustees to consider whether to exercise a discretion in favour of a particular beneficiary.

If any person had a right which "extended" to the whole or any part of the income of any property, and that right ceased upon their death, then estate duty was due and owing to the Commissioner. If the right of the deceased or any other person did not "extend" to any part of the income, then it was not an interest within the meaning of the tax provisions. In short, an "interest" of a beneficiary within the relevant text law could exist, although the trustees did not cause any benefit to accrue or arise to a particular beneficiary.

Having determined that the twins had an "interest", the second issue to determine was whether that interest "extended" to the whole or a part of the income of the trust property. An example was used in order to illustrate the position. If a trust had a dozen beneficiaries then there would be 12 different "interests", each extending to the same income. Taken to its logical conclusion, when any one of the 12 beneficiaries dies, then their interest ceases and there is a "cesser" of an interest which extended to the whole income. If correct, upon the death of each beneficiary, estate duty would have to be paid on the whole trust fund. The same would happen on the death of each and every contingent beneficiary before the end of the discretionary trust. Lord Reid held "that would be a monstrous result which could never have been intended".

Lord Reid thus concluded:

> In my judgment, an examination of the relevant provisions of this legislation leads to the clear conclusion that objects of a discretionary trust do not have interests extending to the whole or any part of the income of the trust fund and it must follow that they do not have interests in the fund within the meaning of S 2(1)(b) ... they do not have interests in possession. It does not seem to me to be a reasonable method of construction to say that you must disregard technicalities when considering what "interest" means and then, with regard to the rest of the phrase "in possession", introduce the technicality that any interest which is not "in expectancy" must be an interest "in possession". To have an interest in possession does not merely mean that you possess the interest. You also possess an interest in expectancy, or you may be able to assign it and you can rely on it to prevent the trustees from dissipating the trust fund. "In possession" must mean that your interest enables you to claim now whatever may be the subject of the interest. For instance, if it is the current income from a certain fund your claim may yield nothing if there is no income, but your claim is a valid claim, and if there is any income you are entitled to get it. But a right to require trustees to consider whether they will pay you something does not enable you to claim anything. If the trustees do decide to pay you something, you do not get it by reason of having the right to have your case considered; you get it only because the trustees have decided to give it to you. Even if I thought the objects of discretionary trusts have interest, I do not find any good reason for holding that they have interests in possession.

121   *Schmidt v Rosewood Trust Ltd*
[2003] 3 All ER 76 (PC)

Complicated trust settlements, as may be created pursuant to international tax planning arrangements, can create many issues. In this case, two trusts — the Angora Trust and the Everest Trust — were settled by Pacquerrette Limited in the Isle of Man in 1992 and 1995 respectively. Rosewood became trustee of both trusts in 1997.

Rosewood acknowledged that Pacquerrette was, in both instances, simply a nominee for Vitali Schmidt, a senior executive director of Lukoil, one of the world's largest oil companies.

Both trusts were largely discretionary. However, Vitali sent letters to the trustee of each of the trusts shortly after their settlement asking that, if he died before the termination of the trust, any portion to which he might have been entitled be held on trust for his son Vadim, the appellant in this case. Rosewood believed neither letter had any effect, as both trusts were discretionary and gave no beneficiary any fixed entitlement to funds other than those chosen to be allocated by the trustee.

Vitali died intestate in 1997 and letters of administration were granted to Vadim in 1998. Vadim was a major beneficiary of Vitali's estate and devoted considerable energies to tracing his father's assets. Rosewood, as trustee of the trusts, failed to provide some information sought by Vadim, and Vadim brought proceedings seeking fuller disclosure of the trust's accounts and information about its assets.

The key issue rested on Vadim's right to trust documents in his role as personal representative for Vitali and as an intended beneficiary after Vitali's death.

In Their Lordships view, the right to seek disclosure of trust documents was an aspect of the Court's inherent jurisdiction to supervise and, if necessary, to intervene in, the administration of trusts. The right to seek intervention did not depend on a fixed and transmissible beneficial interest. The Board regarded a "proprietary right" approach as unsatisfactory, as a beneficiary only had equitable rather than proprietary rights, and the proprietary rights approach only caused confusion as to what were and were not "trust documents".

No beneficiary (and least of all a discretionary one) was entitled as of right to any document which could plausibly be called a trust document. However, as Vadim Schmidt was the personal representative for the deceased Vitali Schmidt, he did have a powerful case for disclosure of trust documents, particularly documents relating to distributions to Vitali, and whether there had been any breach of fiduciary duty in relation to Vitali (such as the possibility of overcharging). Having found that Vadim's rights and claims fell under the Court's inherent jurisdiction, the Board returned the case to the lower Courts.

122 *Foreman v Kingstone*
[2004] 1 NZLR 841 (HC)

Bill Foreman had three trusts and had been married three times. Each trust was a discretionary trust, with all distributions entirely at the trustees' discretion until the relevant vesting day of each trust, at which point the trust fund would be divided among specified classes of beneficiaries.

The plaintiffs were beneficiaries under the various trusts and sought information relating to the trusts. The relevant trustees refused to provide these, leading the plaintiffs to apply to the Court for financial statements, reasons for trustees' decisions, details of distributions, and various correspondence. Apart from copies of the trust deeds themselves, and some other minor information, the trustees resisted further provision of information to the beneficiaries.

The Court noted that the beneficiaries were discretionary beneficiaries only, and the trustees had absolute discretion as to the application of the trust fund. Each beneficiary's interest was "a mere expectancy", and they could not be described as "contingent beneficiaries".

Referring to *Schmidt v Rosewood Trust Ltd* **(121)**, the Court noted that a beneficiary's access to trust documents should be approached as an aspect of the Court's inherent jurisdiction to supervise the administration of trusts, rather than an equitable proprietary interest in trust property. Nevertheless, the trustees clearly had fiduciary obligations to the beneficiaries, including the duty to account to the beneficiaries for the administration of the trust, although not for the reasons for the trustees' decisions. The beneficiaries were therefore entitled to receive information which would enable them to ensure the accountability of the trustees in terms of the trust deed, including the right to trust accounts and financial statements. In turn, the beneficiaries were required to respect the autonomy of trustees in their decision making, and were not entitled to the reasons for the trustees' decisions.

123 *Burns v Steel*
[2006] 1 NZLR 559 (HC)

When Andrew Kirkpatrick died in March 2004, he had no wife or children, but he did own some valuable shares in a company his late father had established. Mr Kirkpatrick left all his shares in the company to his sister, Ms Burns, with the residuary estate being divided between Ms Burns and Kirkpatrick's other two sisters.

The company's constitution provided for rights of preemption in relation to shares in the company. Ms Burns sought to direct the trustees of Kirkpatrick's estate as to how their discretions should be exercised: (a) in relation to how and when the preemption process should proceed; and (b) in their role as shareholders in the company pending completion of the preemption process. The trustees, on the other hand, sought to exercise their own discretions without direction from Burns. The trustees had obtained a legal opinion that the shares were held as bare trustees and that they must follow Ms Burns' directions. Nevertheless the trustees felt they should avoid preferring any one beneficiary over any other.

The Court noted that Ms Burns' interest in the shares was not absolutely vested, as the gift was necessarily subject to the constitution of the company. In addition, the trustees' duties were defined by reference to the company's constitution and a "bare trustee" relationship could not be said to exist, although the overall context of the trustees' obligations and discretions was more important than nomenclature.

Here, the trustees were not mere ciphers; they had active duties as executors and trustees. The trustees were required to hold the shares and undertake the pre-emption process in the best interests of Ms Burns as beneficiary, exercising their own discretion in a conscientious manner. It was for the trustees to decide when, and on what terms, to issue a transfer notice under the constitution. If Ms Burns was dissatisfied, then she could apply to the Court for a review of the trustees' actions, but she could not simply direct the trustees of her own accord.

Ms Burns could not direct the trustees on how to exercise their rights as shareholders in the company. Given the preemption provisions, Ms Burns might never hold the relevant shares, and it was absurd that she should be entitled to obtain in advance rights she might never actually hold. She was however entitled to dividends under the terms of the will.

124   *Wrightson Ltd v Fletcher Challenge Nominees Ltd*
[2002] 2 NZLR 1 (PC)

Employee superannuation schemes can involve large amounts of money, and the ownership and administration of such schemes can give rise to a range of interesting legal issues. In this case, the employees of Wrightson signed on to the scheme of its parent company Fletcher Challenge in 1983. Fletcher Challenge Nominees Ltd (FCNL) was trustee of the scheme. Wrightson ceased to be a wholly owned subsidiary of Fletcher Challenge in 1993 and withdrew from the Fletcher Challenge scheme in 1995.

This constituted a partial dissolution of the scheme. FCNL proposed that it would distribute to the new Wrightson scheme a share of the moneys held by FCNL to meet members' benefits, but not a share of the surplus fund, which would be retained by FCNL. Wrightson's members, obviously wishing to share in this surplus fund, brought proceedings against FCNL as trustee.

Clause 4.2 of the scheme's trust deed provided that if a member such as Wrightson left the Fletcher Challenge scheme, the plan would be dissolved as to such part as the trustee determined to be appropriate to the relevant participant — a rather broad trustee discretion, to say the least! The High Court found that a "share of fund" approach should be taken, and that a proportionate share of the whole trust fund (including the surplus) should be distributed.

The Court of Appeal took a different approach. It held that members of the plan were only entitled to a share of actual benefits, not to any surplus, and noted that provisions in the trust deed requiring proportionate distribution of the benefits fund and surplus on the *winding up* of the fund did not apply to partial dissolutions caused by an individual participant's withdrawal from the scheme before the final winding up. The Privy Council agreed, and held that FCNL's discretion as trustee was, although not completely unfettered, broad enough not to require it to distribute a share of the trust fund surplus to any withdrawing participant.

125   *Gailey v Gordon*
[2003] 2 NZLR 192 (HC)

This was not the end of Fletcher Challenge's fund issues. In 2000, the Fletcher Challenge Energy Employee Educational Fund (the trust) was set up with assets of around $11m. In 2001, the Fletcher Challenge company which had settled the trust was to be sold overseas, and the trustees sought direction from the Court, under s 66 of the Trustee Act 1956, in relation to a proposal that the trust be wound up accordingly. Two employees of Fletcher Challenge who were eligible for benefits challenged this proposal.

The first issue was whether the Court was restricted to either granting or declining the specific orders sought by the trustees, or whether the trustees' discretion on the relevant matter was surrendered to the Court, who could then make a completely different order in the interests of the beneficiaries. Distinguishing *Marley v Mutual Security Merchant Bank & Trust Co Ltd*

[1991] 3 All ER 198, a Privy Council decision in a Jamaican case, and *Re Allen-Meyrick's Will Trust* [1966] 1 All ER 740, the Court held that the trustees had sought specific directions and had not intended a blanket surrender of their discretions to the Court. The beneficiaries themselves had no jurisdiction to apply to the Court under s 66 of the Trustee Act, and there had been no actual decision to wind up the trust and therefore no ability for an application under s 68 of the Trustee Act.

Ultimately, the Court found that the company restructuring meant there were no longer any employees of the relevant company to be beneficiaries of the trust. Persons made redundant were not beneficiaries of the trust. There were no beneficiaries left and that left "no real alternative" to winding up of the trust. In addition, the trustees had not acted unreasonably (there being some discussion of whether *Wednesbury* unreasonableness may apply to trustees — see *Associated Provincial Picture Houses Ltd v Wednesbury Corporation* [1948] 1 KB 223). The trustees were therefore directed to proceed with the winding up.

126   *Re Motorola New Zealand Superannuation Fund*
[2001] 3 NZLR 50 (HC)

Motorola had a superannuation trust scheme for the benefit of those employees who were members. There were three accounts: a number one account containing employee contributions, a number two account containing employer contributions, and a reserve fund containing other income and capital.

The trust invested in AMP funds, and when AMP was demutualised in 1998 the trust received a windfall of 12,800 AMP shares. This allocation of shares was based on the membership of the Motorola fund as at December 1996 (not as at 1998); however, membership of the fund had decreased significantly in this time. When the trust sold the shares, $327,095 was realised. A dispute arose as to whether these proceeds should be distributed to members who had resigned since 1996, those who were members in 1996 and remained members, or those who were current members, but had joined since 1996. The trustees resolved in 1999 to amend the deed so that past members could receive a share of the proceeds, but some existing members refused to consent to the amendment of the trust deed to enable this distribution. The trustees then sought directions as to whether they had the power to amend the trust deed to distribute to all classes involved in the dispute, or were required to distribute to any particular class.

After noting that there was no rule that an express trust could not be subject to a constructive trust, the Court noted that the trustees received the share proceeds subject to the terms of the trust deed and not subject to any constructive trust. There was nothing unconscionable about the express trust, and the requirement that only current members benefit from it (including the share proceeds) was simply the "rub of the green".

127   *Buschau v Rogers Communications Inc*
       [2006] SCJ 28, [2006] 1 SCR 973 (SCC)

In 1974, Premier Communication Ltd set up a pension plan trust for its employees (the Premier Plan). The Premier Plan was expected to continue indefinitely, but could be terminated by the company at any time, with the benefits of the plan to continue being paid to retired members, and the balance of the assets to be distributed among the remaining members.

In 1980, Rogers acquired the Premier Communication business. In 1984, the Premier Plan was closed to new employees and in 1992 the Premier Plan was merged with a number of other Rogers' plans into an overall plan known as the RCI Plan. This was not supported by former Premier employees remaining part of the original Premier Plan.

In 1995, members of the Premier Plan initiated proceedings to seek return of the trust funds paid over to Rogers in 1985 and a declaration that the funds belonged to the Premier Plan members, The British Columbian Court of Appeal ruled that the merger of the plans was valid, but that this did not prevent the Premier Plan's existence as a separate trust — which, in the BCCA's view, meant the beneficiaries could use the rule in *Saunders v Vautier* **(118)** to terminate the trust and obtain the proceeds. Following an application to terminate the trust by the Premier Plan members, the matter came before the Supreme Court of Canada.

After considering the social and economic implications of pension plans, the SCC turned to the rule in *Saunders v Vautier*, allowing the beneficiaries of a trust to modify or extinguish the trust without reference to the wishes of the settlor or trustees. The Premier Plan members argued that this rule allowed them to wind up the trust, even though the rules stated that only the employer could terminate it.

The SCC, however, agreed with Rogers that the rule in *Saunders v Vautier* did not apply to pension plans. Apart from the fact that pension plans were strictly regulated by Canadian statute, which prevailed over the *Saunders* rule, the existence of the trust in this situation was dependent on the existence of the

Premier Plan. The trust and the plan were seen as "indissociable". Further, the plan was established to benefit the *employer's* interests, and as a management decision it should not be challenged, unlike a common law trust, which once created generally excluded the settlor's interests.

Finally, while the dissolution of a family trust would generally be gratuitous, in the sense that advancing the date of entitlement would have no real social consequences, the early distribution of a pension trust could affect the financial security of beneficiaries on retirement and would defeat the purpose of the trust. In the SCC's view, at para 97:

> The introduction of the *Saunders v Vautier* principle without qualification or restriction into the private pension system would constitute a very significant derogation from an employer's right to voluntarily choose to offer or continue a pension plan. An employer motivated by labour market factors to create and maintain a pension plan for its employees for the business benefits it may derive may not be so motivated when a plan instituted for such reasons can be terminated by the unilateral action of members and other beneficiaries, without consideration of the employer's business interests.

Notwithstanding the statutory, cultural and jurisprudential differences between Canada and New Zealand (including the fact that Kiwisaver funds, while likely to grow significantly in future, are distinct from the Premier Plan in that they involve employee as well as employer contributions), the comments in this case may well influence pension plan cases here in future.

- Victoria Stace "Supreme Court of Canada holds that the rule in *Saunders v Vautier* does not apply to pension schemes" (2007) 13 NZBLQ 121.

128   *Johns v Johns*
[2004] 3 NZLR 202 (CA)

The LR Johns Family Trust was settled in 1967. Stephen Johns, a son of the settlor and one of the beneficiaries under the trust, brought proceedings in 2000 alleging breach of trust and breach of fiduciary duty. There were various transactions between the trust and a company of which the trust was shareholder which were alleged to be at undervalue, mostly during the 1970s, although one relevant transaction had taken place in 1995. The transactions from the 1970s were found to be beyond the six-year limitation period set out in the Limitation Act 1950.

It was noted that Stephen had three interests in the trust property: one as a discretionary beneficiary; one as a residual beneficiary; and one as a beneficiary entitled to income. The Court found that Stephen's interest as a discretionary beneficiary was, following *Hunt v Muollo* [2003] 2 NZLR 322, a "mere expectancy" rather than a real legal or beneficial interest.

The interest as a residual beneficiary was, however, a "future interest" in the trust property, even though the interest was a contingent interest and there was no guarantee there would be any funds remaining on the trust being wound up. The interest in the income was also a "future interest", as Stephen's interest could be harmed by breaches of trust reducing the amount of income available in future years.

Both the latter interests accrued from when possession was taken of the interest, and so were not time-barred. In addition, as the breach of trust claim was not barred by the Limitation Act, it was inappropriate to similarly bar an equitable claim for breach of fiduciary duty.

129   *Hotung v Ho*
[2002] 3 HKLRD 641

Not everything that could be said about the law of trusts has been said, and new issues continue to arise in the Courts.

In this case, Ho Yuen Ki agreed by two declarations of trust that certain shares she owned in two companies were held on trust for three beneficiaries: Michael, Sean and Anthony Hotung. The first declaration, in 1979, meant each beneficiary was entitled to 3334 shares in Hotung Enterprises Ltd. The second, in 1980, entitled each beneficiary to one share in Hotung Investment (China) Ltd. Anthony and Sean requested that Ho appoint them as her attorneys in respect of their shares in the two companies. Ho refused, and Anthony and Sean issued proceedings on the basis that Ho was a bare trustee or a nominee in relation to the shares, that she had no discretions to perform, and that they were entitled to call for a transfer of legal ownership of the shares to them and terminate the trust. It was recognised by the Court that this was a "novel" point without any precedent on point.

The Court drew a distinction between bare and special trusts. A bare trust was where property was vested in one person for the benefit of another without any prescription as to the nature of the trust. In such a case, the trustee must permit the beneficiary to enjoy the property and obey the beneficiary's instructions; for example, property held subject to a bare trust must be transferred to the beneficiary on request. The trustee had no duties other than to follow the beneficiary's instructions. Conversely, a "special" trust (which the vast majority of trusts were), was one where the terms of the trust imposed duties on trustees, and particularly elements of discretion. Following *Saunders v*

Vautier **(118)**, however, a trust could exist where the trustee was required to transfer property to the beneficiaries on request, but until that time had active powers and discretions to exercise. This was, in the Court's view, different to a standard "bare trustee" arrangement, though it was often referred to as such.

The most useful precedent was *In Re Brockbank, Ward v Bates* [1948] 1 Ch 206, where it was found that beneficiaries did not have the right to change the trustees of the trust as they pleased — they must keep the trust on foot with the original trustees, or extinguish the trust. This principle was found to extend to bare trusts as well as special trusts. In other words, the beneficiaries were free to direct Ho as trustee as to her actions, but could not at the same time override the pre-existing trusts (by requiring the powers of attorney) *and* keep the trusts in existence. The beneficiaries, having agreed to keep the trusts in existence and be bound by the trust, must allow Ho to carry out her duties — they could not have all the rights of legal and beneficial ownership through the powers of attorney without assuming the burden of actual ownership. The claim of Sean and Anthony was dismissed.

TRACING

130   *Re Hallett's Estate*
(1880) 13 Ch D 696, [1874-80] All ER Rep 793

Henry Hughes Hallett (one of the world's great alliterative names), was a solicitor who died in February 1878. At his death he was insolvent. On investigation, it was found that during his lifetime Hallett had misappropriated money and property belonging to his clients. One, Mrs Cotterill, had entrusted Russian bonds to the value of £2442 to Hallett, for safe custody. Hallett had clear instructions that when he received interest on the bonds, he was to pay it over to Mrs Cotterill from time to time. Hallett did account to Mrs Cotterill for the income, but in November of 1877, he sold the bonds, and received the proceeds amounting to £1800. The proceeds of that transaction, were paid into an account with a further £770, being the proceeds of the sale of more Russian bonds belonging to another innocent party. The journal entries for the accounts indicated that the £770 had preceded the deposit of the £1800. Hallett continued to operate this account during the rest of the short period of his life, and he drew out substantial sums for use in his own affairs. Hallett withdrew a total of £2600, while the aggregate of the amounts paid in amounted to only £1300. At the time of Hallett's death, the account was £3000 in credit.

Both Mrs Cotterill and the other aggrieved party brought an action claiming that they should be paid out of the credit balance being the proceeds of the sales of their respective bonds. Hallett's bankers on appeal argued that the drawings of Hallett, being greater than the total amount paid into the account, had effectively wiped out any credit which could be found to be in favour of Mrs Cotterill.

Sir George Jessel MR, held that the proceeds of the sale of Mrs Cotterill's Russian bonds had been deposited with Hallett's bankers in a "separate parcel". There was no doubt that Hallett stood in a fiduciary position towards Mrs Cotterill and had improperly sold the bonds and deposited the returns. There was also no dispute that the proceeds of the sale of Mrs Cotterill's bonds had been mixed with Hallett's own moneys at the time of his death. In essence therefore, Mrs Cotterill sought to "trace" the proceeds of the sale of her bonds to Hallett's account, and draw those moneys out of the hands of Hallett's bankers. His Lordship stated that:

You can, if the sale was rightful, take the proceeds of the sale, if you can identify them. If the sale was wrongful, you can still take the proceeds of the sale, in a sense adopting the sale for the purpose of taking the proceeds, if you can identify them. There is no distinction, therefore, between a rightful and wrongful disposition of the property, so far as regards the right of the beneficial owner to follow the proceeds.

In this case, as in many others, the proceeds had been intermingled with Hallett's own moneys. The question was therefore, whether the proceeds of a wrongful sale (in breach of fiduciary obligations) could be traced into an account containing intermingled funds.

The Court held that the moment one can establish a fiduciary relationship, the modern rules of equity relating to the following or tracing of trust of moneys will apply. In this case it did not matter whether Hallett was viewed as a fiduciary, an agent, or as bailer of the proceeds of the Russian bonds or the wrongful sale. Looking at the law relating to the bailing of goods, a bailer could in equity follow the proceeds of the sale of goods wherever they could be distinguished, either when actually kept separate, or when mixed up with other moneys.

A useful analogy was used. Where a trustee (and that term was used to include a person placed in a fiduciary relationship) had intermingled the proceeds of the sale of his or her fiduciary goods, it would make no difference for the purposes of tracing. Thus, if a trustee retained a bag containing 1000 sovereigns, into which either by mistake, accident or otherwise, the trustee had placed a sovereign of his own, there was nothing in equity to prevent the cestui que trust taking 1000 sovereigns out of the bag. It wouldn't matter if it was one sovereign, or 1000 sovereigns of the trustee's moneys which had been intermingled. And so, where the trustee had carried the bag to his bankers, it made no difference to the right of the cestui que trust to trace the moneys into the bankers' account. Effectively, the bankers were in no better position to claim any right to the intermingled funds than Hallett.

Developing the rules of tracing relating to intermingled funds, His Honour referred to the case of *Frith v Cartland* (1865) 2 H & M 417. That case involved a situation where the personal funds of a trustee had been intermingled with trust funds. The trustee had then withdrawn some of the intermingled moneys. In such a situation, equity presumes that the withdrawal of moneys is notionally taken from the funds belonging to the trustee first, rather than the trust. Thus, if a trustee retained in one account £1000 of his own money, and £1000 of trust money, and then subsequently withdrew £500, a Court of equity will presume that the withdrawal of £500 is taken as against the account of the trustee, rather than the trust. It followed that in the instant case Hallett's withdrawals from the intermingled funds were to be presumed as withdrawals of his own money. It followed that Mrs Cotterill's right to trace could not therefore be denied on the basis that some of her moneys had been disbursed. Judgment was entered for her accordingly.

131   *Re Oatway*
       [1903] 2 Ch 356

Lewis Oatway and Maxwell Skipper were co-trustees of the will of Charles Skipper, Maxwell's father. They seemed to find themselves in all sorts of trouble even in the early stages of their office, for in short order the sum of £3000 was lent to Maxwell from the trust funds. This was a flagrant breach of trust. Maxwell did provide security for the loan in the form of a mortgage to Oatway over a property he owned, and also gave him a power of attorney. Maxwell then, somewhat foolishly as it happened, went abroad for a considerable period of time.

Meanwhile the untrustworthy Oatway used the mortgage and the power of attorney to sell Maxwell's property, which netted him approximately £7000. Rather than repaying the trust the £3000 it was owed, and holding the remainder for Maxwell, Oatway put the lot into his personal bank account, which was in credit at the time. He then proceeded to squander the entire credit balance of his account. The only asset he bought was some shares to the value of £2137 in the Oceana Company, which were bought in his name.

Following Oatway's death, Maxwell returned from his travels to discover that the trust was still owed £3000, his property was gone, and that the only asset was the Oceana shares. He brought a summons seeking a declaration as to whether the proceeds of sale of the shares could be paid to him personally, or in his capacity as trustee.

Judge Joyce noted that it was a well-settled principle that a true owner is entitled to seize his or her property in whatever altered form it may be, so long as he or she can prove the identity of the original material. Thus trust money may be followed into land or any other property in which it has been invested. When a trustee has, in making any purchase or investment, applied trust money together with his or her own, the cestuis que trust are entitled to a charge on the property purchased for the amount of the trust money used in its purchase. The Judge felt it was clear that:

> [W]hen any of the money drawn out has been invested, and the investment remains in the name or under the control of the trustee, the rest of the balance

having been afterwards dissipated by him, he cannot maintain that the investment which remains represents his own money alone, and that what has been spent and can no longer be traced and recovered represents the money belonging to the trust.

In this case the balance had been dissipated. The only property remaining which represented any part of the mixed moneys in Oatway's account were the Oceana shares. The trust therefore had a charge upon these for the £3000 paid into Oatway's account. In other words, the shares and any proceeds from their sale, belonged to the trust. Maxwell could not deny the trust's claim to the shares due to his own breach of trust. He, alas, recovered nothing for the loss of his property.

132   *Sinclair v Brougham*
[1914] AC 398

In June 1911 an order was made for the winding up of the Birbeck Permanent Building Society. The object of the society was to enable its members to raise a joint fund out of which they could individually buy or build houses. There were two classes of shareholders: those to whom loans were granted; and those who were mere investors. The investing shares were divided into classes A and B. The main difference between the shares was that the A shares matured after a fixed period, and would be paid off after that period, while the B shares were ongoing. In both cases the shareholder could give notice and withdraw the amount of his or her share.

During the earlier period of its existence the funds which were derived both from shares and from loans by depositors were laid out in mortgages to members. Later, while the society continued its business as a Building Society, it began gradually to increase its deposits and to do the business of a banker.

On the balance sheet of 31 March 1911 the liabilities to shareholders was stated to amount to just over £1m while the liabilities deposited were nearly £11m. Unsurprisingly, the society went into liquidation.

The question which arose was how the liquidator was to dispose of the mass of assets in his hands. The first instance Judge ordered the assets to be applied, first, in payment of costs; secondly, in paying debts properly incurred to outside creditors; thirdly, in paying the unadvanced members or shareholders the amounts due to them in respect of the subscriptions paid; and fourthly, distributing the balance among the customers of the society on deposit or a current account in proportion to the amounts standing to their credit in the books.

The Court's decision was on the basis that the society was not authorised to engage in banking business, and that its action in doing so was ultra vires. Every deposit was therefore ultra vires. The depositors could therefore be subjugated to the rights of debtors. And, if the depositors could identify their money as earmarked, they could follow it under a tracing judgment. If the money was not earmarked, the depositors could not claim to be creditors either at law or in equity, and their only right was to the surplus assets after payment of all legitimate debts.

In the House of Lords the appellant depositors argued that they were entitled to succeed in recovering their deposits, either because their money was "had and received" by the society, or as money which never truly formed part of the assets of the society, and which could be followed into the hand of the society's liquidator.

Delivering the decision of the House, Viscount Haldane stated that a cause of action based upon money had and received could not be sustained. It followed that the depositors in the present case would not succeed unless they were able to trace their money into the hands of the society or its agents as actually existing assets. Holding that there had been no breach of fiduciary duty on the part of the society, Viscount Haldane held that the depositors could in his opinion only claim the value of the depreciated assets, which represented their loss, and nothing more.

In *Westdeutsche Landesbank Girozentrale v Islington London Borough Council* **(80)** the House of Lords came very close to overruling *Sinclair v Brougham*. However the decision still stands, on its own specific facts.

133   *Re Diplock*
        [1948] 2 All ER 318

Caleb Diplock in his will directed his executors to apply his residuary estate "for such charitable institution or institutions or other charitable, object or objects in England as my acting executors may in their absolute discretion select".

After Caleb's death, his executors paid out a total of £203,000 to charitable institutions of their choice. Each payment was made by way of cheque accompanied by letter from the executors, advising the happy recipients that the moneys were paid pursuant to a bequest from Caleb. However, as is often the case with large sums of money, persons claiming to be the next of kin challenged the validity of the charitable bequests, and wrote to each recipient institution a "warning letter", informing them of the challenge and calling on the organisations not to spend or distribute the money which they had received. A number of the next of kin brought actions against the estate which fell into two categories:

1. claims "in personam" based on a right of an unpaid or underpaid beneficiary, to recover money overpaid to another beneficiary or to a stranger to the estate; and

2. claims "in rem" based on the right to trace assets where the proceeds of the payments could be identified in the hands of the charitable institutions.

Some of the accounts of the charities were in credit, others were in overdraft, and in a few cases, the moneys had been expended by investment in maintenance or upgrade of buildings and various purchases. In other words, the moneys had passed from the charitable organisations to third parties for valuable consideration, and often without notice of the claim of the next of kin.

In relation to the "in personam" claims, the Court of Appeal held that it was not able to make an exhaustive formulation of the nature of an equitable claim applicable to every class of case. However, that aside, it was clearly established in a large volume of case law that the existence of an equitable claim "in personam" did exist. Such claims were against a recipient who was paid more than he or she was entitled to receive at the date of payment or who was not in fact entitled to any payment. These remedies would be available to an unpaid or underpaid creditor, a legatee, or in this case, a next of kin. Further, a claim by next of kin would not be defeated merely because:

1. there was an absence of administration of the will by the Court; or

2. the mistake under which the original payment had been made was one of law rather than fact; or

3. the original recipient turned out to have no title at all, and was a stranger to the estate. In this situation, it was the conscience of the recipient upon which the equity acts, and in circumstances such as this case, it was sufficient that the recipient had received some share of the estate to which he or she (or the charitable institution) was not entitled.

A claim by an unpaid beneficiary will always be subject to the qualification that since the original wrong payment was due to the blunder of the personal representatives of the testator, the next of kin's (or beneficiaries') primary claim was against the executors. Therefore, the claim (through tracing) to the charitable institutions was limited to the amount recoverable from the party at fault. In other words, the extent of the claim against the wrongful recipient (in this case the charitable institutions) was limited to the extent to which funds could not be recovered from the personal representatives or executors. In the present case, the amount recovered from the executors under a settlement agreement had to be apportioned amongst the charities proportionate to the grants which they had received. It followed that the maximum recoverable from any individual charity by the next of kin was rateably reduced. Further, owing to an interesting (and seemingly anomalous) development of the law in this area, the charitable institutions were not liable for interest on the principal which they had wrongly received.

In relation to the claims made in rem, the case is a cornerstone of the modern law. Lord Green held that the equitable right to trace into a "mixed fund" was not confined to cases like **Re Hallett's Estate (130)**. *Hallett's* case was an illustration of a much wider principle — that a person's money which had been mixed with that of another or others could be traced into the mixed fund (or mixed assets) where the "mixer" of the funds or assets was an innocent volunteer, provided that:

1. there was originally a fiduciary or quasi-fiduciary relationship between the claimant and the recipient of the money so as to give rise to an equitable proprietary interest in the claimant; and

2. the claimant's money was fairly identifiable; and

3. the equitable remedy available (that was, a charge on the mixed fund or assets), did not work an injustice.

Where the defendant is in a fiduciary relationship to a claimant, and had mixed the claimant's money with his own, the claimant's claim to the mixed funds took priority over the defendant's. That conclusion was reinforced in a situation such as in the present case, where the defendant had notice that the money was in equity the claimant's. Further, where there was a contest or battle between two different claimants to a mixed fund consisting of moneys belonging to both, both claimants would share pari passu (in even shares).

There was a further important qualification to these principles: where a claimant's moneys had been transferred to an individual for value without notice of the claimant's equity, then the claim, and all equities in the moneys, were extinguished. This was to be contrasted with the case of a volunteer who had taken without notice (for instance, by way of gift) and where there was no question of mixing. In such a situation, the volunteer holds the money on behalf of the true owner, whose equitable right to the money continues.

Finally, if the volunteer had innocently mixed the money of his or her own, or received it mixed with his or her own money from a fiduciary agent, then the volunteer must admit the claim of the true owner. That aside, the volunteer is not precluded from setting up his or her own claim in relation to the moneys which he or she has contributed to the mixed fund. The result being, that the volunteer and the claimant share pari passu in the mixed fund, neither being entitled to a priority.

Applying those principles to the instant case, the Court held that where there was a mixing of trust moneys with charity moneys the next of kin were entitled to recover, pari passu from the charity in the case of mixed funds, (subject to a reduction in relation to the amounts recovered from the executors under a settlement agreement). However, where the moneys received by the charity had not been mixed with the moneys of the charity, but had been expended on the alteration or improvements of their own assets (such as erecting buildings or maintenance), or discharging debts of the charity, the trust money could not be disentangled, and if the equitable remedy of tracing by way of charge was permitted, it would cause an injustice. As a consequence, the claims of the next of kin in these situations could not be maintained.

In working out the equity in situations where the moneys had been paid into an active bank account, the rule in *Devaynes v Noble; Clayton's case* (1816) 1 Mer 529 was applicable, and the moneys could be traced. The rule in *Clayton's case* establishes that withdrawals out of the account are presumed to be made in the same order as the payments in, that is, "first in, first out". Where the charity had received trust money and had purchased a specific asset, the charity was prima facie bound by its own voluntary act, and the funds could be traced by the claimant to the asset purchased.

134   *Ontario Securities Commission v Greymac Credit Corpn*
(1986) 30 DLR 4th ed 1

Greymac Creditcorp, as trustee, held over $4m in trust for three trust companies. The money was held in one account in the name of only one of the companies. Greymac then deposited a further sum of just over $1m into that account. Of that amount, $840,000 belonged to an outfit called "Chorny Mortgage Investor Participants". Greymac then withdrew some moneys (without authorisation) and dissipated some of the withdrawn moneys. In the end, there was a shortfall of $1.3m in the account.

An application was brought to determine the entitlement of both Chorny and the trust companies to the balance of the fund.

In the Ontario Court of Appeal, reference was initially made to the "first in, first out" rule enunciated in *Clayton's* case (see *Re Diplock* (**133**)). However, *Clayton's* case had no application to the instant case. Immediately before the unauthorised withdrawals of moneys from the account, the two beneficiaries (the trust companies and Chorny), had a property right in the total fund in proportion to their contribution.

That right did not change because of the transfer; rather, their respective entitlements, in the same proportions, were spread over the moneys retained in the account. Each of the two groups of beneficiaries had an equitable lien on the account to secure the amounts of their total contributions. It was more natural and reasonable to allow the two groups of beneficiaries to continue to share pro rata in the account than to say (applying *Clayton's* case) that it was the trust company's money that was first taken from the account and then that of Chorny.

In principle, the issue was not whether the rule in *Clayton's* case could be used for tracing purposes, as well as for loss allocation, but whether the rule should have any application to the resolution of problems connected with competing beneficial entitlements to a mingled trust fund where there had been withdrawals from the fund. It was held as "a matter of basic concept", that the rule in *Clayton's* should not apply; that it should be confined strictly to the bank/customer relationship. In relation to claims between innocent beneficiaries, the rule was considered to be arbitrary and unfair and the pro rata approach more logical and just. While the rule in *Clayton's* case was convenient, it should not stand in the way of acceptance, as a general rule, of pro rata sharing on the basis of tracing.

135   *Re Securitibank Ltd*
[1978] 1 NZLR 97

This case is notable for several reasons. First, it arose out of the notorious collapse of Securitibank which led to a reform of the securities legislation; secondly, because of the length of hearing before the Supreme Court (a total of 25 days); and thirdly, because of the length of the decision of Justice Barker (just over 120 pages).

Securitibank Ltd was a holding company for a group of companies which came to be called the Securitibank Group. That group engaged in the short-term money market. One of the subsidiary companies, Merbank Ltd, described itself as a "merchant bank" and generally all funds required by clients of the group were provided through Merbank. All securities supporting the various credit arrangements were taken in the name of Merbank. Nevertheless, Securitibank Ltd acted as the "banker" to all the subsidiaries, including Merbank. Securitibank Ltd received unsecured deposits from the public and, among other things, made "money market" advances to Merbank for that company to lend to its clients. Clients who obtained credit "facilities" from the group were required generally to give a mortgage in wide terms over any available real property (and debentures) and were also required to draw "money market" bills in favour of themselves on Merbank, which accepted the bills for a fee. The bills were called "client bills" and were usually discounted to Commercial Bills Ltd, which then sold them to the public. The bills were for short terms, usually 90 days. However the borrowers usually required longer term finance. In these circumstances, when the bills matured, they were "rolled over"; that is, fresh bills were drawn and accepted for the value of the maturing bill plus a sum for discounting the new bill, fresh acceptance fees and any other outstanding charges. The new bills were also generally discounted to Commercial Bills Ltd and that company then onsold the new bills to the public.

In short, the group of companies borrowed short term, and lent long term (a classic "no-no" for banking institutions).

On 2 February 1977 Securitibank, Merbank, Commercial Bills, and three other companies in the Securitibank Group were ordered by the Court to be wound up and the Official Assignee was appointed provisional liquidator of all six companies. The liquidator applied under the then Companies Act 1952 to the Court seeking directions relating to the priority of claims, and a further number of complex matters relating to the liquidator's exercise of his duties.

The case deals with a large number of rather complicated commercial issues, but we shall focus only upon the case's impact in relation to the law relating to tracing.

The issue of tracing arose because a company called Safe Custody Nominees Ltd held the total collection of client bills. Safe Custody held the client bills, inextricably mixed, as a trustee for two groups of beneficiaries (the creditors of both Commercial Bills and Merbank), and the issue was as to how those creditors were to be paid out of the remaining value of the bills.

In the High Court, counsel argued that where a trustee mixed funds of his own with those of a beneficiary, equity requires that the beneficiary is paid out first, so that the total deficiency is borne by the trustee. Further, it was suggested that where a trustee makes money out of two or more beneficiaries, the moneys are applied on a "first in, first out" basis.

In determining the issue of entitlement to the mixed "funds", Barker J relied substantially upon *Sinclair v Brougham* **(132)**. In particular, there was discussion of the two conflicting arguments presented in that case. First, it was said that depositors had parted with their money out and out and could not follow it. On the other hand, it was said that the depositors'equitable property rights were good against the shareholders, who were not bona fide purchasers. The solution adopted by the House of Lords was a pari passu distribution. That conclusion was reinforced by the House of Lords treatment of *Sinclair v Brougham* in *Re Diplock* **(133)**.

Citing fully from both decisions, Justice Barker took the view that:

1. There was an absolute assignment to Merbank under a trust deed;

2. That the deed was not operated according to its terms; and

3. That it was not feasible to reconstruct the dealings of the companies in accordance with the terms of the deed.

The only course open to the Court therefore was to follow *Sinclair v Brougham* and *Re Diplock*. The right of an individual shareholder to make application to trace was reserved in that case. Justice Barker then noted that a similar form of reservation might *in theory* be available in the present case, but it would be unlikely to produce any satisfactory result, because of the virtual impossibility of reconstructing the financial transactions relating to the issue and receipt of bills to and from Safe Custody, Merbank, and Commercial Bills.

136   *Chase Manhattan Bank NA v Israel-British Bank (London) Ltd*
[1981] Ch 105

In 1974 Chase Manhattan mistakenly paid $2m to another bank in New York on account of the Israel-British Bank. Israel Bank petitioned the English Court for a winding-p order for itself and also filed its own bankruptcy petition in New York. Both Courts granted a winding up order. Chase Manhattan brought an action against Israel Bank seeking to trace and recover in equity the money paid by mistake.

Goulding J found that Israel Bank had learned of the mistaken payment two days after the payment was made, and either knew it was a mistake, or was put fully on inquiry by facts which should have indicated the payment might be a mistake.

The initial question was whether the plaintiff was entitled to trace the mistaken payment and to recover the money. His Honour quoted from Gough and Jones, *The Law of Restitution*:

[W]hether a person who is paid money under a mistake of fact should be granted a proprietary claim can arise in a number of contexts. It will be most important where the payee is insolvent and the payer seeks to gain priority over the payee's general creditor.

The English Courts had never had to consider this question. But in the United States it has arisen on a few occasions. The defendant argued that there was no equitable right to trace property unless some initial fiduciary relationship existed.

Goulding J summarised his view of *Re Diplock* (133) as follows:

1. The Court of Appeal's interpretation of *Sinclair v Brougham* (132) in *Re Diplock* was an essential part of the decision and was binding.

2. The Court in *Re Diplock* thought that the majority of the House of Lords in *Sinclair v Brougham* had not accepted Lord Dunedin's opinion in that case, and had rejected it.

3. The Court in *Re Diplock* held that an initial fiduciary relationship was not a necessary foundation of the equitable right of tracing.

4. They also held that the relationship between the Building Society directors and depositors in *Sinclair v Brougham* was a sufficient fiduciary relationship for the purpose of tracing.

Goulding J noted that the fund to be traced need not, as was the case in *Re Diplock*, have been the subject of fiduciary obligations before it got into the wrong hands. It was enough that the payment *was* in the wrong hands. That fact in itself gave rise to a fiduciary relationship.

The Court thus found that the equitable remedy of tracing is in principle available, on the ground of a continuing proprietary interest, to a party who has paid money under a mistake of fact.

In *Westdeutsche Landesbank Girozentrale v Islington London Borough Council* (80) the House of Lords expressed its discomfort with this decision, as it was based to a large extent on *Sinclair v Brougham*.

137 *Re Goldcorp Exchange Ltd (In receivership): Kensington v Liggett* [1994] 3 NZLR 385

In the late 1980s Goldcorp developed a cunning scheme to attract money from New Zealand investors by means of a bullion purchase scheme. An investor would agree to buy gold, silver or platinum at the prevailing market rate, but the transaction was on paper only. Goldcorp was to store and insure the metal free of charge, and the buyer was given a "Non-allocated Invoice" which verified their ownership of the metal. Physical delivery could be taken on seven days' notice.

Large numbers of the public invested money in this scheme with gleeful abandon. All of them were delivered a certificate certifying that they were the registered holder of whatever quantity of fine gold, silver or platinum. The system would have worked quite well had Goldcorp actually bought and stored the bullion. Unfortunately it didn't.

When Goldcorp became hopelessly insolvent it was discovered that the stock of gold, silver and platinum bullion it held was far short of what would have been needed to satisfy the numerous purchasers of the "Non-allocated" contracts. In fact the company's total assets fell well below the amount secured by the primary debenture. This discovery caused great indignation amongst the members of the public whose faith in the promises made by Goldcorp had proved to be misplaced. Their desire for a remedy took this case all the way to the Privy Council.

The claimants fell into three categories, but by far the largest group of these were the non-allocated claimants who had entered into the transaction described above. While these investors had an open and shut case against the company for breach of contract any award of damages would have been meaningless as all the company's funds were going to be swallowed up by the secured creditors. The investors' only real chance of a remedy lay in creating a claim that would enable them to jump the queue and be paid out in priority to the secured creditors. They argued that they had a proprietary right to the small amounts of bullion that were held by Goldcorp, which would allow them to trace to recover the sums they had lost. If this argument was accepted it would mean that any bullion and assets they had a proprietary interest in would no longer be considered the company's property, and would not be distributed among the creditors.

Thorp J rejected the claim of the non-allocated claimants in the High Court. The Court of Appeal reversed this decision by a majority. Cooke P and Gault J found in favour of the non-allocated claimants and went on to hold that the entire amount of the purchase moneys could be traced into the general assets of the company. The receivers and the debenture-holder of the company appealed to the Privy Council.

The Privy Council noted that the issues arising for consideration were:

1. whether any property in the bullion passed to any of the customers;

2. whether the customers retained a beneficial interest in purchase moneys paid to Goldcorp under the contracts of sale; and

3. whether the Court should grant a restitutionary remedy of a proprietary character in respect of that purchase money.

The answers held no comfort to the claimants. It held that the contracts of sale were for unascertained bullion, and the customers could gain no title under the rules relating to the sale of goods, as title can only relate to ascertained goods. Even if the company's collateral promises had created a trust, the Privy Council held that that too would fail since there was no bullion to which the trust could relate. In relation to the rules of fiduciaries in tracing, the Court held that even if the company had been a fiduciary, it had undertaken no more than the promises in the contract, and that there was also no constructive trust.

In relation to an attempt to raise a claim of a proprietary nature, it was argued on behalf of the claimants that Goldcorp stood as a fiduciary to them. At first it was said that because Goldcorp held itself out as willing to vest bullion in the customers and to hold it in safe custody on their behalf, Goldcorp was a fiduciary. The customer, it was alleged, was totally dependent on Goldcorp and trusted Goldcorp to do what it had promised, having no means of verifying this independently. From this the company created an equity by inviting the customer to look on and treat stocks vested in them as their own, and this equity could be recognised only by treating the customer as entitled to a proprietary interest in the stock.

The Privy Council noted that to describe someone as a fiduciary, without more, is meaningless. It considered that no fiduciary duties had been suggested beyond those which the company assumed under the contract of sale together with the collateral promises: namely to deliver the goods if required, and meanwhile to keep a separate stock of bullion to which the customers could look to as a safeguard for performance when delivery was required.

The Court considered that the fact that one person is placed in a particular position vis-à-vis another through the medium of a contract does not necessarily mean that they do not also owe fiduciary duties to that other. The essence of a fiduciary relationship is, however, that it creates obligations of a different character from those deriving from a contract. Many commercial relationships involve just such a reliance by one party on the other as was seen here, and to introduce the whole new dimension into such relationships which would flow from giving them a fiduciary character would seem to have adverse consequences. The Court felt it was possible to say that the customers put faith in Goldcorp and that their trust had not been repaid. But that vocabulary could be misleading: high expectations do not necessarily lead to equitable remedy. Accordingly it was held that no fiduciary relationship existed between the parties. Nothing suggested that the company was obliged to do anything by virtue of being a fiduciary that it had not already, by contract, promised to do.

It was also argued that the Court should declare a remedial constructive trust in favour of the claimants. This, it was argued, would not arise directly from the transaction between the individual claimants and Goldcorp, but would be created by the Privy Council as a measure of justice after the event. This argument was rejected by the Privy Council. The Court held that the conduct of the company was wrongful in the sense of being a breach of contract, but it did not involve any injurious dealing with the subject-matter of the alleged trust. The company had not unjustly enriched itself, and did not act wrongfully in acquiring, maintaining and using its own stock of bullion.

See also ***Elders Pastoral Ltd v Bank of New Zealand* (87).**

138   *Foskett v McKeown*
        [1997] 3 All ER 392

Mr Murphy was a fraudulent property developer who marketed plots of land to be developed in the Algarve, in Portugal. Some 220 purchasers entered into contracts to purchase the land. In total, over £2.5m was paid to him. Although land in the Algarve was purchased, it was never developed. When the time came for the purchasers' money to be repaid to them, it was found that their money had been dissipated. However, not all the money had disappeared into fast living. It turned out that Mr Murphy, in breach of trust, had used £20,000 of the trust moneys to pay in November 1989 and November 1990 the annual premium of £10,000 due under a life insurance policy he held. The life insurance policy was for a total of approximately £1m, but was held on trust for his children. Mr Murphy committed suicide in 1991, and as a result a dispute arose between the two groups of beneficiaries as to who could claim the proceeds of the policy: Mr Murphy's children, or Mr Foskett (suing as a representative of those defrauded in the Algarve property scheme).

The issue was considered by the Court of Appeal. The majority considered that the first issue to decide was whether the property purchasers were able to trace their money into the proceeds of the policy. This question was answered in the affirmative, on the basis that Murphy could be indemnified out of the policy proceeds for payments he had made with trust money to keep the policy on foot. As the trust money came from the Algarve purchasers, they therefore had the ability to pursue that right by way of subrogation.

The next question to be determined was what interest in the proceeds they were entitled to. Did they merely have a charge over the proceeds for repayment of the money used in the premiums, or were they entitled to a proportion of the £1m?

The majority held that they were only entitled to trace to the extent that their money had been used to pay premiums. Lord Scott V-C noted that the normal rule is that a trustee will be accountable to beneficiaries for the benefit the trustee has made out of trust money. This includes a proportionate share in the increased value of any asset bought with the trust money. But this is not the case if the trust money has been spent in improving or maintaining the property of someone else. Here, the proceeds of the policy were held on trust for Mr Murphy's children, who were innocent third parties. Scott VC could see no basis upon which the property purchasers could raise a constructive or resulting trust which could divest Murphy's children of part of their beneficial ownership. Accordingly, the purchasers were entitled only to a remedy by way of a charge over the proceeds of the policy to recover the £20,000 paid as premia, together with interest.

Morritt LJ took a different view of the matter. He felt the basic position was that if a trustee mixes trust money with his own then the beneficiary may, at his option, take a proportionate interest in the property thereby acquired. Similarly, if a trustee mixes the money of one trust with that of another and uses the mixed fund to buy property which appreciates in value the respective beneficiaries may take their proportion of the property.

Morritt LJ felt those principles should be applied in this case. He considered that the £1m under the policy was payable in consideration of all the premia paid, including those made from the purchasers' trust money. If the money of the purchasers and that of Mr Murphy had been mixed before the payment of the premiums then the purchasers would have been entitled to a proportionate share of the proceeds whether they were in competition with the trustee, or other volunteers (Morritt LJ was obviously thinking that Mr Murphy's children fell into the position of volunteers here). Accordingly, he held that common justice required the purchasers should have the right to participate in the asset which came from the use of their money, together with other moneys, namely the entire proceeds of the policy.

The House of Lords then considered the matter, and a majority of Their Lordships essentially came to agreement with Morritt LJ: where a trustee wrongfully used trust money to provide part of the cost of acquiring an asset, the beneficiary had the option as to whether to claim a proportionate share of the asset, or to enforce a lien upon it to secure the personal claim against the trustee for the misapplied money.

COMPLETELY AND INCOMPLETELY CONSTITUTED TRUSTS

139   *Milroy v Lord*
(1862) 4 De G F & J 264

Thomas Medley was very close to his niece Eleanor Dudgeon. He had paid for her education, and she lived with him until his marriage in the summer of 1852. Upon his marriage Mr Medley assured his niece that he was making a settlement to provide for her future.

Mr Medley did indeed make a deed in April 1852 which purported to transfer 50 shares owned by him in the Bank of Louisiana to Samuel Lord (his good friend and new father-in-law) on trust for Eleanor. The shares were transferable only by entry in the books of the bank. Unfortunately, no transfer of the 50 shares was ever made into the name of Samuel Lord, but the dividends received were paid by Samuel to Eleanor, and following her marriage to Andrew Milroy in 1855, to them both.

In November 1855 Thomas Medley died, leaving in his will a legacy of £4000 to Eleanor. After his death Samuel Lord delivered to Medley's executor the certificates for the 50 Louisiana Bank shares. The Milroys sought a decree declaring their interest in the shares. This decree was granted at first instance, but the case then went on appeal to the Court of Appeal.

Turner LJ noted that in the circumstances of the case it would be difficult not to feel a strong disposition to give effect to Medley's settlement, and noted that he had spared no pains to find the means of doing so. However he found himself unable to do so. The Judge noted that it is well-settled law that in order to render a voluntary settlement (that is, a gift) valid and effectual the settlor must have done everything which is necessary to be done to transfer the property and render the settlement binding. This will differ from case to case according to the nature of the property to be transferred. There are two ways of doing this:

1.   actually to transfer the property to the person for whom they intend to provide, or to transfer the property to a trustee to hold on their behalf; or

2.   by declaring themselves to hold it in trust for the persons for whom
      they intend to provide.

One of these modes must be utilised to render a settlement binding, for there is
no equity in the Court to perfect an imperfect gift. Turner LJ then noted that
the authorities go further to hold that if the settlement is intended to be
effected by one of the two means above, the Court will not validate it by
applying the other mode.

Applying these principles to this case it was found that there was never any
legal transfer of the 50 shares to Samuel Lord. As the shares were never
legally vested in him no valid and effectual trust was made. The gift was
imperfect, and could not be perfected.

This case sets down the general rule by which a valid trust may be constituted:
by transferring the property to trustees, or by a declaration that property is
held on trust.

If the settlor declares that he or she will hold property himself or herself as
trustee for intended beneficiaries, then the requirements of the three certainties
must be satisfied — in particular the certainty of intention: see *Jones v Lock*
(12); *Paul v Constance (16)*.

140   *Re Rose: Rose v Inland Revenue Commissioners*
[1952] 1 All ER 1217

Derek Rose owned a number of shares in Leweston Estates Co Ltd. On
30 March 1943 he executed two transfers of his shares, one of which was in
favour of his wife and another person to be held by them upon trust. The
transfers were registered by Leweston Estates Co Ltd on 30 June 1943.
Mr Rose died on 10 April 1948. The Inland Revenue claimed estate duty was
payable on the share transfer as the transfer took place within five years before
his death. This raised the question of when the transfer was completed —
when it was executed by Mr Rose, or when it was registered by the company.

At first instance Roxburgh J decided against the Inland Revenue
Commissioner. He appealed to the Court of Appeal. Lord Evershed MR noted
that the authority in this area was *Milroy v Lord (139)* and noted that in his
judgment its general proposition was too broad and involved too great a
simplification of the problem. He did not think that the case compelled the
Court to hold that where the settlor has done everything which, according to
the nature of property comprised in the settlement, it was necessary to be done
in order to transfer the property, the result necessarily precluded a finding that,

pending registration, Mr Rose was trustee of the legal interest for his wife and the other intended trustee. His Honour then went on to quote a passage from the lower Court decision, dealing with the same questions. He cited and approved the following quote from Jenkins J:

> Those cases, as I understand them, turn on the facts that the deceased donor has not done all in his power, according to the nature of the property given, to vest the legal interest in the property in the donee. In such circumstances it is, of course, well settled that there is no equity to complete the imperfect gift. If any act remains to be done by the donor to complete the gift at the date of the donor's death, the Court will not compel his personal representatives to do that act and the gift remains incomplete and fails ... In this case, as I understand it, the testator had done everything in his power to divest himself of the shares in question ... he had executed a transfer ... he had handed that transfer together with the [share] certificate to [the trustee]. There was nothing else the testator could do.

Thus, if the testator has done all that they have to do to transfer property, the gift will stand. This passage was adopted as a correct statement of the law by Lord Evershed MR. If it was correct, he did not think it could be asserted on the authority of *Milroy v Lord*, or as a matter of good sense and logic, that there was a gap between the execution of the transfer, and the company's registration of it, where Mrs Rose had no rights in relation to the shares. It was therefore held that as Mr Rose had done all that he had to do by the earlier date the transfer was valid and effectual in equity from 30 March 1943, and accordingly the shares were not assessable for estate duty.

141 *Fox v Harvey*
[1968] NZLR 394

William Harvey, known to his family as "Uncle Bill" took out three policies in his own name on the lives of three of his grandnieces and nephews. He then presented the parents of the children with the policies, and notes expressing that they were to be 21st birthday presents.

When Mr Harvey died questions arose as to who owned the life insurance policies. The defendants (the executors and trustees of Mr Harvey's will) claimed that the gifts of the policies were incomplete and imperfect because the assignments of the life insurance policies had not been registered as required by the Life Insurance Act 1908. It was submitted for the recipients that in each case there was a valid equitable assignment by way of a gift of the policy to the child concerned, and that the gift was complete and enforceable against the trustees.

The matter was heard before Tompkins J in the Supreme Court. *Milroy v Lord* **(139)** was his starting point. The question here was whether Mr Harvey had done everything necessary to perfect the gift to his young relations, or whether the gift was incomplete by reason of his not having complied with the formalities of the Life Insurance Act. Unless the recipients could register the assignment of the life insurance policies without the help of their deceased uncle, and without needing him to do anything further, the Judge did not think that they could succeed. In this case the Court found that all three policies could be completed and registered by the infants concerned. Accordingly the Judge ordered that all three policies be registered, and the proceeds paid to the children.

142   *Pascoe v Turner*
[1979] 2 All ER 945

Samuel Pascoe was a small businessman in Cornwall. In 1961 or 1962 he met Mrs Pearl Turner, a widow recovering from her husband's death. Initially they became friends, and Mrs Turner helped Mr Pascoe in his business activities. Once their relationship became more formal she took his young son under her wing. In 1963 she moved into the plaintiff's home, first as his housekeeper but later as his de facto partner. In 1965 they moved to a new house in Camborne in Cornwall, and lived there for the next few years.

In 1973 Cupid aimed his arrow, with disastrous effect. Mr Pascoe began to have an affair with a Mrs Pritchard, and informed Mrs Turner that their relationship was over. He did however tell her in front of some of her friends that she had nothing to worry about as the house and everything in it was hers. Mrs Turner stayed on in the house, and spent a large amount of her money on redecoration, improvements and repairs.

Following a quarrel in 1976, Mr Pascoe decided to throw Mrs Turner out of the house. He filed a claim for possession of the premises. Mrs Turner counterclaimed for a declaration that the house and its contents were hers, and that the plaintiff held them on trust for her. The Judge at first instance found the plaintiff had made a gift to her of the contents of the house, and that a beneficial interest in the house had passed to her by way of a constructive trust. Mr Pascoe appealed to the Court of Appeal.

Lord Justice Cumming-Bruce felt that the situation was not quite so simple. He felt the Court at first instance was right to hold that Mrs Turner owned the contents of the house, but that the long and short of the events in 1973 was that Mr Pascoe had made an imperfect gift of the house. There was nothing in the facts from which the Court could infer a constructive trust. In the event it remained an imperfect gift, and Cumming-Bruce LJ cited the words of Turner LJ in *Milroy v Lord* **(139)**: "There is no equity in this Court to perfect an imperfect gift". So matters stood in 1973 and if the facts had stopped there Mrs Turner would have had no remedy.

But, as the Court noted, the facts did not stop there. Mrs Turner had set about improving the house in the years she lived there by herself. She had contributed a large amount of her meagre income to improving the property. All the while Mr Pascoe stood by, not only watching but encouraging and advising, without a word to suggest that she was wasting her money and her personal effort on his house.

The Court felt that this was a case of estoppel arising from the encouragement and acquiescence of Mr Pascoe. This operated as an exception to the rule in *Milroy v Lord*, in that equity could not be satisfied here without compelling Mr Pascoe to give effect to his promise and Mrs Turner's expectations. He had so acted that he must perfect the gift. Accordingly there was a declaration that the estate in the property in Camborne was to be vested in Mrs Turner. Mr Pascoe was ordered to execute a conveyance forthwith at his own expense.

143 *Wellington Harness Racing Club Inc v Hutt City Council*
[2004] 1 NZLR 82 (HC)

This case concerned an area of 35 ha in the surrounds of Lower Hutt called Hutt Park, which had been used for horse racing since the 1850s, and subsequently for athletics, camping, golf, and public entertainment.

As at 1854, the land had been owned by the Crown.

The Public Reserves Act 1854 permitted setting aside lands for "Public Utility", and the Wellington Provincial Council's Hutt Park Ordinance 1857 provided that land *could* be reserved for a public park and race course. The trustees controlling the land were authorised to lease it for horse racing, and other public purposes open to all persons. However, no land was reserved under that Ordinance.

In 1866, Governor Grey granted Hutt Park to the superintendent of the Wellington province "In trust as a Race Course and for purposes connected therewith". This grant was stated to be under the Public Reserves Act 1854, and not under any Ordinance.

Another Local Ordinance, the Hutt Public Park and Race Course Act 1866 (HPPRCA 1866), made provision for Hutt Park to be managed by a body corporate of certain trustees. By the Hutt Park Act 1907, however, the HPPRCA 1866 was repealed, the trustees discharged from all trusts, and the land, subject to all existing rights, was "vested in trust for recreation purposes" in a committee. A further 1982 Act vested the land in the Lower Hutt City Council as a reserve for recreation purposes. The land was therefore controlled by various entities at different times, ending up under the jurisdiction of the Hutt City Council.

The Wellington Harness Racing Club Incorporated (WHRC) leased about one-third of the area of Hutt Park from 1979. The WHRC was operating at a loss by the 1990s, primarily because there was less public interest in racing, and the maintenance costs on its facilities and rates had increased. Notwithstanding this, the WHRC sought to buy the land it was leasing in 1993, although the offer was not accepted, as Hutt Park was seen to be of political importance as a recreation reserve. By mid-1995, the WHRC was facing liquidation, and with arrears of rental arising, it sought to surrender its lease. The council considered its redevelopment options, and a working group recommended that the harness racing track not remain.

The WHRC issued proceedings to protect the historic harness racing facilities, in particular, seeking a declaration that the council was bound by a trust created by an 1866 Crown grant of land. The basis of this argument was that the 1866 Crown grant set up a "trust" in the private law sense, and that nothing in the subsequent legislation had extinguished this, as each statute had protected existing rights in the land. The Crown was the settlor, the public were the beneficiaries, and the obligations of the trustees were those generally existing in law.

The Court acknowledged that the term "trust" had a specific private law meaning, but commented that the use of the term in this situation had to be understood in the context of the Public Reserves Act 1854. In the Court's view, this use of the word "trust" was best understood in the sense that the Wellington superintendent could not use the land for his own benefit, or for any improper purpose. But there was no "trust" in the free-standing, technical equity sense, which stood apart from the statute creating it. The argument that there was a "trust" in the equitable sense was a case of taking one word completely out of its context. In addition, even if there was a trust, it had been extinguished by the 1907 Act or other statutes.

Sham Trusts and Alter Ego Trusts

144   *Prime v Hardie*
[2003] NZFLR 481 (HC)

Mark Hardie and Kiri Prime started a relationship around July 1992 and had a daughter in 1994. In 1993, Mark purchased a property, which was transferred to the Hardie Trust later that year. The trustees of the Hardie Trust were Mark and a third party. In 1996, Kiri, the daughter and a son of Kiri's began living with Mark in that property, although, from September, Mark, Kiri and the two children moved to a replacement property owned by the trust. The trust also owned two rental properties. The trust was largely funded by Mark, and owed him a debt of over $1m.

The relationship ended in 2002, but up to this time, Kiri spent most of her income on the home and family and carried out most of the household duties. Kiri and the children left the house in difficult circumstances: Mark had proposed marriage and suggested the family move to Australia following a job offer there, when in fact there was no job offer.

Kiri argued that her contributions to the dwelling the family lived in were enough to establish a constructive trust, on the principles set out in *Lankow v Rose* **(98)**. The Court noted that while Kiri's contributions met the test for a constructive trust, there was some difficulty as the property was owned by the Hardie Trust. It was not pleaded that the trust was a sham, but the Court felt it clear that the trust was Mark's "alter ego". Mark was the trust's principal beneficiary, he borrowed money to allow the trust to purchase assets, and paid interest and other outgoings on the trust's properties so in the circumstances, it was appropriate that a constructive trust be imposed on property held by a trust. However, a distinction could be made between the family home and other assets of the trust. The expectations in relation to the family home were clearly different, and Kiri had clearly made a number of contributions to the home. Her contributions to the rental properties were insufficient to establish a constructive trust. The Hardie Trust was therefore ordered to make payment to Kiri in relation to the family home.

145   *Glass v Hughey*
[2003] NZFLR 865 (HC)

Glass and Hughey began a de facto relationship around February 1997 and separated around September 2001. A residence in Kohimarama was purchased in late 1997 and two daughters were born in 1998 and 2000. Hughey had been bankrupted in 1992, but had plans to develop a franchised recruitment business. A number of different companies were incorporated for the business' operations and the business was restructured on a number of occasions during and after the period of the relationship. During the restructuring, Hughey's trust came to own the bulk of the shares in the principal company.

The end of the relationship was shortly before the Property (Relationships) Act 1976 came into force, so the constructive trust principles in ***Lankow v Rose* (98)** were agreed to apply. Glass was found to have contributed to Hughey's franchise/recruitment business through training and other non-essential matters; nevertheless, these had helped the business and were sufficient to establish a constructive trust. It was argued by Glass that the constructive trust began prior to the transfer of the shares to the trust and remained fixed to the shares after transfer, a view with which the Court agreed. Glass also argued that the trust which owned the shares in the principal company was a sham, as Hughey controlled the business and ran it as if it were his own.

The Court held that the trust "should be regarded as a sham or more particularly as [Hughey's] alter ego".

This view was based on the decision in ***Prime v Hardie* (144)**, and also a range of Australian family law decisions, which had made it clear that the Courts will disregard trusts which are a spouse's alter ego or a sham to ensure that a family property claim is not unfairly defeated. It was also supported by a shareholders' agreement in relation to the principal company, which acknowledged that shares might be transferred to an entity nominated by Hughey. This agreement made it clear that the shares, in being owned by the trust, were to be Hughey's property and prevented Hughey arguing in the relationship property claim that the shares were owned by his trust rather than himself.

146 *Begum v Ali*
Family Court Auckland, FP 2001-004-866, 10 December 2004, Judge O'Donovan

Begum and Ali were married in 1988, at which time Ali owned a property in Ponsonby. This became the matrimonial home, and was transferred to the Shorab Ali Trust in 1995. There was some dispute over whether a matrimonial property agreement existed, but ultimately the Court determined there was none. The relationship ended in 2000, although there had been problems for some years and the parties had previously lived apart.

Begum claimed to have no knowledge of the creation of the trust or the transfer of the property to it, a claim accepted by the Court. The Court noted that at the time the trust was established and the property transferred to it, no one seemed to have advised Begum, even though she clearly had an interest in the home as matrimonial property. Begum had no beneficial or other interest in the trust, which was found to reflect a conscious decision by Ali.

The Court found a complete lack of formality in relation to the trust, with the transfer from Ali to the trust being at a level below market value and there being no records as to any activities of the trust following the transfer of the property.

The Court found that the transfer of the property to the trust was not a genuine disposition, and really no more than a fiction. Referring to *Prime v Hardie* **(144)** and **(145)**, the Court noted that it could determine that property owned by a trust was available for division under the Property (Relationships) Act 1976 (PRA) because the ownership and control exercised over the trust by one party was such that the trust should be regarded as that person's "alter ego". In this case, the Court was satisfied that the trust was the "alter ego" of Ali and "a sham", and therefore the Court could disregard it. The Court came to the same result in its consideration of s 44 of the PRA

147 *Genc v Genc*
[2006] NZFLR 1119 (HC)

Tracy and Serdar Genc met in 1994 and were married in 1999. In 1997, Mr Genc established the Genc Family Trust. Mr Genc's solicitor was the settlor and Mr Genc and the solicitor were trustees, with Mr Genc having the power of appointment and removal of trustees. The Genc Family Trust purchased a property from Mr Genc, acknowledging it owed him a debt, although this property was sold in 1998 and a replacement property purchased. When the relationship ended in 2002, Mrs Genc sought to look behind the trust arrangements, arguing that the trust was a sham, or the alter ego, of Mr Genc, and that it should be set aside for the purposes of determining a just division of relationship property.

There was evidence that Mr Genc had established the trust because he worked in the volatile restaurant industry and wanted a trust to protect his assets. The trust's records were impeccable.

The Court observed that while Mr Genc had acted from time to time as though the trust was an extension of himself, this did not of itself provide evidence that the trust was a sham or the alter ego of Mr Genc, or suggest that it should be set aside — after all, it had been noted in *Miller v Stewart* [2000] NZFLR 433 that family trusts are often run in a manner that is unconventional when compared to traditional concepts of trust administration. Looking to the test in *Snook v London & West Riding Investments Ltd* [1967] 1 All ER 518, the Court observed that the Genc Family Trust was not a sham, as there was no common intention on the part of Mr Genc and his solicitor that the trust documents created any obligations other than those which they gave the appearance of creating.

The Court referred to the decision of the Family Court of Australia in *In the Marriage of VR & N Gould* (1993) 17 FAM LR 156, where Fogarty J drew a distinction between a "sham", which had the characteristics of being a counterfeit, façade, or false front; and an "alter ego" which was "the puppet" of a person, although did not approve or adopt this test. *Prime v Hardie* **(144)** and *Glass v Hughey* **(145)** were distinguished on the basis that they involved situations where relationship property was settled on the trust during a de facto relationship, and the Property (Relationships) Act 1976 did not apply. Here, there had been no de facto relationship prior to marriage and the transfer to the trust was of separate property. In this case, the trust was not set aside on sham or alter ego principles.

148   *Official Assignee v Wilson*
[2006] 2 NZLR 841 (HC)

Gary Reynolds was adjudicated bankrupt in 1992, resuming various entrepreneurial activities in 1995. He settled a trust in 1996 to purchase a property in Invercargill for $64,000, with his solicitor, and his de facto partner's mother as trustees. The property was transferred back to Mr Reynolds in 1997 at the same price the trustees paid for it. There was no written agreement of sale, although the trustees asserted that an oral agreement had been made in late 1996 as Reynolds and his partner wished to undertake some renovations that the trustees did not wish to pursue. The Invercargill property was then used as security, along with other properties, for various loans. The trust purchased a property in Queenstown in 1999, with the Invercargill property included in the mix of mortgages and guarantees.

The Invercargill property was eventually sold, but Mr Reynolds was, by this time, in default on some loans. He was adjudicated bankrupt again in 2001 with few assets and over $500,000 in debt. The IRD was the major creditor. The Official Assignee noted the value of the Queenstown property and decided to take a closer look at the trust and its relationship to Mr Reynolds' bankruptcy. After examining Mr Reynolds and the trustees, the Official Assignee (OA) decided that the trust was a sham. The OA was of the view that the Queenstown property was held for Mr Reynolds rather than the stated beneficiaries, and issued proceedings. The trust's record-keeping was far from perfect: no accounts had ever been prepared; there were no resolutions or records of meetings; there was no valuation for the transfer of the Invercargill property back to Mr Reynolds in 1997; and Mr Reynolds had lived in trust property without paying any costs other than outgoings.

The OA argued that the trust was a "sham". The Court noted that for a "sham" to exist, the law required that the parties to the creation of the sham must have a common intention that the documents do not create the legal rights or obligations which they purport to create (*Snook v London & West Riding Investments Ltd* [1967] 1 All ER 518, a case concerning hire purchase arrangements rather than a trust). Here, the Court found that there was no common intention to create anything other than what the documents actually said, and so no sham existed.

The OA then argued that a trust could be an "alter ego trust", which was not a "sham" but where the trustees were mere puppets of the settlor — drawing on **Prime v Hardie (144)** and **Glass v Hughey (145)** as authority. The Court rejected this submission, finding that a trust that was the alter ego of a natural person could indicate that the arrangements were a sham, but common intention must still be shown. In the Court's words at para [58]:

> The underlying common intention requirement for a sham has been consistently adopted by the Court of Appeal and is clearly binding on this Court. If alter ego trusts were to be automatically recognised as shams that underlying requirement would be negated. The result would be that a halfway house between a conventional sham trust and a valid trust would be created. ... to adopt a halfway house would be to effectively rewrite the traditional understanding of a sham.

In the Court's view, while finding that the trust was Mr Reynolds' alter ego would be very relevant to whether a sham had been proved, it did not of itself meet the common intention test. *Prime v Hardie* and *Glass v Hughey* were distinguished on the basis that they were family property claims based on a constructive trust, and in neither case was the difference between a sham and alter ego trust considered in the judgment (para [59]). In other words, an alter ego trust could indicate a sham, but was only a factor to be taken into account in applying the test in *Snook*.

The Court found that the trust had clearly been formed in the light of Mr Reynolds' risky entrepreneurial activities and previous bankruptcy, but that its creation was valid, notwithstanding some infelicities in its drafting (the trust was for the benefit of Mr Reynolds' family, but Mr Reynolds and his partner were not actually named as beneficiaries). To the Court, the deficiencies "were nothing more than drafting lapses". The Court also accepted the trustees' evidence as to the legitimacy of their decisions. It was "thoroughly ~~satisfactory and worthodox~~ ~~that there was no written agreement or written~~ evidence of the oral agreement. However, the reasons for the sale remained genuine and the sale transaction itself was, in the Court's view "completely genuine".

Overall, it was clear that the decisions of the trustees were heavily influenced by Mr Reynolds, but they were not his puppets, and the trust was not his alter ego. Some decisions made by the trustees were perhaps unwise, and may in some circumstances have given rise to a breach of trust claim. The lack of record-keeping was not prudent for trustees, and there was some intermingling of trust and personal affairs. But none of the transactions, or the trust, was a sham, as there was no common intention that the decisions of the trustees did not create the legal rights and obligations which the relevant documents gave the appearance of creating.

- Jessica Palmer "Dealing with the emerging popularity of sham trusts" [2007] NZ Law Rev 81.
- Thomas Gibbons "Alter Ego Trusts" [2007] NZLJ 316.

149   *In the Matter of the Esteem Settlement (Abacus (CI) Limited as Trustee) Grupo Torras SA and Culmer v Al Sabah and Four Others ("In Re Esteem Settlement")* [2003] JLR 188

Tax havens such as Jersey create fascinating trust problems. The judgment in this case extended to over 500 paragraphs, with not all the issues relevant to New Zealand law. However, the case contains many interesting insights into the notion of "sham" trusts.

Grupo Torras (GT) was a company owned by the Kuwait Investment Office (KIO). Sheikh Fahad was chairman of GT and KIO, and between May 1988 and October 1990, Fahad and others conspired to defraud GT of some US$430m, of which Fahad took $120m. GT obtained judgment against Fahad, but by the time of judgment he was personally insolvent. A number of trusts settled by Fahad had significant assets, however, of which the Esteem Settlement (with Abacus as trustee), received contributions of over £4.4m from Fahad. Certain of these assets were traced back to Fahad and granted to GT, but other assets had been contributed to the trust before Fahad began his fraudulent actions and so were "clean".

Action was brought by the plaintiff for these assets on a number of bases, including that the trust was a "sham" as Abacus always held the assets the assets as bare trustee for Fahad, that the veil of the trust should be lifted, and that the Esteem Settlement should be made the subject of a remedial constructive trust.

The Court noted the standard definition of a "sham" in *Snook v London & West Riding Investments Ltd* [1967] 2 QB 802, that a common intention between the parties was required for a sham to exist. It was argued that in the case of a trust, only the intention of the settlor was relevant, as acceptance by trustees was not essential to the creation of a valid trust. The Court disagreed, finding that the intentions of both settlor and trustees were relevant, and that for a sham to exist, both settlor and trustees must have intended that the arrangements not be genuine. There was no evidence that the trustee in this case had such an intention.

Another cause of action was based on the principle of "donner et retenir ne vaut", that for a gift (or, by analogy, a disposition to a trust) to be valid, the donor must not continue to control the relevant asset. This was seen by the Court to be very similar to the argument that the trust was a sham, as if the trustee was simply the nominee of the settlor, and the settlor retained control of the assets, the trust would be a sham; on the other hand, if the trustee was a bona fide trustee, then the maxim could not apply.

A further argument was that the veil of the trust should be pierced, like the piercing of the corporate veil of a company in certain instances. However, the Court noted that a company is by its very nature a separate legal entity from its shareholders; while a trust is really a description of the obligation owed by trustees to beneficiaries in respect of certain assets. The beneficiaries had an interest in the trust assets quite unlike any company arrangements. A trust could be a sham or be genuine, but even if a settlor exercised continuing control over trust assets, the trust could not ignore the terms of a trust unless it was a sham. "Piercing the veil" could not apply to trust law.

The Court then turned to the question of whether a remedial constructive trust could be imposed over the trust, with Abacus being required to hold the assets on trust for GT (or the trustee in bankruptcy). The Court cited the distinction between institutional and remedial constructive trusts in *Fortex Group Ltd (in rec and liq) v MacIntosh* **(93)**, with a remedial constructive trust depending on an order of the Court for its existence. This had been applied in New Zealand, but not in all common law jurisdictions. The Court determined that the imposition of a remedial constructive trust was probably not available under Jersey law, but that even if it was, there was no evidence of the kind of unconscionable behaviour required before one could be imposed.

The Court was also invited to find that, even if none of these causes of action were successful, it was unjust that the assets in the Esteem Settlement remained for Fahad's benefit when his creditors were unpaid. The Court commented that people were entitled to settle trusts and to rely on the protections they gave, there being "an important public interest in the ability of persons to rely upon apparently valid transactions".

150   *Shalson v Russo*
      [2005] Ch 205, [2003] EWHC 1637 (Ch)

Russo was an Italian who practised a number of frauds, including inducing £19.45m from Shalson. WIB was a bank, incorporated in Antigua and Barbuda, which was under Russo's de facto control, although most shares were held under the Brookscastle trust. WIB had an account with PKB, a Swiss bank, to which Shalson's money was paid. Another victim of Russo was Jean-Claude Mimran and his companies, who claimed to have been swindled out of at least US$7.5m, and who also paid into WIB's account with PKB. Mimran pursued a claim against Russo's trust arrangements on the basis that Russo's settlement was a sham.

The facts of how Shalson and Mimran came to contribute so much money to Russo's ventures need not be examined in detail, but it is clear Russo's frauds were carefully set up — WIB's customers, for example, included the Government of Antigua. Much of the case focused on a tracing claim by Mimran, but the Court also considered issues relating to constructive and sham trusts.

It was argued that moneys paid by Mimran to WIB were immediately subject to a constructive trust. The Court disagreed with this submission, arguing that the fraud created a contractual right to rescind arrangements, rather than a constructive trust — with comments in **Westdeutsche Landesbank Girozentrale v Islington London Borough Council (80)** that a "stolen bag of coins" is (by way of example) subject to a resulting trust being expressly disapproved.

Argument was also made that money Mimran advanced to Westland (via WIB) was subject to a *Quistclose* trust, on the basis that it was paid for a particular purpose and so held on trust for that purpose. The Court noted that clear agreement and specificity as to the use of the relevant money was required before a *Quistclose* trust could be imposed, noting the comments in **Twinsectra (42)** that a general purpose will not be sufficient to create such a trust.

A further argument made by Mimran was that Russo's trust arrangements were a sham. The decision in **In Re Esteem Settlement (149)** was made while judgment in this case was pending, and the Court decided to follow the approach in *Esteem*, ruling that in considering whether a trust is a sham, the intention of settlor alone is not sufficient: the trustees must also intend that the arrangements not be genuine. In this situation, Russo's trustees had acted honestly and genuinely at all times, and had exercised independent control over trust assets (notwithstanding Russo's efforts to the contrary at times), and so a sham could not be found.

PERPETUITIES

151   *Cadell v Palmer*
(1833) 1 Cl & F 372, 6 ER 956

Henry Bengough died in April 1818, days after executing his final will and testament. It may have been better for all concerned if he had died a little earlier, for his will established a trust of mind-crunching complexity that was destined to occupy some of the finest legal minds in Great Britain for a long time. In brief, his trustees were directed to hold his property upon trust for a period of 120 years, if 28 persons (being his nieces; nephews; grand-nieces; grand-nephews, and others) or any of them should live that long, and then for a further absolute term of 20 years from the death of the last of them.

The will was challenged by Mrs Bengough who argued that the machinery was an attempt at a perpetuity, and should be declared void (the notion of a perpetuity is that property is held on trust perpetually, never to vest absolutely in an owner. Such an arrangement is frowned upon because it encourages the removal of land and other forms of property from circulation in the economy). The basis for this was the further term of 20 years. While it was acknowledged by the widow's counsel that authorities supported a period of a life in being plus a further 21 years, it was claimed that the 21 years were only available to guard against infants inheriting estates absolutely. It was argued that it was not a principle of general application.

Argument raged in the House of Lords. Authorities dating back to the early 1600s were dusted off and considered. Eventually Baron Bayley, with the express support of the Lord Chancellor, delivered their unanimous conclusion. He cited numerous venerable authorities before concluding:

> [W]e consider ourselves warranted in saying that the limit is a life or lives in being, and 21 years afterwards, without reference to the infancy of any person whatsoever. This will certainly render the estate unalienable for 21 years after lives in being, but it will preserve in safety any limitations which may have been made upon authority of the dicta or text writers I have mentioned; and will not tie up the alienation an unreasonable length of time.

The rule then is that a limitation will not infringe the perpetuities rule if the vesting is suspended for 21 years beyond a life or lives in being. Beyond that period it would be void.

152   ***Duke of Norfolk v Howard***
      (1863) 1 Vern 163; 23 ER 388

Despite its age this case remains one of the classic statements of the justification for the rule against perpetuities. The case was an appeal from a decision that a trust was void for infringement of the rule. The Lord Keeper of the Appellate Court reversed this decision, and stated:

> A perpetuity is a thing odious in law, and destructive to the commonwealth: it would put a stop to commerce and prevent the circulation of the riches of the kingdom; and is therefore not to be countenanced in equity. If in equity you should come nearer to a perpetuity than the rules of common law would admit, all men, being desirous to continue their estates in their families would settle their estates by way of trust; which might indeed make well for the jurisdiction of the Court, but would be destructive to the commonwealth.

The decision was eventually overturned on appeal to the House of Lords, but the Lord Keeper's statements have been remembered.

153   ***Re Villar: Public Trustee v Villar***
      [1929] 1 Ch 243

The testator, Mr Villar, died in September 1926. In his will he left his property to the Public Trustee to administer on certain trusts until the end of a period of twenty years following "the day of the death of the last survivor of all the lineal descendants of Her Late Majesty Queen Victoria who shall be living at the time of my death". The Public Trustee commenced inquiries to discover exactly how many people this encompassed.

After much difficulty it was discovered that in 1922 there were about 120 descendants who were living in England, Germany, Greece, Russia, Sweden, Denmark, Norway, Spain, Yugoslavia and Romania. This did not include difficult questions, such as the fact that no one at the time knew whether Tsarina Alexandra and/or her children were alive or not. At about this stage the Public Trustee's office threw up their hands in despair and sought an order declaring the bequest void.

The Court of Appeal shared the Public Trustee's sentiments, but held the trust valid. The testator had defined the period of restriction as a period lasting for the duration of the lives of an ascertainable number of persons, plus a further twenty years. The Court could not take into consideration the difficulties that would be faced in tracking these persons and discovering when the last of them died. The trust could only be declared void if the rule against perpetuities was infringed, and here it was not. With a few obiter comments about trusts which benefit nothing but the vanity of the testator, the Court upheld the testator's will.

Since the passing of the Perpetuities Act 1964 the New Zealand position is slightly altered. Under the Act a settlor or testator has the ability to specify that the duration of the period before the disposition vests shall be a period not exceeding 80 years. However if they don't so specify the old rule of a life (or lives) in being, plus 21 years, still applies.

See also *Re New Zealand Dairy Board* **(24)**, which considered the rule.

154 *Perpetual Trust Ltd v Roman Catholic Bishop of Christchurch*
[2006] 1 NZLR 282 (HC)

Perpetual Trust was the executor and trustee of Zoe Armstrong, who died in 1986 leaving the bulk of her estate to the ZM Armstrong Charitable Fund (the fund), which was, in the trustee's discretion, to pay up to four-fifths of the income in any year to the Roman Catholic Bishop of the Christchurch Diocese for work with the Aged (cl 4(b)). Any income not paid out was to be accumulated and added to the capital of the fund (cl 4(c)).

Some years later, Perpetual Trust sought directions as whether cl 4(b) constituted a valid charitable trust and as to whether cl 4(c) was void, and, if void, whether the Bishop could receive the income or whether there was an intestacy in respect of the accumulation.

Clause 4(b) was for the relief of aged people which the Court found had been a clear charitable purpose since the Charitable Uses Act 1601 (UK). The delegation to the Bishop was to a specific and identifiable individual who was confined to exercising his powers and the use of the moneys for charitable purposes. The clause was therefore valid.

The Court noted that s 21 of the Perpetuities Act 1964 (permitting the accumulation of income only if that income could later be disposed of) did not apply to gifts to charitable trusts. However, in this case, the *capital* was never to be disposed of or used by any charity. Clause 4(c) was therefore void. The Court was, however, able to read into the will a general charitable intention to give the entire income (including accumulated income) to the charitable purpose of providing relief for the elderly.

The Court then used its inherent jurisdiction to delete the restriction that only four-fifths of the income could be used as a charitable gift and removing cl 4(c). With this change, the whole of the estate and its income could be used for the relief of aged persons.

SUCCESSION — WILLS

See generally the Wills Act 2007 and Nicola Peart "Where There is a Will, There is a Way – A New Wills Act for New Zealand" (2007) 15 *Waikato Law Review* 26.

Formal and statutory requirements

155   *Re Stewart*
High Court, Auckland A389/85, 17 December 1991, Tompkins J

The issue in this case was as to the validity of Mrs Stewart's will. The will consisted of three handwritten pages which were numbered but not fastened together in any way. Page one contained the recital and made various dispositions. The second page continued the last gift made at the end of the first page, made another gift, and the execution and attestation. The third page went on to make further provision as to the disposition of Mrs Stewart's estate, including the residue of her estate.

Tompkins J began by considering the requirements contained in s 9 of the Wills Act 1837 (as amended in 1852). Section 9 provides, inter alia, that a will shall be deemed to be valid where the signature of testator is in such a place underneath, beside or opposite the end of the will, that it is clear on the face of the will that the testator intended to give the will legal effect, but that no such signature "shall be operative to give effect to any disposition or direction which is underneath or which follows it".

He then went on to consider the approach taken by the Courts to the construction of wills. Generally, the Courts will apply a presumption in favour of validity where there is no doubt of the testator's intention. However, the Court should not distort the meaning of the statute in order to effect testamentary intention.

The first issue in the present case was whether the three pages of the will constituted a single testamentary document. The old rule that where a will was contained on separate pages of paper, the pages must have been attached in some way at the time of execution, no longer applied. Previous authorities had established that it would be enough if there was a sufficient nexus between the three sheets to establish that they were a single testamentary document. The evidence given by one of the attesting witnesses did not establish that three pages were present at execution, but did establish that there were more than one and that the pages were held together at the time of signing. Further evidence given by a handwriting expert established that all three pages were written on paper from the same stock, with the same pen, and by the same person. Finally, after the testatrix's death, the three pages had been found folded together in her handbag. On the basis of this evidence, Tompkins J concluded that the probability was that all three pages were present at execution and that they were being held together. Therefore they were held to constitute a single testamentary document.

The second issue was whether the third page of the will should be regarded as an integral part of the will, and incorporated in the probate, or whether it was inoperative as a disposition or direction which is underneath or which follows the signature, in the terms of the statutory provision. Tompkins J reviewed the authorities in this area and then stated that it was established that the words on the page after the signature were written before the will was signed, and therefore in a temporal sense, the attestation *followed* all of the pages. Additionally, the fact that the pages were numbered tended to establish that the third page should be considered part of the body of the will preceding the signature and should be read as incorporated therein. Moreover, the fact that page three contained the clause disposing of the residue of the estate meant that the first two pages were incomplete on their own. Therefore, it was held that the contents of page three should be regarded as incorporated into what was on pages one and two, validated by the signature at the foot of page two. The will was granted probate in solemn form.

156   *Re Cook's Estate*
[1960] 1 All ER 689

The testatrix, Emma Edith Cook, had made a will which began "I, Emmie Cook ... declare this to be my last will". The will concluded with the words "Please Leslie, be kind to Dot, Your loving mother". Leslie was Mrs Cook's son, and Dot her daughter. The issue before the Court was whether the expression "Your loving mother" constituted a signature within s 9 of the Wills Act 1837.

The Court accepted counsel for the plaintiff's argument that the authorities established that where the words used by the testator were intended to represent the name of the testator, then the provisions of s 9 would be satisfied. It was clear in this case that the testatrix intended the words to refer to herself. The Court cited authorities which established that the testatrix need not sign her actual name, provided that the mark used was intended to refer to the testatrix.

157   *Casson v Dade*
(1781) 28 ER 1010

The testatrix, Honora Jenkins, had gone to her solicitor's office to make her will. As the office was very hot, and the testatrix prone to asthma, she and her witnesses went to her carriage outside the office to execute the will. The testatrix signed the will, and the witnesses went back inside the office to attest it. The testatrix watched the will being attested by the witnesses through the carriage and office window. The Lord Chancellor held that the will was validly attested.

158   *Re Colling*
[1972] 1 WLR 1440

The testator was in hospital at the time he made his will. He asked the patient in the bed next to him and a nurse at the hospital to witness his signature. The other patient was present for the whole signing of the will, but the nurse left the testator during signature to attend to another patient. When she returned, the testator and the other patient acknowledged their signatures to her and she signed the will as a witness.

The Court considered the question of whether the writing completed by the testator whilst the nurse was present was sufficient to constitute a signature within the meaning of s 9 of the Wills Act 1837. Ungoed-Thomas J recognised that in some cases, the strict application of s 9 could defeat the testator's intention. Nevertheless, he stated that that the requirements of the section are established as strict and technical. The authorities had established that the meaning of the word "signature" in s 9 was either the name, or some mark intended to represent the name of the testator. The part of the testator's name which had been written before the nurse's departure clearly did not fall within either category. Therefore the will was declared to be invalid, and an earlier will of the testator was granted probate. The Judge expressed his regret at this result, stating that it patently defeated the intention of the testator, but felt compelled to reach this conclusion.

159   *Re Young*
[1969] NZLR 454

The first issue regarding execution in this case was whether two pages of a document marked "My Will" both constituted the testator's will. The first page was paper-clipped to the second, which was signed by the testator and attested by two witnesses. The second page was marked "Page Two" and referred to material contained on the first page.

Tompkins J stated that in order for unsigned pages to form part of a will, there must be some proof that the pages formed a single testamentary document when the will was executed.

The first witness could not recall whether two pages were produced at the time of execution. The second witness stated that when he signed the will, the second page (which he signed) had been covered by another sheet of paper of a similar type. It was held that there was a sufficient nexus between the two pages as to show that they constituted a single testamentary document, as it was probable that at the time of execution, the two pages were either paper-clipped or pressed together.

The second question was whether the will had been properly executed. Both witnesses confirmed that the testator had called them into his office, asked them to witness his signature, and had then signed his name in their presence. The first witness stated in her affidavit that the testator had signed his name after she had signed hers, but in her evidence said that she could not remember whether she had signed her name before or after the testator. The second witness gave evidence that he had signed the will after the testator had signed his name, and that shortly afterwards, he saw the document on the counter by the first witness' desk.

The fact that the will was signed by the testator and regularly witnessed by two witnesses gave rise to the presumption of due execution. Tompkins J held that the vague and inconclusive evidence of the first witness was not sufficiently strong to overcome that presumption.

160   *McLaren v McLaren*
[1919] GLR 287

The testator was a victim of the influenza epidemic which struck New Zealand in 1918. He had died in the Martinborough Town Hall which had been converted into an emergency hospital during the epidemic. Probate was opposed by the testator's widow who preferred to take her share in the testator's estate under intestacy rather than by the will, under which she would receive the whole of the income from the estate provided that she did not remarry.

The testator had been admitted to the hospital on 21 November and was very ill. A neighbour of the testator arranged for the testator's solicitor to visit the testator, and the solicitor arrived at the hospital with a will form on 22 November. The solicitor suggested that the testator make a will, and after some initial reluctance, the testator agreed to do so. The solicitor gave evidence that he had a rational conversation with the testator lasting some 20 minutes, and that he then left to prepare the will according to the instructions he had received. He returned with the prepared document and gave it to the testator to read. According to the solicitor the testator signed the will, and the solicitor went to fetch two witnesses.

On the evidence available, it appeared that neither witness actually saw the testator sign the will. The significance of this, stated Chapman J, would depend on the more general history of the testator's condition. A person in good health could legitimately sign their will apart from the witnesses, and could acknowledge their signature to the witnesses by the mere act of inviting the witnesses (either expressly or impliedly) to witness it.

The evidence indicated that the testator had not invited the witnesses to witness the will, and that he remained "inert" throughout the attestation of the will. Further evidence was brought to show that close to the time of execution of the will, the testator had been in a delirious state.

Chapman J stated that the test for validity of the will was whether, when looked at as the act of the testator, the whole transaction could be regarded as one act to which the testator fully and actively assented. In this case, as the testator neither invited the witnesses to sign their names, nor actively acknowledged the solicitor's invitation, and given the evidence as to the real medical condition of the testator at the time of execution, it was held that he did not have sufficient testamentary capacity during the witnessing of his will.

- See Wills Act 2007, s 11.

Gifts to attesting witnesses

161   *Re Bravda*
[1968] 2 All ER 217

The testator wished to leave the whole of his estate to his two daughters. He made a handwritten will which was signed by two independent witnesses, the second of whom was fetched at the testator's request that she be called to be "the other witness". At the request of the testator, both of his daughters then signed their names at the foot of the will, directly underneath the word "witnessed" and above the signatures of the independent witnesses. The testator asked that they add their signatures "to make it stronger". Neither of the daughters added their address to the will, as the other witnesses had done.

The two daughters applied for a grant of probate, and the validity of the will was challenged by the testator's second wife, from whom he had been legally separated. The issue was whether the daughters had signed the will as attesting witnesses. If they had, s 15 of the Wills Act would prevent them from taking under the will. It was held at first instance that the evidence showed that the daughters signed merely to please their father, rather than as witnesses. On appeal, Willmer LJ said that on the face of the will, it appeared that the two daughters had signed as witnesses, and that this raised a rebuttable presumption against them. The question, then, was whether the plaintiffs had adduced sufficient evidence to rebut the presumption.

The fact that the daughters had not added their address was considered to be largely insignificant, as they both resided in the testator's house, and there was no question that they would be difficult to locate after their father's death. The Court did not accept that the testator's recognition of the need for a second witness to be called established that the testator knew that two witnesses were needed for the valid execution of the will, or that the words "to make it stronger" supported the plaintiffs' case.

In holding that the plaintiffs' evidence was not sufficiently strong to overcome the inference raised by the face of the will, the Court expressed regret that the clear intention of the testator (that the daughters should be the sole beneficiaries of the will) would be defeated by a refusal to grant probate. Nevertheless, it was held that no other decision could be reached, without doing violence to the facts as evidenced in the plaintiffs' affidavits.

- See Wills Act 2007, s 13.

Incorporation by reference

162 *Re Karsten*
[1950] NZLR 1022

Rona Karsten made a will leaving all her estate to her friend Esther, to be distributed as Esther "has direction from me". After Rona's death, Esther found an envelope addressed to her, containing unsigned notes in Rona's handwriting, which appeared to set up her wishes to the disposal of her estate. Apparently these were written out by Rona after the will was signed, and then attached to the will.

The question before the Court was whether Rona's notes had any effect, given that the estate had been given to Esther in trust, with no trust expressed on the face of the will.

The starting point was the decision in *Blackwell* **(4)** where the English House of Lords had noted that a testator cannot reserve to himself or herself a power of making future unwitnessed dispositions by merely naming a trustee and leaving the purposes of the trust to be supplied afterwards. Following from this it has been established that if an unattested document is to be incorporated in a will it must have been in existence at the date of will; it must have been referred to in the will as a document then existing; and it must have been described in the will sufficiently to allow it to be identified. Here where the trust was not fully declared (as the document could not be incorporated), and where no trust had been declared orally after the will was signed, or by a paper not executed as a will, the trust had no validity. Esther necessarily was a trustee for the next of kin, not those named in the directions.

163 *In bonis Truro*
(1866) LR 1 P & D 201

When Lady Truro died on 21 May 1866 she left behind her a will dated 15 September 1865, and a codicil dated 10 October 1865. Her will stated that she left a substantial amount of her property to her husband, including a number of items "as are contained in the inventory signed by me and deposited herewith". The inventory of items left to her husband had been signed on 21 September 1865 — six days after the will was executed. Thus the list had presumably not been drawn up until after the will was signed. The question was whether the list could be allowed to form part of the will.

One of the requirements to allow a document to be incorporated into a will by reference is that it must have been a document existing at the time when the will was signed. The list did not fall into this category in this case. However, Lord Wilde in the probate division of the English Courts had no difficulty in holding that the whole problem could be solved here by looking at the codicil, which "republished" the will. After considering a number of cases he stated the general rule that "republication" of a will is tantamount to the making of that will afresh: the will so republished is a new will. He also felt it was plain that the republication of the will which a codicil effects may add something to a will which formed no part of it when executed, and which is not to be found in the codicil itself.

Therefore in this case if the will was treated as being re-executed on the date of the codicil, 10 October 1865, then the reference to the "inventory signed by me and deposited herewith" now validly referred to a document in existence when the will was republished. It now referred with sufficient distinctness to a document then existing, and thus the list could validly be included with the will.

Mental requirements

Animus testandi

**164   *Corbett v Newey*
        [1996] 2 All ER 914**

A testatrix, a maiden aunt, owned two farms in England. She decided to leave them in her will to her niece and nephew respectively. The residue of her estate was also to be shared between her niece and nephew. She made a will to this effect in February 1989.

After discussions with her lawyers, the testatrix decided that she would prefer to make gifts of the farms to her niece and nephew while she was still alive, and amend her will accordingly. This new will was also to be changed to leave the residue of her estate to her niece's children.

With this in mind the lawyers were instructed to draft a new will, and two deeds of gift. The will was however completed before the deeds of gift could be finalised, and a copy of it was sent to the testatrix to be executed in September 1989. The testatrix was quite well aware that if she executed the will, and then subsequently died before the deeds of gift were finalised, her niece and nephew would not in fact receive the farms, as they would be treated as residue under her new will. She accordingly executed the will, but did not date it. She sent it back to her lawyer asking him to date it when the deeds of gift had been finalised and executed. Both she and her lawyer believed, incorrectly, that the will could not take effect until it was dated.

In due course the deeds of gift were finalised, and were dated 25 December 1989. The testatrix's lawyer then dated her will 26 December. Just over a year later the testatrix died, and her nephew challenged the validity of the later will.

The difficulty in this case was the fundamental principle that a will must be executed with the intention, or animus testandi, that, subject only to the death of its maker, it should be of immediate effect after its execution. A will may be conditional, but any such conditions must be explicitly expressed in the will. In this case, no conditions were apparent on the face of the will. Yet it was clear from the testatrix's behaviour and actions that she did not intend it to take effect until after the deeds of gift had been finalised. Would this satisfy the requirement for animus testandi?

The Court of Appeal decided it did not. Waite LJ felt there was no possibility that at the time the testatrix executed the will in September she intended it to take effect. There were no conditions on the face of the will, and it is impossible to have a will, unconditional on its face, be made conditional in its operation through some direction imposed by the testatrix at the time of its execution. Accordingly the only conclusion open to the Court was to hold that at the moment of execution the testatrix lacked the animus to make any valid will — in the sense of a will intended to be immediately operative — at all. Therefore, the September will could not be upheld, and the February will was to be applied. Whether the lawyer was sued is not recorded.

165 *Re Whyte*
[1969] NZLR 519

The testatrix had made a will in 1945 which left the whole of her estate to her husband. In 1968, she gave instructions for the making of a new will, with the same dispositive provisions as the first will, but with a substituted trustee. The provision which bequeathed the whole of her estate to her husband was inadvertently omitted from the second will.

The will was duly executed, but it was not read over to her, and she did not know and approve of its contents. An application was made under the Declaratory Judgments Act 1908 for an order declaring the will to be invalid.

McGregor ACJ held that the will was indeed invalid. Where no suspicion attaches to the document, the execution by the testator is usually sufficient evidence of the testator's knowledge and approval. However, where the manner in which the will was read over is called into question, or where the will was not read over, the presumption of due execution may be rebutted. In this case, there was clear evidence that testatrix had not read the contents of the will. It was essential in every case that the testator should know and approve the will's contents. Therefore, an order was made declaring the will to be invalid.

166   *Banks v Goodfellow*
(1870) LR 5 QB 549

The testator died, leaving a will which left all of his property to the daughter of his only sister. The issue at trial was whether the testator had the requisite mental capacity to make a valid will.

The Court found that it was unquestionable that the testator had, at times, been of unsound mind. He had been incarcerated in a mental asylum for some time, and even after his discharge from the asylum, continued to have delusions:

> He had conceived a violent aversion towards a man named Featherstone Alexander, and notwithstanding the death of the latter some years ago, he continued to believe that this man still pursued and molested him; and the mere mention of Featherstone Alexander's name was enough to throw him into a state of violent excitement. He frequently believed that he was pursued and molested by devils or evil spirits, whom he believed to be visibly present.

The evidence also showed that the testator had managed his own financial affairs, although it was admitted that, at times, he was incapable of making a will.

The Court found that the testator had the requisite animus testandi at the time the will was made. In coming to this decision, Cockburn CJ held that the appropriate test for cases of psychosis was that which applied in cases where the testator was mentally impaired; that is, that the testator must have comprehended the extent of the property to be disposed of, and the nature of the claims of those he was excluding. Although there was a considerable body of evidence to show that he had been insane for periods both prior to and after the execution of the will, the delusions had no actual impact upon his ability to make a will, and would not have influenced the decisions he made in disposing of his property. Therefore, the testator had the requisite animus testandi at the time of execution, and the will was upheld.

167   *Parker v Felgate*
(1883) 8 PD 171

The testatrix became terminally ill, and consulted her solicitor, Mr Parker, as to the making of her will.

She was concerned about the possibility of her father and brother becoming bankrupt, and (having previously advanced money to them) instructed Parker to provide for legacies of 500 guineas to her father and 250 guineas to her brother. She wished to leave the remainder of her estate (approximately 2750 guineas) to a Hospital for Sick Children.

The testatrix became very ill before the will was finally prepared, and as Parker was away at that time, the will was prepared by his partner, Mr Ponsford, following the instructions given to Parker and a draft will prepared by Parker.

The will was taken to the testatrix in hospital. She was told that the document was her will, and asked whether she wished another woman who was present to sign it.

The question considered by the Court was to what extent the testatrix had been capable of understanding what was going on. Hannen P stated that it would be enough if she was capable of understanding, and understood, simply that she was executing her will for which she had given instructions to Parker. It was not necessary that she be able to remember details of the instructions which she actually gave, or even to recall each clause if it had been read to her.

It was held that the testatrix did have the requisite degree of understanding, and probate was granted accordingly.

Undue influence, fraud and duress

168   *Hall v Hall*
(1868) LR 1 P&D 481

The plaintiff in this case was the wife of the testator who applied for probate for a will which left her the whole of his property which was valued between 15,000 and 20,000 guineas.

The brother of the testator called evidence that this will had been made solely as a result of violence and threats on the part of the plaintiff and that it did not express his late brother's real testamentary intentions.

In delivering his decision that the will was a product of undue influence exerted by the plaintiff, Lord Wilde stated that:

> To make a good will a man must be a free agent. But all influences are not unlawful. Persuasion, appeals to the affections or ties of kindred, to a sentiment or a gratitude for past services, or pity for future destitution, or the like, - these are all legitimate and may be fairly pressed on a testator. On the other hand, pressure of whatever character, whether acting on the fears or the hopes, if so exerted as to overpower the volition without convincing the judgment, is a species of restraint under which no valid will can be made.

169   *Tanner v Public Trustee*
[1973] 1 NZLR 68

In this case, the will of Ellen Ruth Budd which was the subject of the application for probate had been drawn by one of the beneficiaries under the will, a Mr Tanner, whose wife was also named as a beneficiary. The respondents were various charities, which were to take less under the new will than under a previous will of the testatrix. One of the respondent charities was omitted from the new will altogether. The Tanners had been beneficiaries under the previous will, but the new will significantly increased the provision for them.

Macarthur J reviewed the relevant authorities, and cited Lord Hatherly in *Fulton v Andrew* (1875) LR 7 HL 448 at 461, stating that where a person is both a beneficiary under a will, and has been instrumental in its preparation, that person will be under a greater burden than usual in seeking to prove the will. In this situation, that person would have the onus of showing the righteousness of the transaction. Therefore, Macarthur J considered that the Court should not pronounce in favour of the new will unless the suspicion which attaches in cases of this nature was removed, and the Court was satisfied that the document expressed the true will of the deceased.

It was not disputed that Mrs Budd remained alert and had sufficient testamentary capacity at the time of the making of the will. This fact, however, did not preclude further inquiry by the Court.

Tanner had been in the employ of Mr Budd for many years, and had bought the business from Mr Budd when he retired. He was married to the Budds' niece. After the death of Mr Budd, Tanner continued to be involved in the affairs of Mrs Budd, and a power of attorney in his favour was executed, in order that he could manage the sale of her house when she went into a rest home. There was evidence that prior to the power of attorney he had had Mrs Budd's authority to operate her bank account. On Tanner's advice a gift of the "net proceeds" of the sale had been made to Mrs Tanner. This amount was then employed in Tanner's business, without Mrs Budd's knowledge. Mrs Budd also agreed to lend Tanner £10,000, free of interest.

In 1966, Tanner visited Mrs Budd in the rest home, and they discussed the provisions of her previous will. He then went to the Public Trust Office with a note of the instructions for a new will. The solicitor from the Public Trust Office then visited Mrs Budd, and found that although she was alert and well, she was not able to give consideration to alteration of her will. The solicitor asked for a medical opinion as to testamentary capacity, and was told by a doctor that Mrs Budd was capable to make her will, and that she had said she wanted to make changes to her previous will. Another officer of the Public Trust then visited Mrs Budd with the newly prepared will, but she was feeling unwell, and, judging that she did not have sufficient understanding, he left her with the instruction to telephone the Public Trust when she was feeling better.

It was arranged with Tanner that a Public Trust Officer should visit the home on the next morning. The Public Trust cancelled this appointment, and Tanner then went to see Mrs Budd's solicitor, Mr Young, stating that he was tired of Public Trust procrastination. Mr Young and a senior partner of his firm then decided to visit Mrs Budd without Tanner. They found her cheerful and alert, and quite firm that she did not wish to alter her will. Tanner arranged for the Public Trust to deal with the matter. Further discussions about the will took place between Tanner and Mrs Budd until the new will was finally completed. Tanner typed the will himself, and arranged a friend of his to accompany him to the rest home for the execution of the will. Mrs Budd was in good health, and had the contents of the will read over to her and was asked whether she wanted to add anything. She said that she did not, and with her agreement, Mr Curtis called in the matron. Mrs Budd signed the will, which was then attested by Mr Curtis and the matron.

The Court found that the applicants had failed to discharge the onus of proving the righteousness of the transaction. Factors which were considered important in reaching this conclusion were the difference between the dispositions made under the old will and the new will; the fact that other visitors to Mrs Budd had given evidence that she did not wish to change her will (which threw the authenticity of the instructions given to Tanner into question); Mrs Budd's complete trust and confidence in Tanner; a statement made by Tanner to the effect that he thought the old will did not make sufficient provision for Mrs Budd's relations; the fact that Tanner kept the 1966 will a secret (except from his wife) until after Mrs Budd's death; and the fact that Mrs Budd received no independent advice in respect of the making of the 1966 will. The will was declared to be invalid.

170   *Re Naumann*
High Court, Dunedin A17/83, 16 December 1991, Robertson J

Mrs and Mr Naumann (the testatrix and her late husband) had farmed in South Otago for many years. Before the death of Mr Naumann, his health had prevented him from farming, and the McTainsh family (friends and neighbours of the Naumanns) had leased the Naumann land. The lease had initially been on a formal basis, but later on an informal basis, as Mrs Naumann told the plaintiff (the son of the McTainsh family, who had been farming the Naumann land after his father) that she intended to leave the property to him.

In 1975, Mrs Naumann made a new will which, except for some small bequests, left the farm and residuary estate to the plaintiff absolutely.

In 1976, Mrs Naumann made a further will in favour of a Mr Duncan Mackenzie, a man with whom she had been acquainted for less than four months. Aside from small bequests, the whole of her estate was left to Mr Mackenzie.

The plaintiff challenged the will on the ground that upon making it, Mrs Naumann lacked testamentary capacity and had been under the undue influence of Mr Mackenzie.

The plaintiff's evidence included evidence of the testatrix's doctor and the doctor who had attended her after her admission to Timaru hospital that Mrs Naumann had become increasingly vague and a little confused, with some loss of perspective and appreciation, and that she was increasingly concerned with the past. The lawyer who had drawn up the will gave evidence that although he had expressed surprise at the alteration, Mrs Naumann had appeared to be in control of what she was doing.

Robertson J remarked first that when any person makes a will at the age of 92 years, the Court "must be vigilant as to the circumstances". On considering the evidence, he held that Mrs Naumann had lost a proper appreciation of present circumstances.

> She became simply putty in the hands of a man who came along, was prepared to say what she wanted to hear and thereby to inveigle himself into a position in which the deceased was no longer able to make sensible and proper judgments about her affairs and her overall position.

Therefore, the later will made in favour of Mr Mackenzie was held to be invalid, and the Court directed the executor of the earlier will to seek probate of that will.

Mutual wills

171   *Lewis v Cotton*
      [2001] 2 NZLR 21 (CA)

Lloyd Cotton acquired a farm at Mangapai in 1949, and married Dawn in 1956, subsequently acquiring further farm properties. The farms became vested in Cotton Farms Limited during the 1970s. Lloyd held a controlling interest of A shares, but Dawn and a trust she controlled also held some B shares.

Lloyd and Dawn had three children: Susan, Graeme, and Dianne. Lloyd and Dawn had made wills together in 1983 and Lloyd had made a further will in 1994.

Under Lloyd's 1983 will, Dawn obtained the income of his estate for life and Susan a beach house and a legacy of $25,000. Dianne was to have the option of acquiring part of the farm and stock. The rest of Lloyd's estate was left to Graeme, as from 1976 Graeme had worked full-time on the farm. It was found to be Lloyd and Dawn's intention that Graeme have a privileged position in relation to the farm assets. Under Dawn's 1983 will, Lloyd obtained a life interest in her estate, with the residuary going to Graeme. After signing this will, Dawn's trust transferred some B shares to Graeme, and following Dawn's death, Graeme came to hold all the B shares in Cotton Farms Limited.

Lloyd's 1994 will declared an intention that Susan receive part of the farm (owned by Cotton Farms Limited) without payment. The beach house was left to the three children equally, and other gifts also given to Graeme and Dianne.

Dawn Cotton died in 1987 and Lloyd Cotton died ten years later. By the time of Lloyd's death, all three of the children were in a good financial position.

There were two key issues in this case: first, whether Dianne was entitled to provision from Lloyd's estate under the Family Protection Act 1955; and secondly, whether the 1983 wills were "mutual wills", in which case Lloyd could not change his will following Dawn's death. Both issues deserve some attention.

The High Court took the position that the windfall to Graeme through receiving control of the shares in Cotton Farms Limited had led Dianne to her claim, rather than any real need for maintenance. On this basis, following *Williams v Aucutt* **(184)**, Dianne's claim under the Family Protection Act must fail — a proposition with which the Court of Appeal agreed.

In addition, the High Court observed that both Lloyd and Dawn had made prior wills and was aware they were revocable in light of changing circumstances. On appeal, it was argued that it had been the intention of Lloyd and Dawn that Dianne receive part of the farm and that this had been an integral part of Lloyd and Dawn's joint estate planning — in other words, that the 1983 wills were mutual wills.

In discussing the doctrine of mutual wills, the Court of Appeal compared the notion of a secret trust, deriving from joint wills signed by two testators but read as separate documents (*Denyssen v Mostert* (1872) LR 4 PC 236). It was noted that joint wills were so rare in modern times that they might point strongly towards a mutual intention that neither should revoke. While a will was, by its nature revocable, the consequence of a promise of non-revocation might be that the trustees of the replacement will would be required to hold the assets on constructive trust under the terms of the revoked will.

The promise under mutual wills was that either: (a) the wills would not be revoked at any time; or (b) that one person's will would not be revoked secretly during the other's lifetime, or at all after the other's death. Consideration for the promise to make mutual wills was unnecessary, but could be found in the mutual promises and execution of the wills. The promise not to revoke could be explicit or implicit, but must be more than mere coordination of the wills or agreement to draft the wills in a particular way — there must be proof of an agreement intended to bind the two testators to a future course of inaction (*Gray v Perpetual Trustee Co Ltd* [1928] AC 391).

The Court held that many husbands and wives would make wills by agreement without intending to bind themselves not to revoke them. In modern times, such a commitment was seen to be unlikely and undesirable, and too inflexible in light of changing taxes and estate duties. The Courts would be slow to find "mutual wills" just because the wills corresponded. In the circumstances, there was no evidence of any arrangement between Lloyd and Dawn that the 1983 wills would not be revoked, and the mutual wills claim failed.

- See Wills Act 2007, s 30.

Revocation

172 *Re Archibald*
[1992] 2 NZLR 109

The testator had made a will on 23 September 1975, leaving the sum of $10,000 and all his chattels, including motor vehicles, to his wife, and the residue of his estate to pay the net annual income arising to his wife during her lifetime, and after her death, to any of his children who might survive him and reach the age of 25. Later, on 26 May 1978, he executed another will which was drawn by another solicitor who was unaware of the earlier will. By that will, he directed that all debts and expenses be paid, and the whole of his remaining estate go to his wife absolutely. Subsequently, however, he went back to the solicitor who had drawn up the first will, and executed a codicil on 29 August 1984, which was expressed as being the first codicil to the 23 September 1975 will. That codicil revoked the appointment of two people as executors and trustees, who were both executors under the first will, but only one of whom was an executor under the second will. It appointed in their place the testator's four sons. The second clause of the codicil stated that "in all other respects I confirm my said will". Two later codicils were executed by the testator. Each of these referred to the 1975 will and were expressed as codicils to that will.

After the death of the testator, the testator's sons as executors substituted by the 1984 codicil, sought probate in solemn form of the 1975 will and the three codicils. The executors under the 1978 will were described as defendants, although they neither opposed nor consented to the application for grant of probate.

Tipping J stated that two issues fell to be considered in deciding which of the testamentary instruments should be admitted to probate. The first was whether the codicils, particularly the first, revived the 1975 will. The second was whether the codicils, particularly the first, had the effect of revoking the 1978 will.

In considering the first issue, he found that it was clear that the effect of the 1978 will was to revoke the 1975 will. However, the terms of the first codicil, particularly the revocation of the appointment of the two executors appointed under the *1975* will, were evidently intended to refer to the 1975 will, and not the 1978 will. The reference to the 1975 will as being the last will and testament of the testator was an error made by the testator who, at the time of execution of the first codicil, had been focusing his mind on the 1975 will. He then considered whether there was sufficient intention, on the face of the codicil to revive the 1975 will. Under s 22 of the Wills Act 1837, no will which has been revoked shall be revived other than by re-execution or by a codicil properly executed and showing an intention to revive the same. In this case, the words of the 1984 codicil, "in all other respects I confirm my said will" must be taken to have intended to revive the 1975 will.

Tipping J held that the clear implication was that the revival of the 1975 will must have revoked the 1978 will, as their terms could not possibly stand together.

173   *Re Panapa*
[1993] 1 NZLR 694

The testatrix made her will on 4 September 1991. Clause 2 of the will stated that "this will is made in anticipation of my marriage to Wayne Arda Charles Hakaraia and the contents of this Will are to apply after my marriage to the said Wayne Arda Charles Hakaraia". Clause 3 of the will stated that Hakaraia was to receive the whole of the testatrix's estate, subject to payment of her debts, if he were alive fourteen days after the death of the testatrix.

The testatrix was to marry the applicant on 6 September 1991, but she died on 5 September. The issue was whether Wayne Hakaraia (who was alive 14 days after her death) should receive the estate under cl 3 of the will. This entailed consideration by the Court of the true construction of cl 2. The applicant submitted that that Hakaraia's interest under the will was not conditional upon the marriage taking place.

Williams J first discussed the law relating to conditional wills. It is clear that a will may be drafted so that it will only have effect upon the occurrence of some contingency. In determining whether a will is conditional in character, the whole language of the document and the surrounding circumstances should be taken into account. Where the contingency is related to some imminent danger to the testator, it will be necessary to consider whether the will is *dependent* on the occurrence of the contingency, or whether the occurrence is merely a reason for the making of the will.

In the present case, the purpose of cl 2 was clearly to avoid the provision in s 18 of the Wills Act 1837 that everyone's will is revoked upon the occurrence of their marriage. Section 13 provides an exception to this rule in the case of wills stated to be made "in contemplation of marriage", and Williams J considered that the words "in anticipation of", used in the present case, would have had the same effect as the statutory language.

It was clear that, had cl 2 of the will stated only that the will was made in anticipation of the intended marriage, the will would not be conditional upon the marriage occurring. The authorities established that a condition must be expressed or clearly implied before dispositions made in contemplation of an event would be taken to be conditional on the happening of that event. In the present case, the further statement that the contents of the will were to apply after the intended marriage had taken place was considered by Williams J to have been merely added for emphasis or further explanation of the first part of the clause. It did not imply or express that the happening of the marriage was a precondition for the operation of the will.

Moreover, the terms of the will were not ambiguous, and no examination of extrinsic evidence was necessary. However, Williams J did state that the extrinsic evidence strongly supported the view that the will was not conditional upon the marriage.

- See Wills Act 2007, ss 16 and 18.

Family Protection Act 1955

174   *Little v Angus*
       [1981] 1 NZLR 126 (CA)

The testatrix died in 1975 leaving two children from her first marriage, which had ended in divorce in 1955 (her second marriage had ended by the death of the testatrix's husband some time previously). The two children of the first marriage, Mrs Little and Mr Angus, were the only persons to whom the testatrix owed a moral duty. As at the date of the appeal hearing, the estate was valued at over $223,000; it had been around $162,000 at the High Court hearing.

The testatrix's last will of 1974 left all but $4480 to Mr Angus, with the balance going to Mrs Little. The will stated that no further provision was made for Mrs Little as the testatrix had assisted her during her lifetime. Following an application by Mrs Little under the Family Protection Act 1955 (FPA), the trial Court ruled there had been a breach of moral duty (a point conceded by Mr Angus) and ordered that Mrs Little be given one-quarter of the estate. Mrs Little appealed.

The financial position of Mrs Little and her husband was reasonable, but not affluent, and there were some health problems in the family. There was also some evidence that the testatrix had ignored her children somewhat when they were young. Mr Angus was in modest but not penurious financial circumstances.

In giving the judgment of the Court of Appeal, Cooke J noted at p 127 that the principles and practice of FPA claims were well settled:

> The inquiry is as to whether there has been a breach of moral duty judged by the standards of a just and wise testator or testatrix; and, if so, what is appropriate to remedy that breach. Only to that extent is the will to be disturbed. The size of the estate and any other moral claims on the deceased's bounty are highly relevant. Changing social attitudes must have their influence on the existence and extent of moral duties. Whether there has been a breach of moral duty is customarily tested as at the date of the testator's death; but in deciding how a breach should be remedied regard is had to later events ... the Court will not substitute its discretion for that of the Judge at first instance unless there be made out some reasonably plain ground upon which the order should be varied.

The Court noted that Mrs Little had not sought half of the estate, and that whatever was remaining would be ample to provide for Mr Angus and his dependants. The Court also found that the poor health of one of Mrs Little's children and the deficiencies in her upbringing were relevant. It was also seen as desirable to approach the claim of a married daughter "more liberally" than may have been the case in the past.

The Court ruled that Mrs Little should receive one-third of the estate.

175   *Re Leonard*
[1985] 2 NZLR 88 (CA)

John Leonard died in 1978 at the age of 89 with seven children. By his last will, dated 1969, he left $4000 and some items of furniture to each of his three daughters. There was also provision for a house property to pass to them in equal shares subject to a life interest to his wife; however, she predeceased him and the property was sold before his death — meaning that the bequest failed.

The deceased also had other assets, the most significant being two dairy farms and a run-off. One farm was left to two sons in equal shares; and the other was left to the other two sons in equal shares. The four sons also received equal shares of the residuary estate. Although initially valued at $384,000, the value of the estate at the time of the Court of Appeal hearing was $745,000.

The children were by this time all in their 50s or 60s and in comfortable circumstances, but two daughters, Gertrude Gosse and Doreen Terry, brought proceedings under the Family Protection Act 1955 (FPA) for greater provision under the will. In the High Court, their legacies were increased from $4000 to $40,000. This decision was appealed by three of the brothers on the basis that the daughters were in so strong a financial position that the testator had no moral duty to provide for them; or alternatively, no duty beyond the $4000 each was granted in the will.

Both daughters had been dutiful and had similar net worth (with their husbands) of approximately $175,000–$185,000 each. The High Court noted the deceased's desire to look after his sons in their farm work, but commented that John Leonard was out of touch with changes in social attitudes, and regarded his daughters as "off his hands" once married. The brothers were in less need of maintenance, and the FPA was not intended to favour only people of modest means. What maintenance and support was needed was a relative question in light of the circumstances and the size of the estate. The Court of Appeal agreed with this approach, and agreed that there had been a breach of moral duty. The High Court's ruling of $40,000 to each daughter was upheld and the appeal dismissed.

176   *Re MacIntosh*
(1990) 7 FRNZ 580

The plaintiff in this case (claiming under the Family Protection Act 1955) was the only child of Mrs MacIntosh, the testatrix, who died in 1988.

The extent of the estate was about $85,000. By her will, the testatrix left $2000 to the plaintiff, some jewellery to the testatrix's sister, and the residue of her estate to four charities. Prior to her death, the testatrix had no connection with any of the charities.

Applications under the Family Protection Act 1955 were also made by the plaintiff's children (the grandchildren of the testatrix).

Tipping J observed that the plaintiff had been "an extremely dutiful and caring daughter to both her parents" and had devoted a considerable part of her time and energy to their welfare. He described the $2000 gift as a "mere token" and remarked that in practical terms she had been entirely excluded by the will.

He went on to note that the testatrix had been affected by the death of her husband, and had become a very different person in the last two years of her life, often suffering from depression. She had made an earlier will which had left a small bequest to her grandson, and the balance to her daughter, but had changed the will in 1987 (a year before her death) to practically exclude her daughter.

The testatrix had chosen the charities which were to benefit under her will from a volume describing various charities made available by her solicitor. Ironically, the Blind Foundation, which might have been expected to benefit (her husband having been blind for a number of years and having had a close connection with the Foundation) was not included amongst the beneficiaries under the will.

Counsel for the plaintiff submitted that the circumstances indicated a clear breach of moral duty by the testatrix.

Tipping J summarised the relevant test as being:

> [W]hat should a wise and just testatrix have done, in all the circumstances? The question of breach is determined at the date of death and quantum at the date of the hearing. The concept of needs and the concept of maintenance under the legislation include not only financial considerations but moral and ethical considerations as well.

The plaintiff was, at the date of her mother's death, in bad health. She had no income of her own, and her husband had only modest assets. Tipping J found that there were no other moral claimants, nor was there any question of estrangement: the evidence showed that the difficulties which arose between mother and daughter were primarily a result of the changes in the mother's personality towards the end of her life. There was a strong moral duty on the part of the testatrix, which she was obliged to fulfil before there was any room for generosity to charities with whom she had no connection. Additionally, the quantum of the grant under the Family Protection Act should be determined by reference to the substantial assistance given by the plaintiff and her husband to the plaintiff's parents.

The grandchildren of the testatrix supported their mother's claim but argued that if their mother did not receive the whole estate, they should receive the remainder in lieu of the charities. Tipping J found that there was no moral duty owed by the testatrix to provide for the grandchildren, particularly as they could ultimately expect to benefit from the provision made to their mother.

The gift made to the plaintiff was increased from $2000 to $60,000, and costs were awarded in favour of both the plaintiff and the grandchildren.

177 *Re McLean*
[1991] 8 FRNZ 321

The testator had worked in Papua New Guinea until his death from Hodgkin's disease in 1986. His estate totalled $200,000. By his will, he left a total of $53,332 to his former de facto partner of four and a half years, his mentally handicapped son, and his daughter from a previous marriage. The residue of his estate was divided equally between his parents and his sister.

The former de facto partner claimed under the Family Protection Act 1955. The High Court decision was based on a finding that the testator had owed her no moral duty. This finding was overturned in the Court of Appeal, where it was held that a moral duty was owed both to the appellant and to the two children, but that no such duty was owed the testator's parents or his sister.

The appellant had begun to live with the testator when she was 16. She had no educational qualifications, and her employment prospects were limited. Further, the appellant had had greater responsibilities than usual in a de facto relationship, as during the relationship, the testator continually suffered from the symptoms of Hodgkin's disease which included frequent bouts of vomiting.

The appellant gave evidence that the testator's persistent drinking and refusal to seek medical help led her to end the relationship after four and a half years. The appellant subsequently entered into another de facto relationship, and at the time of the hearing, was living in Australia with her de facto partner and their two young children in modest circumstances.

Richardson J held that the appellant was owed a moral duty by the testator. Although de facto partners and former de facto partners cannot usually claim under the Family Protection Act, the Court could consider the moral claim of such a person where testamentary provision had been made for her or him. In this case, the circumstances pointed to the existence of a moral duty, as the appellant had been very much worse off at the end of the relationship than she had been before it. Her education and prospects had been adversely affected, and she had given up four and a half years at a crucial stage in her life.

Richardson J concluded that the daughter and son of the testator should each receive one-third of the residuary estate, and that the remaining third should go to the appellant, subject to the payment of legacies of $7000 to each of the testator's father, mother and sister.

178   *Re Bendien*
(1991) 8 FRNZ 108

The testatrix died in 1985 at the age of 55. She left $5000 cash to be divided among the three children of her first marriage, the residue to go to her second husband. One month after the granting of probate, the children's solicitor notified their intentions to claim under the Family Protection Act. The husband entered into negotiations with them but no settlement was reached.

The husband unilaterally executed a deed of trust under which the house and the proceeds from the sale of a large proportion of the chattels would be held on trust for the children. The house was transferred to the trustees, and $48,700 gifted off the purchase price. The husband intended to gift the remainder of the purchase price or to forgive it by will. The trustees were given discretionary powers of advancement where it was judged that a beneficiary was sufficiently in need. In a letter to his stepchildren, the husband stated:

> Your mother clearly expressed her intention that her property is to be used as a backstop and safeguard for her children and is definitely not to be use as simple spending cash.

The children filed their application under the Family Protection Act shortly after the establishment of the "Anna Bendien Trust", and it was unclear whether they were aware of the trust before filing. At the time of the hearing, the value of the assets held by the trust was about $100,000.

Wylie J first considered the relative means of the parties, and concluded that although none of them were particularly needy, they were all in modest circumstances, and all had a legitimate claim. He then found that on the basis of the face of the will only, the testatrix had breached her moral duty to her children.

He then considered the separate issue of how the breach should be remedied, or indeed, whether it should be remedied at all. The testatrix would have satisfied her duty had she left her husband a life interest and the capital to her children upon his death. Although this was now not possible, given the creation of the trust, Wylie J thought that the husband had in fact, gone a long way towards meeting that objective. The only respects in which the situation differed were that the 2006 date stated to be the "final date of appropriation" could be before or after the death of the husband and that the trust deed did not provide for equal division of the trust assets between the children. However, it was reasonable in the circumstances to assume that if the husband died before the 2006 date, the remaining trustees would advance the date, and that, in the absence of any compelling reasons for uneven distribution, the children would receive equal shares of the trust assets. Further, Wylie J was willing to accept that the trustees' discretion to advance money at any stage where a beneficiary was particularly in need, would be exercised wisely. He concluded that:

> [A]lthough looking at the will in isolation the [children] have established a breach, that breach has been sufficiently remedied out of the assets formerly belonging to the deceased by the subsequent actions of Mr Bendien, provided that ultimately the capital of the trust is distributed justly and wisely.

179   *Re Tonge*
High Court, Whangarei, M 23/8621, 13 March 1990, Robertson J

Mrs Tonge had a son and granddaughter. She also had a substantial estate worth more than $600,000 on her death. When Mrs Tonge's will was read her son was somewhat surprised to find that no bequest had been made to him or his daughter at all, and that his mother's entire estate had been left to the RSPCA. It seems that Mrs Tonge had once made some mention of this idea, but Mr Tonge thought his mother must have been joking. She was not.

Mr Tonge and his daughter brought proceedings under the Family Protection Act. Robertson J began by noting that the duty of the Court, so far as possible, is to consider whether a testator has been guilty of a breach of a moral duty which a just and loving testator would owe to the claimants. In the present case the Judge noted the son was aged almost 40, and while in no particular financial difficulty, was in need of maintenance and support. He had lived for some years in Australia, but was not estranged from his mother, and in fact maintained no more or no less than the normal degree of contact one would expect between a parent and child living in different countries.

The granddaughter was 22 at the time of her grandmother's death. She was married with one child, and not in paid employment. She and her husband owned a car and some furniture and effects, but had virtually nothing in the way of savings. It was clear that her financial need was great.

Robertson J considered that given the size of the estate, the personal circumstances of the son and granddaughter, and the fact that the whole estate was left to a charity with which Mrs Tonge had had no particular connection, it was clear that a wise and just mother and grandmother in her position would have made a more substantial provision for her only child and grandchild before leaving her entire estate to charity. Thus it was held a breach of moral duty had been established. In the circumstances the Court was satisfied that the appropriate balance would be met if Mrs Tonge's estate was divided into 12 equal parts with six parts going to her son, one part to her granddaughter, and the remaining five parts to the RSPCA.

181   *Re Sepsy*
High Court, Dunedin, CP 65/87, 12 August 1994, Robertson J

When Jozsef Sepsy was killed in an accident in 1986 he had been married for two years, and had one child, Steven. His wife, Adrienne Sepsy, had two children from a former relationship, William and Susan, who were 12 and eight. Adrienne and Jozsef had begun living together some two years prior to their marriage, and from this time Jozsef had become the effective father for the two young children. This was reflected in the will he had made at this time in which he left his entire estate to Adrienne, or to William and Susan if she did not survive him. This will was however automatically revoked on Jozsef and Adrienne's subsequent marriage and Jozsef had not made a new will before his death.

Jozsef's estate totalled approximately $115,000. As he had died intestate, under the Administration Act 1969 Adrienne received $70,000 and Steven $35,000, to be held on trust for him.

The Administration Act makes no provision for stepchildren, and thus William and Susan had no entitlement to their stepfather's estate. Accordingly an application on their behalf was made under the Family Protection Act.

The matter was considered by Robertson J who took the opportunity to note that the position of stepchildren reflected changing social norms. He noted that the unusual circumstances of this case highlighted the need for a comprehensive rationalisation of the various pieces of legislation in this area. Robertson J held that there was a moral duty upon Jozsef towards his two stepchildren, and felt that it would be quite artificial not to take into account Mr Sepsy's clear intention to provide for William and Sarah in his earlier will. The Judge could see no basis to differentiate between the three children, and ordered the fund presently held on trust for Steven to be held for the benefit of himself and his stepbrother and sister jointly.

182   ***Williams v Aucutt***
          [2000] 2 NZLR 479 (CA)

The Hendersons were married in 1936. Mr Henderson died in 1975, and Mrs Henderson in 1996. They had two daughters: Susan, born in 1937, and Christine, born in 1946. At the time of her death, Mrs Henderson's estate was worth around $920,000: around $380,000 for her house, $120,000 for contents, and $420,000 for deposits and shares. The assets of Susan and her husband were greater than this at the time of death, while Christine's joint assets with her husband considerably lower.

By Mrs Henderson's last will (made in 1992), she made a number of gifts. Susan received some CSR shares, and a painting and other articles. The grandsons were also granted gifts, but the greater part of the estate was left to Christine. Clause 9 of the will stated that greater provision was made for Christine because Mrs Henderson considered Christine to be in a much worse financial position than Susan. Both daughters were found to have been dutiful to their parents in different ways. The High Court found that Mrs Henderson was entitled to distinguish between her daughters on the basis of financial position, but that there had been a breach of moral duty on the basis that Susan had been very involved in Mrs Henderson's life, and that ample provision could be made for Christine without denying Susan so much of the estate, particularly given that Mrs Henderson's estate was worth much more than she thought. The estate was split 25/75 between Christine and Susan.

The Court referred to ***Little v Angus*** (**174**), noting that changing social mores are important, and ***Re Leonard*** (**175**), noting that mere unfairness was not sufficient to allow a claim. In discussing s 4 of the Family Protection Act 1955 (FPA), the Court noted that there had been some criticism of decisions which made awards on the basis that adult children had some "right" to inherit, particularly where this would disadvantage a surviving spouse. The Court also referred to *Re Shirley* (an unreported Court of Appeal decision from 1987), where a claim by adult children had failed on the basis they had no needs requiring assistance from the deceased.

The Court of Appeal commented that the Courts did not actually have to find "need" in order to provide for support, as "support" under the FPA was more wide-ranging than simple "maintenance" and extended to comfort, the involvement of the claimant in the life of the deceased, and similar moral and ethical matters. It was observed that the Courts should not rewrite a will merely because it might be unfair to a particular family member, and it was for the claimant, not a beneficiary, to justify a certain share of the estate. In reviewing the affidavit evidence, Blanchard J also gave a clear warning to families not to try to air each other's dirty linen in the Courts, "It is a comparatively rare case where denigrating the character and motives of a family member will assist the cause of another in the eyes of a Judge trying a family protection proceeding"(para [71]).

Susan's share of the estate under the will was around 5 per cent of the total, and the Court of Appeal agreed with the High Court that Mrs Henderson, while giving considerable thought to the division of assets, was probably unaware of the full extent of her estate at the time of her death. The fact that her last will was made some years before her death was implicitly relevant. The High Court's award was seen to focus too much on the disparity in the gifts as between the children, rather than on any moral claim of Susan. That said, in the Court's view, the bequest of the CSR shares to Susan was not adequate overall and provision was made for a further $50,000, giving her around 10 per cent of the estate.

183   *Re Hardie*
[2002] NZFLR 229 (HC)

Joseph Hardie died in 2000 aged 90, his last will having been drafted in 1993 with no provision for his three sons Ronald, Malcolm and John. Under this will, all Joseph's chattels were left to his second wife, a large debt owing by his Family Trust to him was forgiven, and the residue was left to his Family Trust.

Ronald, Malcolm and John were Joseph's sons from his first marriage, which lasted from 1934 until 1954, although the divorce was not finalised until 1962. Joseph later remarried, his second wife dying four months before his death. Joseph's sons had little contact with their father after the divorce, although some familial relations were established in adulthood. Joseph's Family Trust was established in 1954, with the three sons as beneficiaries.

By the time of Joseph's death, Ronald was 64 and had some health problems. He had been a permanent resident in the UK for some 40 years, and had net joint assets with his wife of around NZ$850,000. Malcolm was a lawyer in Hamilton; he and his wife had net assets of around NZ$480,000. Malcolm was also in poor health.

Ronald and Malcolm, with no benefits accruing under the will, applied for provision from Joseph's estate under s 4 of the Family Protection Act 1955. John, a trustee of Joseph's estate and also of Joseph's Family Trust, made no claim.

Following *Little v Angus* **(174)**, the Court noted that the key issue in a Family Protection Act claim was whether there had been a breach of moral duty by the testator; following *Re Leonard* **(175)**, the existence of a moral duty was to be considered in light of all the circumstances and social attitudes of the day; and following *Williams v Aucutt* **(182)**, a grant of maintenance required proof of financial need, while the need for support was a question of intangibles, including relationships, contributions and support by the children to the testator, and the family's history.

Ronald and Malcolm argued that Joseph intended that his Family Trust be wound up and his assets distributed upon his death; the Court did not agree, taking the view that the Family Trust could distribute not just to Joseph's sons but also to his grandchildren.

The key question, in the Court's view, was whether Joseph had breached his moral duty to Ronald and Malcolm. The Court's answer was that he had. Ronald's and Malcolm's finances were modest, and both were in poor health. Both had supported their mother through some difficulty after her separation from Joseph, and both had enjoyed good relations with Joseph in adulthood. It was not enough that Ronald and Malcolm were beneficiaries of Joseph's Family Trust (see *Re Wilson (deceased)* [1973] 2 NZLR 359), as there was no enforceable right to trust assets or income and relied on the discretion of the trustees, including John. Ronald and Malcolm were each awarded $350,000 for both maintenance and intangibles, though this sum was to be paid in instalments.

184   *Keelan v Peach*
[2003] 1 NZLR 589 (CA)

In 1929 Hamama Walker customarily adopted Sam Keelan, then a baby, by whangai (Maori customary adoption). Hamama had a natural son, Hirini Poihakena (Poihakena), when Sam was about 15 years of age. Poihakena later adopted a son, Jason.

Hamama died in 1970 leaving a will and codicil granting the net income from the estate to Poihakena during his lifetime with the remainder to those of Poihakena's children who reached 21. There was no provision for Sam, but Sam was given some land of little economic value.

Sam died in 1986 and Poihakena in 2000. Ngawini, the daughter of Sam and his executor, brought proceedings under the Family Protection Act 1955 (FPA), arguing that Sam had made significant contributions to Hamama's property and that Jason should not be able to liquidate all of Hamama's estate.

The key issue at hand was whether Ngawini had standing for a claim. Section 3 of the FPA allowed for certain persons, including children or grandchildren, to bring FPA claims. The question therefore arose as to whether whangai were "children of the deceased" for the purposes of s 3(1)(b) of the FPA. The High Court ruled that a whangai was not a "child" for these purposes, and that Sam (and by extension Ngawini) had no claim. The matter was appealed to the Court of Appeal.

The Court of Appeal considered the history of family protection legislation in New Zealand, going back to the Testator's Family Maintenance Act 1900, and found that the policy of the FPA was to set out a clear scheme of those eligible to claim under it — the Court being "virtually compelled" to the conclusion that it could not add to the list by stealth. Further, s 19 of the Adoption Act 1955 provided that Maori customary adoption was not legal adoption for the purposes of that Act. While some flexibility was allowed in respect of what maintenance should be provided (*Little v Angus* (174)), for example, recognising that changing social attitudes could affect the Courts' understanding of moral duties), the question of *who* could claim was restricted by the wording of the FPA. While the Court had some sympathy for the plaintiff's position, whangai were found not to fall within the definition of "child" in the FPA and the appeal was dismissed.

185   *Auckland City Mission v Brown*
[2002] 2 NZLR 650 (CA)

Mr Miller moved to New Zealand from Denmark in 1955 with little in the way of savings. He worked hard, both at his business and his investments, and accumulated some considerable wealth. He and his wife divorced in 1975, by which time they had had two daughters: Freda, who died without issue in 1993, and Inge, who was married with three children. By the time of his death in 1999, Mr Miller had around $4.5m in assets.

His last will of 1996 made the following gifts:

    (a) $25,000 for gravesite flowers for himself and Freda for ten years after Mr Miller's death;

    (b) $400,000 to Suzanne Walker, a close friend, and $50,000 to her daughter Michelle;

    (c) $250,000 plus a car to a loyal employee;

    (d)   various chattels to his housekeeper and nephew;

(e) to Inge, certain shares, investments, chattels and the forgiveness of part of a loan;

(f) $500,000 to the Cancer Society;

(g) a commercial property to be held in trust for the maintenance of his grandchildren; and

(h) two-thirds of the residue to the Auckland City Mission and one-third to the Salvation Army.

Inge obtained approximately $110,000 under the will and made a claim under the Family Protection Act 1955.

The High Court assessed the family's total wealth, and noted that the family had no special health problems, and that the trust income to the grandchildren would amply meet their educational needs. Inge and her family had previously lived next door to Mr Miller, and had incurred considerable expense renovating their house in accordance with his wishes, with minimal contribution from Mr Miller. In addition, while Mr Miller had provided some support to Inge and her family, including a trip with him overseas, he was "frugal by nature" and, as with Suzanne and Michelle, Mr Miller did not assist Inge in any direct financial way. Mr Miller's solicitor gave evidence that Mr Miller had avoided provided direct gifts to Inge as he did not hold a high opinion of Inge's husband and believed that assisting her children would indirectly assist the husband.

It was common ground that Mr Miller had breached his duty to Inge under the Family Protection Act 1955 and the key issue was what further provision should be made. The Court was however critical of the personal attacks made between parties on the affidavit evidence.

The High Court ruled that there had been a breach of moral duty. Inge had been a dutiful daughter, and had an independent right to be freed from the shackles of economic necessity. Mr Miller had never properly discharged his duty as a parent to Inge and had left almost $3m (or 60 per cent of the estate) to charities which had no moral claim which could compete with Inge's. In the High Court's view, a wise and just testator would have wanted to see Inge and her family adequately housed, would have forgiven her all indebtedness, and would have wanted to provide her with an income independent of the business dividends she would receive through the gift of shares. While the charities had believed an order for $650,000 appropriate, the High Court ruled that Inge should be paid $1.6m from the residuary of the estate, in addition to the gift to her under the will.

On appeal, the Auckland City Mission and Salvation Army argued that the award of $1.6m was excessive; went well beyond what was required to remedy any breach of moral duty; failed to give proper attention to changing social attitudes to the support of adult children; ignored the testator's intentions, and effectively rewrote the will. Inge's solicitors argued that the award should stand, and that the litigious approach taken by the charities should not be condoned.

The Court discussed *Williams v Aucutt* (182) at some length, noting that a Court should not rewrite a will just because it is perceived as being unfair to a particular person, and that the onus is not on a beneficiary to prove its entitlement. In the Court of Appeal's view, the High Court had not considered that any award to Inge should be limited to the amount required to repair the breach of moral duty. In the Court of Appeal's view, the charities were worthy beneficiaries and had every right to defend a challenge to the will. The Court considered Mr Miller's moral duty and ordered that Inge should receive $850,000, plus forgiveness of all debt, from the residuary estate.

186   *Re Powell*
[2000] NZFLR 269 (HC)

George Powell was, in the latter part of his life, a farmer of 466 isolated acres at Karioi near Ohakune owned by the George Powell Trust. George married twice but had no children.

John Powell was born in 1910, and although George was not named as John's father on his birth certificate, John was raised by George and his second wife Sarah as though her was a son.

George made his last will in 1937 and died in 1940. The bulk of the estate was held on trust for a life interest to George's widow, then to John, and then for the benefit of children under the care of the Wanganui orphanage by providing the benefit of country life, a self-supporting farm, and the opportunity to contribute to the farm. Notwithstanding these intentions, the trustees of the estate also had the right to sell and convert to money any part of the trust estate, and to apply any income from the estate for the benefit of the children of the Wanganui orphanage. In addition, any widow or any children of John were to have the right to ask the orphanage for assistance (whether allowance or employment); and after the end of the life interests, surplus income was to be used for the benefit of the orphanage.

John married twice. His second marriage, in 1952, was to a woman who already had two children, who were later adopted by John. John died intestate in 1977, leaving little in his estate. Letters of administration were not applied for until 1995, when John's children became aware of the George Powell Trust. By this time, the trustees of the George Powell Trust were relatives of the children, and the Wanganui orphanage had ceased to exist, with the benefits of the trust now going to intellectually handicapped children. At the time of the hearing in 2000, the George Powell Trust had total assets of around $800,000.

A key issue was whether a Family Protection Act 1955 claim could be heard, on the basis that the estate of George had not been fully distributed. In the Court's view, the administration of George's estate ended when John died and the remainder vested in the George Powell Trust. It was also not proven as to whether John was George's son. Given that George's will referred to John as "John Powell (known as my son)", and there was no other real evidence as to paternity, the Court was not convinced that John was George's son.

In addition, John's children were posthumous grandchildren of George and, following *In re McGregor (Deceased)* [1961] NZLR 1077, this kind of order was seldom warranted, and was not in this case as George would not have foreseen John's remarriage and adoption of his second wife's children. The Court did not allow a Family Protection Act claim.

There were also some further issues. The first was whether the trustees of the George Powell Trust should be given leave to sell the land owned by the Trust — the trustees having applied for leave to sell it under s 64 of the Trustee Act 1956 and s 33 of the Charitable Trusts Act 1957. It was acknowledged that the orphanage trust no longer looked after orphans, and that cash would be a most useful benefit. The Court was happy to order sale.

The final issue was whether, under s 66 of the Trustee Act, each of John's children could be granted orders to receive one-third of the George Powell Trust's assets, there being no scope for a claim under the Family Protection Act, and George having expressed a desire to assist John's family when in need. However, this was seen in direct conflict with the decision in *Baptist Union of New Zealand v Attorney-General* [1973] 1 NZLR 42, as it was clear that George's intentions were charitable. The Court would not therefore grant an order that two-thirds of the estate be distributed for non-charitable purposes.

187   *Flathaug v Weaver*
        [2003] NZFLR 730 (CA)

Ludvig Kritian Stein Flathaug was a Norwegian who fled to England during World War II to escape the German occupation of Norway. He married Muriel in 1943. After the war ended, they lived in Norway for a short time and had a son they named John. They moved back to England in 1947 and had a second son, Nils.

In 1952, the Flathaugs came to know the Hewletts, an English couple who had married in 1942 and had two sons as well. They came to know each other very well, in fact, as Mr Flathaug and Mrs Hewlett entered into an exclusive relationship, and in 1955 Mrs Hewlett became pregnant with Jane Weaver, the claimant. Jane's birth certificate stated that Mr Hewlett was her father, and he acted as her father until his death in 1977, but Mrs Hewlett's evidence was that Mr Hewlett (and Mr Flathaug) accepted that Mr Flathaug was the father.

In 1966, the Flathaugs and their sons moved to New Zealand. The couples decided to go their separate ways, and there was little contact between the families until 1979 when Mr Flathaug visited England. At that time, Jane commented on her close physical resemblance to Mr Flathaug and it was revealed to her that Mr Flathaug was her biological father. From then on, the relationship between Mr Flathaug and Jane was emotionally quite close and there was contact at various times until Mr Flathaug's death in 2000.

Mr Flathaug's will left his entire estate to the Flathaug Family Trust and forgave all debts the trust owed to him. At the time of death, Mr Flathaug's estate held two properties worth $520,000 and a debt from the trust worth around $260,000. The trust was a described as a standard family trust, with Mr Flathaug's sons and their children the beneficiaries. Mrs Flathaug and Jane were not beneficiaries. The trust held assets of around $890,000.

John died several weeks after his father, leaving three children, two of whom were adults. John had few assets when he died and the financial position of his surviving partner and her son were poor. Nils and his family were in a comfortable financial position.

Mrs Flathaug made claims under the Property (Relationships) Act 1976 and the Family Protection Act 1955. In the trial Court, she was entitled to an equal division of relationship property, which totalled around $1.1m. Once this was done, the balance of the estate was $550,000, and the trial Judge awarded her additional property and assets.

Jane was married with three children, with equity in her and her husband's joint property of UK£150,000. The trial Court found she had not had a disadvantaged childhood, nor any financial deprivation. There was evidence that Mr Flathaug had agonised over provision to Jane, but had eventually decided that provision to her during his lifetime was sufficient. The trial Court found that Mr Flathaug had breached his moral duty and made an order for $90,000 to Jane. Mrs Flathaug then appealed.

The Court of Appeal agreed that Mr Flathaug had breached his moral duty to Jane. No moral duty arose before Jane became aware who her biological father was, as Jane benefited from a unified and stable home. However, the discovery that Mr Flathaug was her biological father must have come as a shock and was itself a legitimate consideration for evaluating the moral duty. The joint efforts of Mr Flathaug and Jane to build up a relationship in the years following this event also warranted recognition from Mr Flathaug's estate.

In addition, the entitlement of John and Nils and their children to benefit under the family trust was relevant, even though the trust was completely discretionary as the intent (and likely reality) of the trust was to provide for them. Also, although less significantly, John and Nils were likely to benefit from Mrs Flathaug's estate when she died.

Overall, then, a moral duty was owed by Mr Flathaug to Jane, but it was important to remember that only a limited relationship existed between the two. There was no shared family life or mutual sacrifice. The emotional bond between the two was important, but was less than between a parent and child who had shared a lifelong relationship. The sum to Jane was reduced to $40,000.

188   *Re Stewart*
[2003] 1 NZLR 809 (HC)

Valmay Stewart died in 2000, and probate was granted to Price and Hall (two solicitors) as executors and trustees of her estate. The only beneficiaries named in the will were Sandra and Terry, who were granted the net estate over the course of 2000 and 2001.

In mid-December 2001, Colin and John Smith (the plaintiffs) became aware of Valmay's death and brought proceedings under the Family Protection Act 1955 (FPA), arguing that the executors and named beneficiaries deliberately avoided notice being given to the plaintiffs of Valmay's death, that their right of action was concealed from them, and that the named beneficiaries' receipt of the assets was subject to a constructive trust.

Valmay had been informally fostered by the parents of the named beneficiaries, and at a young age married a man much older than herself. The two children of the marriage were the plaintiffs. Valmay left the marriage when the children were young and lived with another man, who had been a boarder. She chose not to have any contact with the plaintiffs but maintained a close relationship with the named beneficiaries as her foster-siblings.

On Valmay's death, no death notices were published and no notices were published under s 35 of the Trustee Act 1956. It became clear that Valmay had expressed the wish that the plaintiffs not be contacted, and that the executors had followed this wish.

The plaintiffs were out of time for an application under the FPA, but sought an extension on the basis of a breach of fiduciary duty by the executors to potential statutory claimants as the executors were aware of the existence of the plaintiffs as Valmay's children and had concealed knowledge of Valmay's death. The executors denied they had any duty to seek out potential claimants or to disclose Valmay's death to any person.

The Court noted that the primary obligation of an executor is generally to give effect to the wishes of the deceased as expressed in his or her will. There was an obligation of even-handedness to potential claimants who had indicated the possibility of a claim, but the question here was whether there was a duty on the executors to be even-handed where the plaintiffs themselves were unaware of their potential claim.

In these circumstances, though, the executors were aware of the plaintiffs' potential claim, even if the plaintiffs were not. The executors were required to be proactive, otherwise, they would be favouring the named beneficiaries over other potential claimants and would not be acting even-handedly. The duty was, however, proscriptive rather than positive: the executors must not conceal the death from potential claimants but, in the absence of mandatory statutory language, could not be seen to have a duty to positively advise all potential claimants. The concealment was found to be constructive fraud, and this was sufficient to allow the plaintiffs what would have normally been a time-barred claim.

The named beneficiaries were also found to be likely to have had sufficient knowledge of the fraud for the Court to find the potential for a tracing order against the assets already distributed to the named beneficiaries. The right of the plaintiffs to a claim was upheld, but no substantive orders were made.

Law Reform (Testamentary Promises) Act 1949

189 *Hawkins v Public Trustee*
[1960] NZLR 305

Mr Hawkins was a self-made and intensely ambitious farmer. Being sadly disappointed in his son, he found in his daughter's oldest child a person whom he considered to be a capable and worthy successor to himself and to his name. His grandson of course bore his mother's married name, and so it was particularly important to Hawkins that his grandson should take his name. Thus, in 1936, when the grandson was 21, Hawkins senior promised him that if he changed his name and "stuck by" his grandfather he would inherit all his property. In reliance on this promise the grandson took on the trappings of a father/son relationship: he took the name of Hawkins and worked on and managed his grandfather's farms.

In 1946 Hawkins senior informed his grandson that he was unable to carry out his original promise, but now proposed to leave him a quarter-share in the estate. After some thought the grandson acquiesced. However, when he discovered in March 1953 that his grandfather's will left him a small annuity only, he left his grandfather's farm and went farming on his own account.

On his grandfather's death the grandson made a claim under the Law Reform (Testamentary Promises) Act 1949 claiming that he was entitled to the quarter-share of the estate that had been promised to him in 1953. The Act gives the Court jurisdiction to grant relief where there has been a failure to carry out a promise to reward by testamentary disposition a claimant who has performed work or services for the deceased.

Shorland J accepted that it was clear that the original promise had been made, and that this had been changed to the promise of a quarter-share of Hawkin's estate in return for the grandson's services. He found that the grandson had left his grandfather's employment only upon learning that his grandfather had decided not to honour this promise. In the opinion of Shorland J this did not deprive the grandson of his right to claim. The fact that the promisee does not intend to honour their promise excuses further performance. The Court also held that services had been performed to support the promise by the fact of the adoption of the name of Hawkins; the entry into a father/son relationship; and working in the employment of Hawkins senior. The Court held that the claim had been satisfied, and awarded Hawkins junior the sum of $5500.

190   *Re Welch*
[1990] 3 NZLR 1

Albyn Stewart was brought up solely by his mother until he was eleven, when she married Mr Raymond Welch. From that time Mr Welch treated Albyn as his son, and the family enjoyed a close relationship. The Welches had no other children, and Mr Welch had indicated that he intended to make a will leaving most of his property to Albyn. Mr Welch died intestate. Albyn then bought proceedings against his stepfather's estate seeking an order under the Law Reform (Testamentary Promises) Act 1949.

Albyn's claim met with the success in the High Court but the executor of Mr Welch's estate appealed. It was argued that there was enough evidence of services and the requisite promise to give the Court jurisdiction to to make an award, but the executor claimed that the award was too high. The Court of Appeal agreed and fixed the award at $20,000. Albyn then appealed to the Privy Council seeking the restoration of the High Court judgment.

The Privy Council noted that the scope of the Act had to be strained somewhat to bring such a situation within its ambit. There was a distinction between the concepts of services performed as part of life in a close family group, as existed in this case, and those seen in *Hawkins v Public Trustee* **(188)**. The Privy Council agreed with the Court of Appeal who had considered that here there was nothing more than a family relationship between a stepfather and stepson who got on well with each other. They could see no evidence that the alleged promises were ever seen by either party as a reward for services rendered, and felt that in any event much of the evidence of services was tenuous. The Court felt that the award made by the High Court went beyond the true scope of the Act as any award should not be more than reasonable recompense for services rendered. The appeal was dismissed.

- Nicola Peart, "*Re Welch*: The Boundaries of the Testamentary Promises Act" [1991] NZLJ 77.

191   *Re Archer*
[1990] 3 NZLR 737

Mrs Archer was a widower with no children or close relatives. She did however have the friendship of the Hibbs family. From 1969 until Mrs Archer's death in 1984 Mrs Hibbs and her two sons, John and Donald, visited her weekly. The boys mowed her lawns, looked after her garden and did other work around the house while Mrs Hibbs cleaned the house and looked after Mrs Archer. Mrs Archer often told the Hibbs family that they were in her will and indicated to them and others that she would be leaving her property to them.

However, following Mrs Archer's death in 1984, no will including provision for the Hibbs family could be found. The only will that could be located had been drawn up in 1952, and left Mrs Archer's entire estate to two of her friends.

Hillyer J was satisfied that Mrs Archer had made promises to Mrs Hibbs, and that in response to this Mrs Hibbs and her family had rendered substantial services. The Judge found that the promise was made to reward the Hibbs family not only out of love and affection, but also for their services. The Judge then had to decide on reasonable remuneration. Here he found that the Hibbs' claim could not exceed the sum of $200,000 as that was the limitation that their solicitor had imposed in correspondence with the executors of Mrs Archer's estate. Despite a dispute between Mrs Hibbs and her solicitor over his actions in imposing this limitation, the Court could not award more than this sum.

The Court was also not prepared to accept an argument raised by the executors that John and Donald Hibbs could have no claim under the estate as no promises had been made directly to them. Hillyer J felt that an implied promise had been made for the services they had rendered, and this founded their claim.

192   *Powell v Public Trustee*
[2003] 1 NZLR 381 (CA)

Frank Birdling died in 1999, with his last will from 1964 leaving his entire estate to his nephew (Menzies). Frank had, in 1996, sought to amend this will by replacing Menzies as sole beneficiary with Alma Powell, but this amendment was not valid as it was not witnessed. Alma brought a claim against the estate of Frank under the Law Reform (Testamentary Promises) Act 1949 (LTPRA) for work and services during the last nine years of his life. She had worked on his home and farm, and also provided companionship, although there was some concern about the precise nature of her work as she had exaggerated her diary entries. There was also third party evidence that Frank intended to leave his estate to Alma.

The trial Judge awarded Alma $30,000, a relatively small part of an estate valued at $500,000 at trial, and Alma appealed.

The Court of Appeal noted, with reference to s 3 of the LRTPA, that the main criterion for relief is reasonableness, although an assessment of the value of the work by a promisor with capacity should not be lightly departed from (*Re Welch* (190)). The companionship provided by Alma to Frank was significant and was to be considered as services worthy of reward, though any reward was difficult to quantify.

The Court also looked further into the value of the estate and found that Frank's farm, the main asset, was worth around $350,000. The Court of Appeal agreed with the High Court's assessment that Menzies had no strong moral right to inherit the property based on his association with Frank. While Alma had benefited from Frank's companionship too, this was not to diminish her contributions; and while her false diary entries counted against this, the Court of Appeal's view was that this should penalise her costs, not her claim.

While acknowledging that the trial Judge's findings were discretionary and should not be lightly overturned, the Court of Appeal found that the High Court had given insufficient weight to the intangible aspects of Alma's companionship with Frank and had awarded a sum that was too low. The Court of Appeal awarded Alma $120,000, which it acknowledged was less than the original value of the promise, but believed it to be a very reasonable sum in the circumstances.

193   *Ryan v Public Trustee*
[2000] 1 NZLR 700 (HC)

Miss Sherlock was born in 1909 and died in 1993, with her most recent will of 1973 leaving her estate to her sister Vera. Unfortunately Vera had died in 1985, and Miss Sherlock therefore died intestate. The Public Trustee, as executor and trustee, determined that 72 relatives would benefit on intestacy, including the plaintiff, who had visited Miss Sherlock regularly following Vera's death.

It had become apparent in the late 1980s that Miss Sherlock was suffering from hallucinations and delusions, and with the plaintiff's involvement, the Public Trustee had been appointed manager of Miss Sherlock's property under s 31 of the Protection of Personal and Property Rights Act 1988 (PPPRA). Miss Sherlock wrote a letter to another relative in 1992 indicating she was intending to make a new will. The plaintiff also took Miss Sherlock to an appointment with the Public Trustee in 1992 where the Public Trustee was given handwritten will instructions. After Miss Sherlock's death, however, it became apparent that a new will had been prepared and never signed — hence Miss Sherlock's intestacy.

The Court found that the plaintiff had a valid testamentary promises claim, as her actions had gone beyond normal kinship and had been carried out at some sacrifice to herself. This had also been confirmed by the instructions to the Public Trustee and, with testamentary promises analogous to contract (*Public Trustee v Bick* [1973] 1 NZLR 301), Miss Sherlock's capacity was found to be sufficient to make this kind of promise. The PPPRA also did not prohibit this disposition.

The Court also found that the Public Trustee knew of the PPPRA order and so, following *Gartside v Sheffield, Young & Ellis* [1983] NZLR 37, owed a duty of care to the plaintiff (as an intended beneficiary under Miss Sherlock's intended new will) to investigate whether or not Miss Sherlock had testamentary capacity. This duty had been breached and damages were payable, equivalent to the one-sixth of the estate the plaintiff would have received if Miss Sherlock had executed a valid will.

FIDUCIARY DUTIES

194   *Dickie v Torbay Pharmacy (1986) Ltd*
[1995] 3 NZLR 429 (HC)

The plaintiffs were doctors practicing together in Auckland in the form of an "associateship", sharing common rented premises and expenses, but each retaining his or her own fee income. Across the road from the rented site was a former car dealer's lot (the NZMC site) which some third parties, one of which was Mainzeal, were interested in developing for a time.

Buchanan, an accountant, operated out of premises nearby and had a friend, Johnson, who was a pharmacist operating a pharmacy in a different area. Johnson and Buchanan had some common investment interests. Buchanan became interested in developing the NZMC site to house the doctors and other professional tenants, and approached Mainzeal about undertaking a joint development project. Mainzeal reacted positively, and Buchanan then approached the doctors about their interest in the site. No fixed plans were made, but intentions for a co-venture between the doctors and Buchanan led to Buchanan being the main spokesperson for himself and the doctors in negotiations with Mainzeal.

Because of difficulties in negotiations with Mainzeal, Buchanan decided to put a "back-up" agreement in place to ensure the NZMC site would not be lost if the Mainzeal deal fell over. This back-up deal involved entering into a conditional agreement to buy the NZMC site directly from its owners so the site could be developed by Buchanan and the doctors. To avoid having Mainzeal become aware of this, Johnson (through his company Torbay Pharmacy) agreed to enter into the back-up agreement as nominee for Buchanan and the doctors.

Difficulties arose, and the doctors claimed that by mid-1993, Johnson was holding himself out to be a participant in the development venture rather than simply a nominee. The doctors did not want Johnson as partner and would not proceed. Johnson and Buchanan stood together and proposed to transfer the NZMC property to their joint company Redmount. The doctors lodged a caveat, then allowed the transfer and registered a further caveat. The essential question at hand was whether Johnson/Torbay Pharmacy was simply a nominee of the doctors and Buchanan, or whether the doctors had agreed to

Johnson becoming a co-venturer. There was a clear conflict in the parties' understanding of the facts, with Buchanan understanding that the doctors (through Sinclair, a representative) had agreed to Johnson becoming part of the project, while the doctors thought they had made it clear that they did not want Johnson as a co-venturer at any stage.

On the facts and evidence, the Court preferred the view that the doctors had not agreed to Johnson as a co-venturer, and in presuming him to be one, Buchanan had overreached himself. It was also far from clear – even unlikely – that Sinclair had the authority to bind the doctors and Buchanan should have sought agreement from all doctors, not just their representative. Buchanan did not have the authority to involve Johnson in the venture beyond Johnson being a nominee for the purchase. Johnson's remedy for anything said by Buchanan was against Buchanan, not the doctors.

In this kind of co-venture, Buchanan and the doctors clearly had fiduciary obligations to each other, involving mutual good faith and reliance. While in normal circumstances Redmount might be seen to hold the property as constructive trustee for the doctors and Buchanan, Buchanan had clearly acted against the interests of the doctors. In determining the appropriate remedy, the Court favoured the view that a party guilty of misconduct should not be able to take advantage of that conduct. The Court therefore ruled that Buchanan and Johnson should be refunded any deposit paid, plus interest, and that Buchanan should receive an allowance for his involvement in the project up to the time the doctors terminated it. The doctors were granted ownership of the NZMC property and were allowed to continue with their development without Buchanan.

195   *Mothew v Bristol & West Building Society*
[1996] EWCA CIV 533, 24 July 1996

Mothew was an English solicitor who acted in respect of a purchase of a property in Romford for £73,000 in 1988. The purchasers of the property had applied to the Building Society for a loan of £59,000 to finance the purchase, and had warranted to the Building Society that the balance of the purchase price was being funded by them personally. The solicitor was also required to certify to the Building Society that this was the case. The purchasers intended to fund the balance of the purchase price themselves through the sale of another property, which was then mortgaged to Barclays Bank (the bank). When the purchasers came to sell their existing property, however, it became apparent that they had a small debt outstanding, which they agreed with the bank could be secured by a second charge over the Romford property.

Mothew attended to this second charge but did not advise the Building Society, which clearly he should have done. Two mortgages were registered against the Romford property.

The purchasers defaulted on their loan from the Building Society and the Building Society sought to enforce its security, but proceedings only realised £53,000 from the sale of the property. The Building Society sued Mothew for breach of contract and negligence (admitted by Mothew), and also for breach of trust. The latter claim was most significant as the Building Society argued that issues such as remoteness and causation were not relevant to a claim for breach of trust or breach of fiduciary duty. The trial Judge found that a constructive trust arose in respect of the loan moneys paid to the solicitor to settle the purchase, found the solicitor in breach of trust, and made orders for payment of £59,000 less the sum received by the Building Society on the sale.

The English Court of Appeal noted that the word "fiduciary" was often thrown around with some carelessness. Not every claim arising out of a fiduciary relationship was necessarily a breach of fiduciary duty. A breach of fiduciary duty involved disloyalty or infidelity rather than mere incompetence. The Court noted that the Building Society was fully aware that Mothew was also acting for the purchasers, and any potential conflict that arose was of the Building Society's own making. Mothew had failed to fulfil his duties to the Building Society, but was not in breach of fiduciary duty. In addition, while Mothew knew he was a trustee of the loan money for the Building Society, on the facts he did not know he had misled the Building Society. Therefore, he would not have been aware that his actions would end his authority. Neither would be aware of the consequent obligation to return the loan moneys to the Building Society. Mothew was not in breach of trust.

196   *Chirnside v Fay*
[2007] 1 NZLR 433 (SCNZ)

From 1997, Chirnside and Fay were involved in a project to develop a commercial property. In 1999, Chirnside entered into a conditional agreement to purchase the site as a trustee for a company to be formed. By this stage, there had been regular discussions between the parties as to the project, although no formal joint venture agreement had ever been concluded. The project was made feasible by the attraction of a major tenant in 2000, and Chirnside made the agreement unconditional. Chirnside then excluded Fay from the venture and carried out the development through a company he controlled, keeping Fay off the scent with a combination of delays and untruths. When Fay found out about Chirnside's actions, he brought proceedings for breach of fiduciary duty and sought an account of profits.

There were four different judgments, the two main ones both traversed the question of a definition of "joint venture"; and the question of fiduciary obligations between joint venture parties. Elias CJ observed that the project to develop the site was essentially a single transaction partnership, and the fact the parties may have expected to make more formal arrangements in future through a corporate structure or partnership did not alter the nature of the relationship formed at the early stages of the project. The major judgment in the case was that of Blanchard and Tipping JJ, delivered by Tipping J, of the view that the High Court's finding of the existence of a commercial joint venture was reasonable on the evidence and should not be challenged. They then commented that "most joint venture relationships can properly be regarded as being inherently fiduciary because of the analogy with partnership", and went on to observe that "all fiduciary relationships, whether inherent or particular, are marked by the entitlement ... of one party to place trust and confidence in the other". A joint venture could also arise without all contractual terms between the parties being finalised.

In Blanchard and Tipping JJ's view (para [91]):

> A joint venture will come into being once the parties have proceeded to the point where, pursuant to their arrangement or understanding, they are depending on each other to make progress towards the common objective. Each party is then proceeding on the basis that he or she is acting in the interests of all or both parties involved in the arrangement or understanding. A relationship of trust and confidence thereby arises; each party is entitled to expect from the others loyalty to the joint cause, loose as the formalities of the joint venture may still be.

The Court went on to note that the appropriate remedy for a breach of fiduciary duty was an account of profits. Where one party had breached its duty but sought an allowance, the onus was on that party to show the Court that an allowance should be made without the allowance constituting unjust enrichment. The allowance to Chirnside made in the High Court was reduced by the majority.

- Bram van Melle "Fiduciary duties and joint venturers" [2007] NZLJ 32.
- Jessica Palmer, "Fiduciaries and remedies" [2007] NZLJ 36.